Democracy and Teacher Education

This book connects the dilemmas educators experience in daily practice with key theories, research and policy about democracy, ethics and equity in education. Illustrated through vignettes from practising teachers, as well as suggested questions and supplementary readings for each chapter, the authors recognise and explore the complex nature of the insoluble problems that face practising teachers in their everyday lives and how they can be understood in order to address them in a more elaborate manner.

Divided into eight concise chapters, this book provides a much-needed comprehensive exploration of issues within the education discourse, as seen from a global perspective, such as:

- Teachers' understanding of their profession
- Political demands and the complexities of practice
- Schools' democratic values
- Performance and accountability
- Minority needs and majority rule
- Countering radicalisation, terrorism and misinformation.

Democracy and Teacher Education is a fantastic resource for students in teacher education programmes, as well as teacher educators, who are looking to develop a critical understanding of the choices made within the education field in a more thoughtful and sensitive manner.

Silvia Edling is a Professor and excellent teacher at the Academy of Education and Business Studies at University of Gävle, Sweden, and specializes in questions concerning democracy, teacher professionalism, ethics, justice and rights in education and higher education.

Geraldine Mooney Simmie is a Senior Lecturer in Education at the School of Education, Faculty of Education and Health Sciences, University of Limerick, Republic of Ireland, where she lectures in Policy Studies. Her research interest is in emancipatory teaching and research, teacher professional learning, ethics, social justice and how education intersects with democracy.

'Keeping alive the idea and reality of teacher education within and for democratic renewal is vital. Edling and Mooney Simmie succeed in doing just that because they focus on issues that prompt the question: how do we do teaching and learning together? Addressing this requires all the resources provided in this book: history, values, knowledge and expertise. The key message is that teachers should be educated and not just trained to deliver data. The authors demonstrate that while professional practice takes place in a dynamic and an often threatening policy context, the unifying constants are values and the importance of valuing the educability of all children.'

Helen Gunter, *University of Manchester*

'At a time when neoliberal capitalism has successfully institutionalised the concept of the individual-to-be-educated as a bundle of market-serving human capitals, *Democracy and Teacher Education* presents a refreshing and hopeful counter-narrative. It makes a compelling and engaging case for democratic and emancipatory education for teachers and teacher educators. It also provides a salutary reminder of Freire's dictum that education is never neutral politically; it operates either for domestication or for freedom.

This is a fascinating and exciting book. It is theoretically rich and practically engaged, accessible and challenging at the same time. It is a welcome and timely reminder of why public education matters and why critical educational thinking and praxis is vital for democratic societies. Both uplifting and engaging, I strongly recommend it to teachers and teacher educators.'

Kathleen Lynch, *University College Dublin*

'At this historical juncture known as the Capitalocene, when education is under attack by the irrepressible forces of neoliberal capitalist retrenchment, this book offers a lifeline to those educators who are drowning in despair, who are too strong to yield but too weak to overcome the barriers erected to prevent democracy from functioning as it should. The authors are skilled social justice educators who, by virtue of their visionary approach to education and democracy, have created a powerful ecology of pedagogical possibilities, that is able to do more than to undermine the rationalism, fatalism and toxic nationalism that has gripped our age but to establish a new praxis of teacher transformation and a politics of hope for a future where democracy is able to live up to its name.'

Peter McLaren, *Chapman University*

Democracy and Teacher Education
Dilemmas, Challenges and Possibilities

Silvia Edling and Geraldine Mooney Simmie

LONDON AND NEW YORK

First published 2020
by Routledge
2 Park Square, Milton Park, Abingdon, Oxon OX14 4RN

and by Routledge
52 Vanderbilt Avenue, New York, NY 10017

Routledge is an imprint of the Taylor & Francis Group, an informa business

© 2020 Silvia Edling and Geraldine Mooney Simmie

The right of Silvia Edling and Geraldine Mooney Simmie to be identified as authors of this work has been asserted by them in accordance with sections 77 and 78 of the Copyright, Designs and Patents Act 1988.

All rights reserved. No part of this book may be reprinted or reproduced or utilised in any form or by any electronic, mechanical, or other means, now known or hereafter invented, including photocopying and recording, or in any information storage or retrieval system, without permission in writing from the publishers.

Trademark notice: Product or corporate names may be trademarks or registered trademarks, and are used only for identification and explanation without intent to infringe.

British Library Cataloguing-in-Publication Data
A catalogue record for this book is available from the British Library

Library of Congress Cataloging-in-Publication Data
A catalog record has been requested for this book

ISBN: 978-1-138-59324-4 (hbk)
ISBN: 978-1-138-59325-1 (pbk)
ISBN: 978-0-429-48952-5 (ebk)

Typeset in Bembo
by Taylor & Francis Books

Contents

List of illustrations   vi
Acknowledgements   viii
Foreword   ix

1. Democracy and teacher education dilemmas, challenges and possibilities: an introduction   1
2. Historical background   23
3. The policy cycle   54
4. Teacher professionalism and democracy   74
5. Knowledge and democracy   99
6. Darwinian strength   121
7. Teacher reflexivity   150
8. Teachers' democratic assignment   166

Index   *182*

Illustrations

Figures

2.1	Soldiers marching in Third Reich	38
3.1	Quality teaching understood as a well-defined toolkit of pedagogies	58
3.2	William compares the teacher's role with a pilot landing an aeroplane	58
4.1	An illusion of Wittgenstein's Duck and Rabbit. It reveals two images depending on where the subjects chooses to focus (see)	91
5.1	Critical understandings of the necessity of a Public Forum in education to question authority	110
6.1	The image symbolizes a 'manly' arm hitting a Jew, with the text 'Der Schlag muss sitzen' (approximately translated as: 'the blow must be perfect')	127
6.2	An example of a propaganda used in the Third Reich picturing violence as something desirable [*Der Schlag muss sitzen*/The hit must be perfect]	132
7.1	Reflection generally tells you what you look like?	157
7.2	The psychiatrist's couch symbolizes the uncomfortable work of critical reflexivity	159
8.1	A cloud/overview of value tensions and hence dilemmas discussed in the book	167

Tables

2.1	An overview of dilemmas discussed in Chapter 2	24
2.2	An overview of a selected number of ideological governing forms together with a brief description of each and who is/are in power	26
3.1	An overview of dilemmas discussed in Chapter 3	56
4.1	An overview of dilemmas discussed in Chapter 4	75
4.2	A summary of themes found in *Visible Learning* and *Excellent Education* as concerns what a good teacher needs to know/handle	88
4.3	A summary of themes found in *Visible Learning* and *Excellent Education* concerning what a good student needs to know/handle	89
4.4	In order to grasp the consequences of various seeing, the following example can be used. In reation to violent cases at an elite boarding school in Sweden school staff and some pupils argued in relation to the left column while the Swedish School Inspectorate argued in relation to the right column	90

5.1	An overview of dilemmas discussed in Chapter 5	100
6.1	An overview of dilemmas that will be discussed in Chapter 6	122
6.2	Examples of how values are split into a dualistic model, where some values are connected to women/femininity and other to men/masculinity	128
6.3	A selection of how the brain works and how it influences learning	138
6.4	An example of how a Gloria Effect is created. Put your hand above the right-side column and think for yourself what kind of thoughts and emotions the left column causes to arise. Take away your hand and add the new information to the previous one. What happens?	140
7.1	An overview of dilemmas discussed in Chapter 7	152

Acknowledgements

We would like to direct our sincere thanks to faculty, staff and colleagues at the University of Gävle, Sweden, and the School of Education, University of Limerick, Republic of Ireland, for their encouragement and support, including some financial supports in writing this book. The production of a book is a collective endeavour. Many thanks also to Helen Pritt, senior editor for Routledge Education at the beginning of the process and for Simon Jacobs who later took over from Helen. Your optimistic spirit, kindness and quick replies were invaluable to us during a complex and time-consuming activity like writing a book. Additionally, warm thanks to Routledge editorial assistants Alexandra Butterworth and Marie Andrews for keeping us on track. Finally, thank you LIBER publications for allowing some select pieces from the book *Demokratidilemman i läraruppdraget* to be freely translated into English for this publication.

Foreword

How do you write a textbook today for student teachers and experienced teachers on the democratic mission of education and teacher education? Over 100 years ago John Dewey's *Democracy and Education* was published and his textbook is still inspiring, but of course there are new dilemmas and challenges that now need to be analysed. And that is what Silvia Edling and Geraldine Mooney Simmie are seeking to do – to address the dilemmas, challenges and possibilities of today. And we need to be aware that the democratic role of schools is not a given in Western democracies today. The dominant mission seems rather to be to ensure that students achieve certain predefined goals in terms of knowledge, not necessarily that they are motivated and made ready for political participation in a good society, which used to be an explicit endeavour in many Western democracies.

In this book, *Democracy and Teacher Education: Dilemmas, Challenges and Possibilities*, the authors develop a multidimensional answer to what Emily Robertson, a prominent researcher in teacher education, referring to the democratic purpose of schools, asked in her contribution in 2008 to the third edition of the *Handbook of Research on Teacher Education*: "What dispositions and abilities can strengthen a democratic way of life? What roles can education, including teacher education, play in developing them?" (Hansen, 2008, p. 6). Robertson's responses focused on how teachers in schools can assist the young in developing the arts of deliberation, negotiation and activism in the name of justice and freedom, and she also addressed how teacher education can help new teachers, through what we can call collegial deliberation, to grasp and teach these arts.

Robertson, citing Parker (2003), writes that deliberation is not just a sharing of perspectives, "but rather discussion with an eye toward decision making" even when the participants are not themselves the primary decision makers. She also underlines that "the point of deliberation is to convert disagreement into agreement about what to do by determining which proposals are supported by the best reasons" (Robertson, 2008, p. 31).

I interpret Edling and Mooney Simmie's contribution as following up the broad tradition of linking teacher education to democracy in the ways developed by Robertson, David Hansen and Hugh Sockett (2008) in the framing chapters of the handbook mentioned, but with certain qualifications, in that they see the classroom and the teacher education seminar as weak publics in which moral judgements take shape.

What Edling and Mooney Simmie also stress in their contribution is that we have to understand that "policy desires cannot and should not be made equal to what takes place in educational settings". What teachers encounter is an ecological, organic and dynamic practice often based in dilemmas, specific challenges that plead for attention, but that lack obvious one-dimensional solutions. Edling and Mooney Simmie also argue that it is important to highlight and explore these dilemmas in order to navigate the terrain of education and teaching in a thoughtful and sensitive way, and that this "sensitivity plays a major role in the complex interweaving of education, a terrain that is often messy and complex". Their central aim in writing this book is to bring about a dialogue examining different practices for addressing dilemmas, related to their reflexive positioning as teacher educators and using examples and starting points from Sweden (Silvia) and Ireland (Geraldine).

There are many similarities between the two countries Sweden and Ireland, but there are also crucial differences. Both countries have historically built state-funded systems, the Swedish one more secular and the Irish one strongly related to the Catholic Church. As will be developed in this volume, the Swedish school system has changed in many ways in recent decades, and schools in both Sweden and Ireland have been heavily influenced during those decades by the epistemic dominance of the OECD.

Irish schools are heavily influenced by the Catholic Church, and according to Edling and Mooney Simmie there are few mentions of the word democracy in education policy documents. It is also stated by the authors that there is nowhere that democracy is explicitly portrayed as a matter of recognition, respect and celebration of difference along the lines of ethnicity, race, religion etc. In Ireland, "the question of difference and 'other' appears to be understood more as assimilation into the existing culture rather than a fluid and dialectical understanding of democracy and plurality". In this book there are empirical examples and references both to the Irish situation and to Sweden.

With regard to Sweden, and as general themes also related to Ireland, the authors begin by analysing three general dilemmas: first, the question of inclusion/exclusion; second, issues that have to do with adjustment/freedom; and third, the dilemmas of legitimisation, implying that democracy is nothing without the active agreement of citizens to the sovereignty of democracy. Previously in Sweden, the idea of a social welfare society was strong, with a common comprehensive school for all from 1962 to 1989/90, but over the last 30 years the idea of free choice of schools has led to a segregation of the Swedish school system and of Swedish society as well. In fact, the school system seems to be perhaps the most crucial element in this process of segregation, and this is the context of the investigation presented in this book.

While Sweden's comprehensive schools were once characterised by an aspiration to develop equality and democracy through education (e.g. Ball & Larsson, 1989), the school system of today (2019), following the introduction of free choice of schools, is characterised by growing groups of students in suburban schools with low achievement. These students generally have parents with low education and incomes, and it is clear from many studies that parents' levels of education and income are strongly correlated to the levels of achievement of their children. Without a group of medium- and high-achieving students, schools with a majority of low achievers are the ones that primarily account for poor school results. The 'schoolmate effect', whereby students from different social classes encounter one another and low-achieving pupils attain better results, is no longer realised as it was with a comprehensive school for all in the decades leading up to 2000.

At the same time, there are fast-growing privately based education providers offering careers in schools for medium- and high-achieving students where, as such a student, you meet students like yourself. It is also evident that these private groups are making big profits because the tax-based funding of their schools ends up in profits, as a result of specific recruitment of comparatively well-behaved students, smaller numbers of teachers, and lower-paid and unqualified teachers (Molander, 2017).

The profits made by these private providers are not ploughed back into the school system as a whole but are distributed to shareholders, putting pressure on the schools to make even bigger profits, but there are also demands from parents to give their children high grades, resulting in grade inflation (Vlachos, 2018). In spite of a majority of the Swedish population being critical of this system whereby tax-based funding generates large profits for shareholders, political attempts to stop or at least limit it are opposed and prevented by the antisocialist parties.

So, what can teacher education do today? What kind of teacher professionalism is needed to ensure that we have teachers for democracy: professional accountability or professional responsibility? The authors definitely lean towards professional responsibility and offer us as readers many carefully developed answers. Each chapter of the book provides us with new perspectives because there are so many different dilemmas and challenges to deal with. In addition, at the end of every chapter seven questions are put forward, both to explore many of the dilemmas in greater depth and to expand the frame of reference for how to act as a professional teacher.

Tomas Englund
Senior Professor in Pedagogy
University of Örebro, Sweden

References

Ball, S. & Larsson, S. (eds.) (1989). *The struggle for democratic education: Equality and participation in Sweden*. London: Falmer.

Hansen, D. (2008). Introduction: Why educate teachers? In M. Cochran, S. Feiman-Nemser & D. J. McIntyre (eds.), *Handbook of research on teacher education: Enduring questions in changing contexts* (3rd edn.). New York: Routledge, pp. 5–9.

Molander, P. (2017). *Dags för omprövning – en ESO-rapport om styrning av offentlig verksamhet* [Time for a reappraisal – An ESO report on the governance of public sector activities]. Stockholm, Sweden: Regeringskansliet, Finansdepartementet.

Parker, W. (2003). *Teaching democracy: Unity and diversity in public life*. New York: Teachers College Press.

Robertson, E. (2008). Teacher education in a democratic society: Learning and teaching the practices of democratic participation. In M. Cochran, S. Feiman-Nemser, D. J. McIntyre & K. E. Demers (eds.), *Handbook of research on teacher education: Enduring questions in changing contexts* (3rd edn.). New York: Routledge, pp. 27–44.

Sockett, H. (2008). The moral and epistemic purposes of teacher education. In M. Cochran, S. Feiman-Nemser, D. J. McIntyre & K. E. Demers (eds.), *Handbook of research on teacher education: Enduring questions in changing contexts* (3rd edn.). New York: Routledge, pp. 45–65.

Vlachos, J. (2018). Trust-based evaluation in a market-oriented school system. Stockholm, Sweden: Department of Economics, Stockholm University, and Research Institute of Industrial Economics (IFN), Working Paper No. 1217.

1 Democracy and teacher education dilemmas, challenges and possibilities

An introduction

We have for several years now being researching and lecturing about issues and transformative possibilities related to democracy and (teacher) education not only in Ireland and Sweden, but also in other countries. It is a joy when a lecture stimulates enthusiasm and stirs people's thoughts into motion. However, it is equally important to pause and think about times when teacher educators, experienced teachers, beginning teachers and student teachers express situations they find difficult to handle and comprehend. In various contexts teachers have always stood face to face with **dilemmas** that they feel a pressure and a duty to solve or which stir strong emotions. By dilemmas we mean specific challenges that plead for attention but that lack obvious and/or one-dimensional solutions (e.g. Edling, 2016).

Educators seldom have one **purpose** with education, but many that coexist simultaneously and often collide with each other. Educators here include pre-school teachers, teachers in various educational contexts, and formal educational leaders. Moreover, educators are not governed by one single act or guideline for education but several, which seldom are crystal clear and perhaps even more rarely harmonize with each other. Besides the multitude of purposes and policies, teachers are forced to act in specific contexts and cultures governed by certain values, norms, and structures that most likely are far from identical to those defined on an official policy level (see Chapter 3 for a more detailed analysis of how this policy cycle plays out) – to mention some examples central to teachers' work (e.g. Ball, Maguire & Braun, 2012).

At the same time, there is a tendency in media debates and popular discussions to claim that the **messiness**, i.e. complexity and multilayered features of education can easily be erased or cleansed away by smart (efficient) magic-bullet solutions. This rather simplistic way of engaging with teachers as solely problem-solvers for an inward view – versus other important roles such as public intellectuals, critical thinkers and problem-posers – risks education and teacher education functioning in an oppressive manner (Edling, 2014). Dilemmas do not simply disappear just because people decide to cut off or ignore some disturbing aspects and highlight others (Honig, 1994). On the contrary, the illusion of order and teleology of certainty created by populist debates distant from teachers' everyday practices, risks leaving teachers feeling disillusioned (Santoro, 2017, Snyder, 2017). Santoro (2017) and Zipin & Brennan (2003) refer to teachers' felt sense of demoralization and the ethical suppression of teachers' agency and voices. Parallel, to a profession that is complex, the mood in society, the ways we understand the social order and the role of the school in securing that social order, and going beyond that social order to allow something new to emerge, is changing rapidly. We discuss this new cultural revolution in greater detail in Chapter 3.

Forces influencing (teacher) education and democracy – an overview

Questions regarding democracy, social justice, and ethics are larger than policy in that they have a long history of engaging people in various ways. These questions cannot and should not be made equal with policy. At the same time the power of policy as one major source to define the content of education and subsequently existing political desires and obligations should not be overlooked. Teachers in many European countries today are directed through various global policy agreements and encouraged to work in favour of a broad approach to democracy where struggle for equal conditions and an acknowledgement of everyone's equal value are emphasized as vital (Council of Europe, 2019). This has not always been the case. Research shows that the task to promote a **broad understanding of democracy** is far from obvious, and requires more than common sense, being kind and respectful or simply stressing that "I follow the policy documents required".

We tend to notice aspects we have **knowledge** about and ignore others and also often act in good faith of being well-informed while our speech and actions are coloured by **unconscious prejudices** (Pillow, 2003). Moreover, work involving values in education can evoke **strong emotions** like anger and resistance, since it questions habits, world-views, and social and power relations that have existed for a long time (Edling, 2018).

Overtime and especially in the past decade, since the global economic recession of 2008 in particular, this national grouping of policy actors has increasingly been undermined by the epistemic dominance of new partnerships between **multinational corporations and supranational agencies** that support economic aims, such as the World Bank, the European Commission and the Organisation for Economic Cooperation and Development (OECD), bolstered by an elite grouping of **neo-conservatives** for a practice turn toward legislation and doing 'what works' (McLaren, 2016; Sellar & Lingard, 2013).

Accordingly, the school system has ever since the building of the nation state been an important tool for the government to shape citizens in ways that secure desired ideals, stability, change and development (Edling & Mooney Simmie, 2017; Mooney Simmie & Edling, 2016, 2018). Arendt (1961, 2001) wrote about this in a seminal essay where she argued that 'crisis in education' is a recurring pattern in history and almost always occurs in response to crises in the economy. At this moment, and since global recession in 2008, we have arrived at a new crisis in the global economy, in education and in democracy – in the ways economic theory and political philosophy advances a new view of what it means to be human, to live in society and the concept of the good life.

The new economic policy of **Human Capital Theory** (HCT) is deeply embedded in the notion that the needs of the individual in education and across all forms of human activity bend in an arc in the direction of national economic competitiveness (Tan, 2014). While there is a fuller explanation of HCT in Chapter 3, it is sufficient here to state that HCT advocates for a market-led discourse of education, a customer-led endeavor of rational choice, fulfilling needs for a predetermined package of outcomes and predetermined components in an era of performativity (Ball, 2003, 2016).

Thus the **policy cycle** in education has become more and more the remit of business-interests and their managers. The subordination of human emancipation and democracy in favour of national economic achievement targets has had a profound effect on the (re)conceptualization of teacher identity and pedagogy, from a former view of the art (and possibly the science) of teaching to a science of teaching that is firmly based on evidence-based modes of clinical and empirical practices (Ball, 2003).

In relation to this the western world operates using a new politics of inevitability where there is no alternative and where politics itself is no longer construed as the art of the possible but rather as a **political science** – requiring none other than straightforward rational planning and a fixation on metrics for quality assurance (Snyder, 2017, 2018). A slow undermining of democracy is not only done using rationalism but includes a multitude of strategies (Browning, 2018) including for example, using platforms such as Facebook to spread fake news and harvest detailed personal profiles of social media users without their consent (approximately 87 million people). This illicitly sourced data was then used to target and influence (psychological) behavior change in various identified groupings of unsuspecting voters, for example, seen in the Cambridge Analytica controversy in relation to the US Presidential election and the Brexit Leave campaign in the UK (see podcast in the supplementary reading by journalist Carole Cadwallader as she asks whether free and fair elections are a thing of the past).

Indeed, we live in a **global era of the spectacle** (Debord, 2012) where clashes between various world-views have more often than not become hidden and where the medium often appears as the message. The Brexit vote in the UK to leave the EU, the election of Boris Johnson as leader of the Conservative Party (and Prime Minister), the election of Donald Trump as President of the USA and theadvocacy for Le Pen as President of France point toward the increasing emergence of authoritarian and right-wing politics as contemporary social phenomena that nurture a desire for simple answers to complex problems, a resurgence of nationalism and a turn to perceived past glories, and the expression of fear and racial hatred against migrants and foreigners.

The position of teacher education institutions as a shaper of future teachers has too been subjected to the era of the spectacle. It is often pictured as a low status institution in media and public debate (Cochran-Smith & Lytle, 1998; Edling, 2014; Labaree, 2000, 2004). Subsequently, teacher education as both a solution for the government to shape people, workers and citizens and as an institution often faces severe bashing from media and public debate, and risks creating dilemmas and tensions for teacher educators that need highlighting.

An example of **media bashing of educators** in the media in Ireland is done through careful selection of spokespersons and those who are considered reputable experts. Published articles on education in national newspapers, TV shows and the media tend to focus on either discussion of examination results, comparison with international league tables (e.g. OECD PISA) or the need to scrap the present national examination system. For the most part, they are written and/or presented by leading economists. It suggests that the views of the economist occupy a higher position than the opinions of educators who are specialist researchers. Recent examples include a full-page article on education written in *The Sunday Independent* newspaper by the economist Dan O' Brien and a TV3 show dedicated to the topic of education hosted by the economist David McWilliams.

In Sweden, educators are often regarded as victims of a bad teacher education and as such are not subjected to teacher bashing (Wiklund, 2006, 2012). Current media debates evolve around an image of teacher education as being ideologically infused, postmodern and purely theoretical rather than getting on with the important task for society of applying the latest cutting-edge knowledge emanating from brain-research and engaging itself in a practice turn for success (Edling & Liljestrand, 2019).

Public education reform policies over the past forty years have come under the spotlight as a spectacular failure in terms of educating people to know, to do, to be and to learn to live together in peace and mutual respect (UNESCO, 2015). In the last decade, reform policies that have advocated inclusion, multiculturalism and social cohesion do not appear to have penetrated deep into the psyche of western learners. As a consequence, there is an urgent need for fresh thinking and **critical debate** in many western democratic countries around issues of cultural and ethnic diversity, citizenship, migration and social inequality in this era of performativity, understood more as a discourse of fear for national and individual economic competitiveness (Ball, 2003; Tan, 2014).

At the same time it is important to remember that social processes taking place today are intimately interwoven with past experiences and come with moral significance and the need for a strong case against perfection and this current **teleology of certainty** (Snyder, 2017, 2018). In the aftermath of the two World Wars in the 20th century, democracy was regarded as an antidote to war, armed conflicts, environmental degradation, inequalities and human rights violations in European and Anglo-Saxon countries (Carr, 2008; Dahlstedt & Olson, 2013, Edling, 2016). Brutalities of the wars were created, not the least, through people's degrading perceptions of others as different/non-humans, evoking the need for securing an ethical dimension in democracy that stresses the importance of everyone's equal value (UN, UNESCO, see Chapter 2).

As a desire to avoid past harms, democracy as it is understood in many countries today is not just about **procedures** such as election, majority rule and voting but has also an ethical dimension which Dewey refers to as a **form of life** that takes into account the moral consequences of plurality expressed through people's everyday practices and ways of thinking and being in the world (Edling, 2016). Whereas democracy tends to be regarded as a hope for a better future, it is at the same time fragile and vulnerable – always on the verge of becoming rather a fixed (police) state and regime (Biesta, 2013; Edling, 2016; Mouffe, 2000, see also Chapter 2).

The examples of forces influencing (teacher) education described above and the efforts needed to create peaceful ways of existing in society often generate dilemmas for teachers and as such need to be taken into account when discussing democracy as an educational content in general.

Democracy and dilemmas

The narrow and broad approach to understand teacher professionalism, described above, can be compared to a narrow and broad way of comprehending democracy. **Democracy** appears at times to be interpreted in **dualistic terms**, i.e. an inclination of dividing the world into two inseparable pieces which are valued in terms of superiority/inferiority. Should democracy be about forms and procedures like voting, majority rule or should it be about what takes place in the flow of human life? Concepts such as **democracy as procedure** and **democracy as a form of life** (Dewey, 1916), **thin** and **thick democracy** (Armando & Apple, 2002; Carr, 2008) and **shallow** and **deep democracy** (Furman & Shields, 2005) all give the impression that democracy stands between these two distinct choices. However, rather than seeing them as **either–or**, black and white alternatives we maintain that it is rather a question about where the scope of the responsibilities linked to democratic aspirations should be drawn. Should democracy solely be about voting, principles and procedures or should it also take into account the consequences, various principles, choices of action, ways of thinking for people's life conditions, which is tightly linked and knotted to issues of plurality?

Another useful way of approaching this is to consider **discourses** in teacher education and to view the overarching emphasis in public policy and the systemic resourcing of teachers and teacher educators to achieve specific learning intentions with young people and student teachers. By discourse we mean the policy intentions and justifications that frame knowledge and which are always interlaced with values and differential power relations and depend on whose interests are being served and legitimated (Mooney Simmie & Edling, 2018). While in former times public (political) policy intentions were strongly connected to the moral goods of teaching and notions of good teachers as reflective practitioners (Santoro, 2017), nowadays, policies are tightly defined within laws and legislation. This **juridification** mandates teachers and school leaders to be compliant with policies and produce predetermined measurable outcomes or risk losing their occupation through non-compliance and fear instilled through statutory obligation and the 'terrors of performativity' (Ball, 2003; Skerritt, 2018).

Gunter (2001) speaks about four discourses of teacher education as: scientific, instrumental, humanistic and critical. A **scientific discourse** puts the focus on gathering data and effect sizes for an evidence-based practice. An **instrumental discourse** speaks to an expedient set of guidelines and handbooks that coach teachers into technical mastery through apprenticeship, observation and most significantly expedient modes of imitation. A **humanistic discourse** speaks to community, relations and the interdependence of teachers and teacher educators through various partnerships and productive forms of mentoring and learning for mutuality and co-inquiry (Mooney Simmie & Lang, 2012, 2018, 2019; Mooney Simmie & Moles, 2011). However, to assure all three discourses as dynamic and dialectical discourses of education and teacher education - rather than risk-management for a teleology of certainty – Gunter (2001) argues that it is the presence of the fourth discourse, the **'critical'** – with **capability** for critical thinking and critical consciousness of diversity issues and social justice – that allows these discourses to be called education and to contain what Biesta (2013) calls the beautiful risk of education (Nussbaum, 2010).

What tends to characterize democracy is the importance, while at the same time difficulty, in handling **plurality** (see for instance Mouffe, 2000; Weedon, 1999; Edling, 2012/2018). We understand plurality as being about various groups in society categorized in terms of social class, gender, ethnicity, ability, sex, religion and so forth and about differences between people as unique subjects (Mouffe, 2000). While difference becomes an important part of democratic ideologies and thus vital to protect, it has, at the same time, a long history of being cast out from society, treated as something disgusting or/and dangerous. For example, difference can be about being fat in societies premiering thin people, being dark in a country of mainly white people, being homosexual when heterosexuality is premiered, but also in relation to other aspects in life like having a different sense of humour that does not correspond with the majority, and even dressing differently than the cultural norm (Edling, 2016).

Whereas plurality is emphasized as valuable to protect in a modern democracy in contrast to ancient times, there is an in-built dilemma that pleads for attention, namely the tensions between treasuring plurality and the need to restrain it (e.g. Benhabib, 2004; Ljunggren, 2012). The political scientist Andreas Johansson Heinö at University of Gothenburg identified three dilemmas linked to democracy in modern societies, using Sweden as a case study. The first dilemma involves the question of **inclusion/exclusion**: who are to be included and excluded [in society and education]? The question has generally been answered with the help of national belonging but in the multicultural countries we now experience with the increase of refugees and globalization, the question becomes more complex. The second dilemma has to do with **adjustment/freedom**: to what extent are those within democratic systems to adjust to democratic values and to what extent is the state to respect their right to freedom? Finally, Johansson identifies a third dilemma which he terms the dilemma of **legitimization**, which implies that democracy is nothing without the citizens' active agreement in the sovereignty of democracy. Previously, the idea of the social welfare society grounded in the logic of nationalism had functioned as a glue, but it is now insufficient to handle social challenges (Johansson Heinö, 2009).

Besides democracy, plurality is at the heart of the notion of **dilemma**, which Bonnie Honig (1994) a political, legal, and feminist theorist specializing in democratic theory elegantly states "[d]ilemmas – situations in which two values, obligations, or commitments conflict and there is no right thing to do – pose the question of difference and the ineradicability of conflict in a specific and ordinarily familiar setting" (p. 568). It is not possible to solve a dilemma by finding what is the right or correct way to act since there are multiple correct ways to act. If the focus in education solely becomes directed upon reducing doubt there is a risk that dilemmas – which have existed, and continue to exist as long as there are humans with various value systems – will end up in the shadows and make it difficult to take deep/broad dimensions of democracy seriously (e.g. Honig 1994, 2009; Mouffe, 2000).

Dilemmas and **controversies** bear significant resemblances. In Robert Stradling's definition from 1984 he defines controversial issues as "Questions that deeply divide a society and which generates contradictory explanations" (p. 121). Vital for Stradling is to keep controversies and contradictions that arise in everyday education alive rather than wait and solely rely on solutions from external experts. Keeping controversies alive means not losing touch with context along with the experiences, knowledge, and values accompanying actors in the setting (ibid.). The concepts **topic, problems**, and **issues** when discussing controversies in education are by Diane Hess (2009) described as tools that can help orient in an otherwise confusing mixture of levels and focus points (p. 37–49). In this book the *topic* democracy and (teacher) education can be regarded as dilemmatic spaces (Fransson & Grannäs, 2011; Honig, 1994) that give rise to certain *problems* in relation to plurality or plural world-views and which in turn raise specific *issues*. Some of these problems and issues are to be discussed in this book.

The majority – if not all – textbooks about democracy and teacher education of the last twenty years focus upon solutions to promote a certain ideal of democracy rather than illuminating unsolvable dilemmas that teacher educators are struggling with in their everyday practices due to the unavoidable presence of plurality and diversity. Rather than overcoming dilemmas in a problem-solving view of evidence-based teaching, instead we argue that dilemmas are important to highlight and explore in order to navigate in the terrain of education and teaching in a more thoughtful and sensitive way. During our lectures and conversations with experienced teachers, teacher educators and student teachers about democracy in education we have encountered concepts, ideas and dilemmas which plead for attention. We aim to create a dialogue between these practice dilemmas, our reflexive positioning as teacher educators and theory and research. In this book Sweden and Ireland are used as starting-points, but the dilemmas have bearing outside the borders of these countries.

Sweden and the Republic of Ireland – background and context

The dilemmas chosen in the book all stem from Sweden and the Republic of Ireland (Ireland). Although the examples might be of value to countries all over the world it still important to provide a brief background of the two countries' teacher education institutions.

Teacher education in Sweden

Teacher education has existed in Sweden ever since the introduction of the elementary school (Folk School) in the middle of the 19th century. The teacher education just like education in general was based on a parallel school system and it was first in 1977 that both small school seminars and school seminars became integrated within higher education (Linné, 1996). Today, Sweden is a **secular country** which means that there is a clear division between religion and the state, rendering religion to be a private rather than public matter (Svanberg & Westerlund, 2008). Sweden has a population of approximately ten million people and has twenty-eight teacher education institutions scattered across the country. Teacher education institutions are strongly regulated by the state, more so than any other higher education institutions. Since 2011, it is possible to select four different teacher education programs, namely: as pre-school teacher, elementary teacher, subject teacher and vocational teacher (e.g. Hallsén, 2013).

Teacher education is governed by various aims and purposes, which require interpretation and which are influenced by international treaties like core values formulated by the Council of Europe, UN's Universal Declaration of Human Rights. Moreover, just as many other countries, Sweden is influenced by the Global Education Reform Movement (GERM), hence adapting to similar educational policy reforms worldwide. As a consequence of this, teacher education in Sweden has established a core curriculum with distinct core subjects (e.g. Edling, 2014; Priestley & Biesta, 2013a; Ross, 2000). Even though various countries do not approach the core in the same way (Priestley & Biesta, 2013b), they are nevertheless similar when it comes to a new dominant stress on economic instrumentalism and individual development (Yates & Collin, 2010). There are seven core elements in the teacher education curriculum in Sweden of which democracy is emphasized in the first one:

- history of the school system, its organisation and conditions as well as the core values of early childhood education, including fundamental democratic values and human rights
- syllabus theory and didactics
- theory of knowledge and research methodology
- development, learning and special needs education
- social relationships, conflict management and leadership
- assessing and analysing learning and development
- evaluation and development processes.[1]

As a consequence of this, teacher education in Sweden has established a core curriculum with distinct core subjects that all teacher education institutions in a country need to incorporate into their program. These are specified in the Swedish Council for Higher Education (2015):

- demonstrate the capacity to communicate and instill core educational values, including human rights and the fundamental democratic values.[2]

Teacher education in Ireland

The first (public) school system of education in Ireland saw the introduction of the elementary school (Primary School) by the British in the middle of the 19th century, a system described as 'payment by results' (Ó'Buachalla, 1988). After Irish independence, in the second decade of the 20th century, education and teacher education sought to quickly establish a system of education that gave recognition and respect for what was deeply felt to be lost in 700 years of British colonial rule – a national identity inextricably linked with (Catholic) religion, the (Gaelic) language and Gaelic games.

The education system adopted is, just as Sweden, described as a publicly aided system where the state pays for teachers' salaries and structural repairs/buildings and the churches; in particular, the majority Catholic Church, provides the schools and holds patronage. By contrast to secular Sweden, the role of the Catholic Church as a major policy player in Irish education has not abated with the ethos and characteristic spirit of schools protected in the Education Act (1998) and where 92% of primary schools and over 60% of secondary schools operate under patronage of the Catholic Church. In a similar way, teacher education institutes were closely associated with the churches who oversaw what was understood as the primacy of the moral goods of education and teaching (Coolahan, 2001; Mooney Simmie & Edling, 2016).

Ireland has a population of more than four and a half million people. It has nineteen teacher education institutions scattered across the country, currently undergoing amalgamation to seven national centres of excellence (Sahlberg, 2012, 2018). Nowadays, teacher education institutions are increasingly regulated by the state, more so than any other higher education institute using a new emphasis on statutory regulation and compliance for new modes of juridification and public accountability.

Under Section 38 of the Teaching Council Act, *Initial Teacher Education* (ITE) programs are provided with criteria and guidelines from the Teaching Council – the professional standards body for teaching established on a statutory basis in 2006. For example, within the criteria and guidelines for ITE program providers for post-primary/secondary teacher education the curriculum is sub-divided into Subject Disciplinary Knowledge and Skills (50%); Foundational Studies and Professional Studies (25%); School Placement in a practicum setting (25%) with fifteen mandatory elements (Teaching Council, 2017):

- Early Childhood Education [Adolescent Learning]
- Inclusive Education [Special Education, Multiculturalism, Disadvantage, etc.]
- Numeracy
- Literacy
- The Teacher as Professional/Reflective Practitioner/Researcher
- Developing a Professional Portfolio
- Parents in Education – Co-operation and Collaboration
- The School as a Learning Community
- Preparation for School Placement
- Teaching, Learning and Assessment (including School and Classroom Planning)
- Differentiation
- Behaviour Management
- ICT in Teaching and Learning
- Legislation in Relation to School and Classroom
- The Teacher and External Agencies

However, there is no direct connection to any explicit view of democracy and plurality other than what is inferred by 'Inclusive Education'. Previous studies we conducted show that there are few mentions of the word democracy in policy documents in teacher education in Ireland (Edling & Mooney Simmie, 2017) and there is nowhere that democracy is explicitly portrayed as recognition, respect and celebration of difference along the lines of ethnicity, race, religion etc. The question of difference and 'other' appears to be understood more as assimilation into the existing culture rather than a fluid and dialectical understanding of democracy and plurality.

Cases of dilemmas

During the years we have encountered numerous dilemmas in relation to the topics addressed in the book and founded on these we have made a selection based on recurring experiences, stories from other teacher educators, synopses of studies undertaken by experienced teachers and school leaders, and written reflections from student teachers in Sweden and Ireland. These dilemmas can both be about events directly taking place at a teacher education institution and events where a student teacher describes their experiences in an education placement setting where they have completed their practice. We have used pseudonyms in all cases of undergraduate student teacher thoughts and reflections.

While dilemmas occur due to a range of different value systems colliding they often tend to occur in a seemingly dichotomous form in real-world settings which means that we have chosen to present them as x versus y but with the intention to keep the tensions between dilemmas alive and in dialogue. Although the dilemmas mentioned in this book are born in specific educational contexts, they can very well be used as a source for discussion in other countries as well. Major themes include the contrast between totalitarian ideologies versus democratic ideologies, and the intimate relationships between democracy and emancipation, plurality, justice, and ethics. Thus, the purpose of the book is to provide a textbook for (teacher) educators, educational leaders, student teachers, beginning teachers and experienced teachers grappling with issues, challenges, dilemmas and possibilities of democracy and (teacher) education in their educational settings. We approach democracy as a (subject) content in education which needs to be closely scrutinized and for this reason we turn to curriculum theory.

Curriculum theory

Concepts such as **pre-school, school, teacher educational institutions** are here understood as organizations where education is carried out (e.g. Ekerwald & Säfström, 2012, p. 3). Accordingly, education is applied here as a broader concept than teacher education, pre-school and school institutions, which makes it possible to regard them from a greater distance and pose questions such as: why are teacher educational institutions, pre-schools and schools structured as they are? Why do teachers choose the content they choose? What kind of social mission should teacher education and schools have? **Curriculum** here has a broad connotation, incorporating perceptions in time forming the content of education and also the conditions for people involved. Drawing on **curriculum theory** we focus on how perceptions coloured by culture and hegemony influence the content, methods, purposes and aims of education (Lundgren, 1989, pp. 20–21) and bring forth the individual's possibilities to act and (proactively) contribute to and shape their society (Englund, 1997).

In this regard, curriculum has traditionally been understood as a selection from culture and has often been depicted as a 'struggle' between various interest groups in society for the soul of the curriculum. This understanding goes well beyond any notion of content and subject disciplinary knowledge and moves into the realm of philosophical and deliberative reasoning and diplomatic negotiation between a wide variety of policy actors, not all with equal power (Ball, 2008; Mooney Simmie, 2012, 2014, 2020; Mooney Simmie & Lang, 2020; Ó'Buachalla, 1988; O'Sullivan, 2005). Interest groups can appear as combinations of policy actors such as the state, students, policymakers, politicians, church-interests, business-interests, teacher unions, researcher interests and parent groups.

While all research needs to be based on evidence we argue that **evidence-based research**, understood as quantitative empirical research based on the philosophy of positivism is far from enough. Within evidence-based research, content tends to be taken for granted and is often regarded as value-free (e.g. Klette, 2007, p. 148) and reduced to instruction and methods (*Didactics*) rather than examining the meaning of content and debating this in relation to various educational purposes. Contrary to this stance the German term *Didaktik* focuses on meaning and selections, how content is taught and learned in education as well as how this changes over time due to context. Within this starting point it becomes important to acknowledge the relational, complex, plural and dilemmatic aspects of education (Edling, 2016).

Different ways of grasping teacher professionalism in (teacher) education

A definition of a good (teacher) educator is dependent upon context and hence what is deemed as desirable characteristics for this profession in a specific society. As such, the first question is not how to make teachers efficient (efficient in relation to what), but what education is about and why this specific way of educating is important (and for whom). Historically two different approaches to teachers' professional responsibilities have dominated in (teacher) education: teachers as **intellectuals** and/or teachers as **technicians** (Ball, 1995), universal or practice oriented teachers (Colnerud & Granström, 2002; Frelin, 2010), and teachers with an **outside-in-professionalism** or **inside-out-professionalism** (Stanley & Stronach, 2013; Edling, 2016, see also Chapter 4).

Although various researchers have labeled teachers' responsibilities differently, the descriptions share many important characteristics. Are teachers expected to merely follow external instructions from experts drawing from large quantitative studies claiming universal solutions for all and/or are teachers also to take into account the dynamics, flow and uniqueness of everyday practice? The former standpoint, teachers as technicians, regards teachers as technicians who only have to comply and follow orders from the outside ripped from their own judgements and the particularity and peculiarity of cultures and contexts. The latter, teachers as intellectuals, stresses that although external (public policy) directives are necessary they are not sufficient, as it is teachers' judgement that needs to be developed (Edling, 2016) and become informed by research. A **research-informed approach**, contrary to an evidence-based approach, is here grasped as a rich combination of philosophical co-inquiry and empirical research, inclusive of quantitative and qualitative research and interpretations of what teachers encounter in their everyday contexts.

Starting from curriculum theory and a research-informed way of approaching education means that a teacher (educator) and student teacher need to start observing how **meaning** is expressed through language-use in a particular context, how meaning is always linked to certain values, how meaning defines what is worth knowing and not knowing, and how you select content in relation to specific educational purposes which automatically positions you to justify your selections and to negotiate what should be excluded (e.g. Bingham & Sidorkin, 2004; Edling, 2016; Englund, 1997).

Thus, the procedure stimulates an awareness of how **content** – understood here as subject disciplinary knowledge, theoretical knowledge, attitudes, skills, values, dispositions and taste – what is taught and assessed in policy terms and in practice settings never just exists as an objective item, but affects people's lives, thereby rendering them to have moral and ethical implications in need of being scrutinized (Edling, 2016; Englund, 1997; Säfström & Månson 2010,. Methods are important here as well, but they are never enough, requiring teacher (educator's) who can not only interpret and analyze what they do but show capability to 'critically read the world' (Freire, 1970).

Juggling different educational purposes

Education carries several major and often competing roles, including providing access to knowledge for **qualifications** for members in a society involving specific knowledge, skills, knowledge based practices, as well as understandings of the wider world generated from that knowledge (see Chapter 5 for a deeper exploration of knowledge and democracy). Education also has an important role in **socializing** young people as citizens into a desired order that is political, cultural or/and social in nature. Finally, education can be said to have a third function, namely **subjectification**, where education is depicted as emancipatory spaces where people can enter as unique subjects, beyond or in the ruptures, gaps and discursive spaces of socialization and qualification (Biesta, 2010, Edling, 2016, see also Chapter 4). In order to be able to navigate professionally in this terrain, teachers' judgement and critical constructive efforts at unearthing hidden assumptions becomes immensely important as the reflexive dangers of symbolic violence are never very far away (see Chapter 7).

Therefore, education can be described to have three very general purposes and desires that at times collide with each other, namely: **economic, personal**, and – in many countries but far from all – **democratic desires**. Indeed, education can be regarded as a vital means to strengthen economic prosperity, secure individuals' personal happiness, aspirations, health and growth, and create a democratic society where at times social justice and emancipation are regarded as important to pay regard to (e.g. Biesta, 2011, p. 63). How these three possible contributions of education are to be understood and brought to life in everyday education and policy is not fixed but dependent on what a society and public (political) policy regards as desirable in a certain context and timeline.

In order to provide teachers capable of juggling various social demands necessary to secure this individual and national economic competitiveness, teacher education has been elevated in all public policies to a key position. **Teacher education institutions** educate future teachers with knowledge, skills, expectations, taste, attitudes etc. that all impact on the processes taking place in school, whilst public (political) policy expectations influence what qualification, socialization and emancipatory spaces for subjectification teacher educational institutions are to offer. In this way, there is a symbiotic connection between school systems and teacher education institutions; it helps remind us that the content of teacher education is never fixed and obvious but stands in relation to the kind of people, workers and citizens the education system wants to advance at any one time (e.g. Hallsén, 2013).

This difference in how to approach teacher professionalism can also be grasped as a tension between **Dolor complexitatis** and **Amor complexitatis**. Complexity exists, in the same way that plurality exists, whether or not teachers and politicians want it or not – the question is whether complexity should be ignored or taken into account:

> We believe that we can never eliminate complexity in education, not even by the most sophisticated educational strategies. Education is about people and therefore education is complex, just as complex as human life itself. The question is how to deal with this complexity in education, and how to benefit from it, even.
>
> (Bakker, et al., 2016, p. viii)

Whereas, the more technical approach to teacher professionalism expressed as an outside-in professionalism is based on a massive reduction and fear of complexity (dolor complexitatis) the practice oriented view, here labeled inside-out-professionalism, stresses the need to embrace and come to terms with complexity (amor complexitatis). The terms dolor (pain) and amor (love/passion) play with emotions linked to teachers' everyday work. Since complexity is entangled in human life any reduction of complexity is a reduction of this human life and pleads for ethical awareness (e.g. Bakker & Montessori, 2016). What aspects of human life should be ignored and taken into account? What is the consequences of reduction for the people involved? How much complexity can we as educators and teachers, student teachers, beginning teachers and experienced teachers handle?

Historically there is a tendency to align with one of two extreme stand-points (Dewey, 1916). For instance, people appear to either love complexity or hate complexity. In contrast to this view we argue for the need for teachers, student teachers, public policymakers and media to leave the safe haven of either–or and subsequently navigate in-between these poles. Moreover, this clearly requires a new sensitivity to dilemmas and controversies that might occur in their everyday work.

One way to grasp this in-between field is to turn to Biesta's (2012) term '**middle ground**'. Existing in a world with others, who do not necessarily reason or act the way I do risks causing resistance and this can be handled in various ways. We can for a start violate or render extinct the object of resistance by actively denying the presence of the Other or by literally killing him/her/them (genocide). This extreme strategy destroys the possibilities of people's differences to enter in the world and subsequently destroys the *social* world itself in favour of a dominating I (singularity of being). Another extreme strategy is to run away and avoid anything that feels strange and hence dangerous. The lack of engagement with others risks causing violence to the self, since a withdrawal from the world implies an impossibility to be seen, heard and become a subject together with others. Both strategies can be compared to dolor complexitatis, i.e. a dislike of and hence an avoidance of complexity.

However, rather than describing the third road as a love of complexities, Biesta pictures it as a rather frustrating place to be in, since it forces people to grow up and engage with that which causes resistance without falling into the temptation of destroying the world or ourselves. This temptation to first set up an Other to possibly imitate and later to rebel against and/or harm the person has been previously studied by René Girard and more recently elaborated by McLaren & Jandrić (2019). It is understood as a primal instinct for human survival, starting off possibly as a positive way of imitating and making progress that can later turn to 'mimetic rivalry' and making scapegoats of those who are somehow different. History has many examples of 'mimetic rivalry' between various peoples, tribes and groups that have resulted in blood sacrifices, murder and genocide (see Chapter 2 and Chapter 6).

The challenge in education and democracy is to keep this in-between field or middle ground vibrant. Hence, instead of being spokespersons for a single interpretation of democracy and (teacher) education or simply state that democracy and (teacher) education is complex and therefore resign in desperation, we aim with this book to pose certain re-occurring dilemmas that teacher educators and student teachers encounter and link these to philosophical inquiry and research findings.

The intention is not to overcome dilemmas or make them disappear but to use them as a source for thinking in new ways that hopefully enable teachers to navigate and act in the terrain of education more productively and sensitively. To put it differently, although some dilemmas never disappear just as complexity, resistance and plurality never do, we believe that an increased consciousness about backgrounds, contexts and connections might function as guides in the otherwise frustrating, passionate, indifferent, scary, and/or joyful field of education.

Conclusion

Central in this book is that official public (political) policy desires cannot and should not be made equal to what takes place in educational settings (Ball, Maguire & Braun, 2012). Educators do not enter a fixed order of things when they start working. Rather they enter an ecological, organic and dynamic practice (e.g. Dewey, 1916) where their scientifically informed knowledge bases along with a sensitivity for the people and contexts they encounter are vital components for shaping education in relation to desired aims and outcomes. This sensitivity plays a major role in the complex interweaving of education, a terrain that is often messy and complex (Mooney Simmie, Moles & O'Grady, 2019) and dilemmatic (Edling, 2016; Fransson & Grannäs, 2011; Honig; 1994).

This messiness arises from a practice where human relations are at its core and where the heart-work of teaching and learning can at times be felt as overwhelming and a strategy to turn toward empirical solutions or technical and instructional methods might feel enticing. Simultaneously, there is enough evidence from research indicating that **universal methods**, methods that function everywhere and hence in all contexts are not sufficient even though they might be a useful support. It is equally necessary that teachers interpret, deconstruct and value the practice they are involved with in order to handle the complex set of purposes and aims along with preconditions that often exist parallel to each other and more often than not collide with each other, creating tensions, contradictions and feelings of dilemmas. In a court case in Sweden it was stated that "it is not reasonable that the personnel, by avoiding interpreting signals can stay unknowing of what is going on between pupils at a school" (Swedish National Board of Education, 2014, p. 28, our translation, in Edling, 2016).

In this introductory chapter, and again in Chapter 4 we will show how this way of reasoning is based on an inside-out-professionalism where teachers freely access discursive spaces and affordances to make well-grounded judgments based on contextual needs, in contrast to an outside-in-professionalism where the role of the teacher is to un-reflexively comply with the latest policies and results from large-scale quantitative studies (Stanley & Stronach, 2013). But what does this really mean? Are teachers to be guided by their subjective world-views and make wild interpretations in their daily work?

No, we are not saying that, not at all. Research about teachers' professional judgment stress the importance of teachers' competences and skills along with their susceptibility in the relational world and communal-orientation of practice (e.g. Frelin, 2010; Kelchtermans, 1993; Schön, 1983). Indeed, it is never about doing whatever we want, since teachers' work, *de facto*, is governed by public policy and specific purposes and aims. Central in teachers work is to systematically understand the pieces of this complex epistemic puzzle, the layers, dimensions, the clashes between theory, research, experience and practice that constitute the profession since they influence teachers' work in constructing educational practice and mindfulness in the present.

However, as teacher educators and researchers we are concerned (see Chapter 3) with what Marcel (2013) calls the heuristic, critical and social aspects of education and with recent public policy developments that narrowly regard teachers' practice as a highly skilled professional practice for an occupation that merely requires interrogation of self and practice and that fails to require capability to critically read the wider world and/or to regard democracy as an organic entity of becoming rather than a fixed social order (Freire, 1970; Nussbaum, 2010).

We understand that teachers can be highly skilled and highly effective, but without understanding why they do what they do and what it is that is rendered efficient (and what is not) – including capability to problem pose as well as problem solve – there is a real risk that public policies and teachers' actions will merely achieve the opposite to what is intended.

This book aims to raise these issues for deeper scrutiny and to make a productive contribution in this regard for all teachers, student teachers, beginning teachers, experienced teachers and school leaders.

The structure of the book

The book is divided into eight chapters and progresses from a historical overview of democracy at the outset toward a deeper gaze at the policy cycle and the mainstream ways that policy when moving from the official state level to the school level is mostly interpreted as a linear rational process of policy implementation. We then move in the direction of teasing out different aspects of teacher professionalism and seeking to ascertain what this might mean, first in terms of teachers' knowledge and reflexivity. We consider the increasing dominance of a strong discourse of competition in education (Chapter 6) and what this means for the field of educational research formerly considered a soft social science that is based on relationships and human encounter. We argue that educators, teacher educators and researchers need to interrogate their reflexive positioning, as good intentions while necessary are never enough (Pillow, 2003). In this regard we eschew the notion that teacher educators and educational researchers can justify any claim that they come from nowhere and can somehow behave as neutral and objective observers. Finally, we draw together the key principles, concepts and ideas considered in relation to teachers' democratic assignment in the final chapter.

The chapter headings are laid out according to the following titles: (1) introduction, (2) a historical background, (3) the policy cycle, (4) teacher professionalism, (5) democracy and knowledge, (6) Darwinian strength and purpose, (7) reflexive strategies for a vibrant democracy, and (8) teachers' democratic assignment for plurality. Chapters 2–7 highlight specific dilemmas which student teachers, experiences teachers, school leaders and teacher educators in Sweden and Ireland have expressed. The final Chapter 8 aims to gather the key concepts and principles discussed in order to navigate more thoughtfully and sensitively in the field of teacher education and practice settings while, at the same time, aiming to provide a tentative conclusion. We now summarize the content of each chapter:

Chapter 2 Historical background

Neither democracy nor teacher education exist outside history and the purpose of this chapter is to explore how democracy has become an important ideology and political governing form in many western democratic countries since the Second World War. The chapter highlights how democracy and democratic ideals are closely interlaced with emancipatory desires, ethics, equity, plurality and a will to establish just and peaceful societies. Hence, democracy as a political governing-form and life-form has never just passively erupted, but has come into being through human struggle and often in tension with totalitarian ideologies existing parallel with democracy, like dictatorship, fascism, and Nazism. This chapter gives an overview of various traditions of democracy and their influence on (teacher) education, linked to concepts such as broad democracy and narrow democracy. At the end, the ideals of democracy are placed in relation to current tendencies taking place in many societies where totalitarian ideologies are revived on a public and political level through democratic elections.

Chapter 3 The policy cycle

Since the advent of schooling as an instrument of the nation state, the education policy cycle has been shaped by economic and political philosophies and has changed direction several times to reflect this. Policy borrowing and comparison between countries has always been a feature. However, what has changed in recent years, particularly since the global recession of 2008, has been the epistemic dominance and speed of globalization and technologization and the interplay between new modes of network governance and superstructures, flows and assemblages. This market-led discourse has gained dominance in education and across all human activity for an 'actuarial' entrepreneurial self for individual competitiveness, new quality management and national economic competitiveness in a new era of performativity. This policy imperative is facilitated by reforms in the direction of 'teacher learning', 'lifelong learning' and 'self-directed' learning, found for example in Sweden, Ireland and Australia. In this chapter we examine dilemmas in relation to the policy cycle – whether policy is understood as implemented in linear rational ways or as policy enactment using complex, creative and critical translations and interpretations. We show how these reforms are not only changing what teachers do but are calling up new types of teachers and teacher educators who are focused on policy compliance and providing evidence of predetermined and successful outcomes.

Chapter 4 Teacher professionalism

In this chapter dilemmas linked to various ways of understanding professionalism at/in (teacher) education and subsequently the democratic assignment are portrayed and discussed from multiple perspectives. Particularly two ways of understanding teacher professionalism are highlighted, namely an inside-out professionalism and outside-in professionalism which are placed in relationship to holistic (broad) perspectives and atomistic (narrow) perspectives. The dilemmas created in the clash between broad and narrow views on teacher professionalism are intimately linked to various scientific traditions, such as natural/medical sciences influenced by positivism and humanism/social sciences influenced by a range of perspectives used for interpreting the social world. Whereas natural sciences are based on four principles: essentialism, dualism, visibility and eliminating doubt (plurality), advocates within social and humanistic sciences maintain that these principles are insufficient and at times harmful towards people and education. The chapter explores how education can be understood as a soft science where the element of unique people and organic practice renders absolute certainty and causality impossible. This pleads for a different platform for education beyond either–or perceptions, and as such allowing space for teachers who can interpret their surroundings based on previous knowledge and a susceptibility for the presence.

Chapter 5 Democracy and knowledge

This chapter considers teachers' specialist knowledge base and the unrelenting push nowadays for credentials and qualifications in education. In particular the chapter addresses the politics of knowledge, such as, how knowledge is connected to differential power and social relations, what is deemed as the most valuable knowledge at any one time, who claims to own this judgement, to whom in society this knowledge is distributed and how and in what ways is this sub-division of knowledge forms (e.g. disciplinary knowledge, theoretical knowledge, professional knowledge) intimately connected with democracy and equity. In former times there was a clear distinction in hierarchy between the dominance of the regulatory discourse (e.g. philosophy, rationalism) and the subordination of an instructional discourse (e.g. skills, measurement, empiricism). This has broken down in the commodification of education and the resulting divorce of knowledge from the knower. In this chapter, we consider some dilemmas and implications of this redistribution of knowledge for teachers in their practices and in public policy.

Chapter 6 Darwinian strength

What is problematized in this chapter are dilemmas created between a desire to promote people's well-being by opposing various forms of violence like oppression, bullying, discrimination and violation and what we have already described as a historical disgust for weakness (see Chapter 2). Ideas about everyone's equal worth, cherishing of plurality, a will not to harm others along with a sensitivity to people's conditions are some central cornerstones in a broad view of democracy. These values awaken a need to be open to others' vulnerability which at times may create reactions of disgust enhanced by current dominant world-views stressing competition, individual strength and autonomy. The chapter explores how the concepts weakness and strength have a history of being treated in a dualistic and narrow fashion and with clear connection to gender, where weakness is linked to feminine values and strength to masculine values. Moreover, the chapter explores how disgust for weakness, drawing on the research of Darwin and Spencer, was applied during Nazism and contributed in the eruption of mass-violence that followed in its after wake. The chapter ends by providing alternative perceptions of weakness and strength in educational situations.

Chapter 7 Teacher reflexivity

This chapter focuses on deconstructing what we understand by a 'critical reflexive' gaze and examines dilemmas in this regard. We draw from work in becoming a critically reflective teacher through accessing lenses of self-interrogation; evaluation with a peer; evaluation with students and the perspectives of literature and research. We view reflective practice as a deeply 'uncomfortable' exercise. We add to the debate in terms of insistence on the power of imagination and the need for educators to question taken-for-granted assumptions underpinning practices, including capability to question authority and to hold power to account. In this chapter we are arguing for teachers to unearth their own positionality and to identify hidden aspects of their own 'habitus' that can often be unconscious and can interfere with the development of an 'uneasy social conscience' required for teaching *for, about, of* and *thro*ugh democracy. We distinguish between reflexive work and new debased modes of self-evaluation in teacher education for the production of a pre-determined package of components for a risk-managed application of expert knowledge generated elsewhere.

Chapter 8 Teachers' democratic assignment

This chapter revisits our earlier definition of teachers' democratic assignment and provides the reader with a synthesis of the key principles and main concepts and ideas threading through the chapters of this book. We show how democracy has been reframed in recent years in policy reforms, at European level, and in particular in Sweden and Ireland. This reframing of democracy as rather shallow is commensurate with a new diminished role of the nation state in a policy cycle dominated by supranational interests. This epistemic dominance is grasped as a new market-led discourse underpinned by Human Capital Theory – for a linear rational view of the human being as a self-absorbed and utility driven animal concerned with her/his own competitive advancement and readily moulded in the direction of national economic competiveness. Our studies examining the changing paradigm shift in teacher education and democracy in Sweden and Ireland have shown how this neoliberal subjectification plays out in national policies and how it is acutely felt in the dilemmatic spaces of teachers' everyday practices.

Supplementary readings: podcasts related to education and democracy.

1   Professor Stephen J. Ball explaining his post-modern take on policy as localised complexity
     21 Years After "What is Policy?" by Stephen Ball, for Discourse: Studies in the Cultural Politics of Education, 06/11/2014
     www.youtube.com/watch?v=xrzXi-_5SHA
2   Professor Maxine Greene speaking to new teachers about her broad democratic view of education and capacity to imagine and change
     Maxine Green – To New Teachers
     www.youtube.com/watch?v=b_raVMnP57w
3   Professor Noam Chomsky. Broadcast on Democracy Now On What's Really Going On! 12/04/2019
     www.youtube.com/watch?v=FvQk1eDS8Ko
4   Philosopher Slavoj ZiZek discusses the fate of Europe with the former Greek Finance Minister and economist Professor Yanis Varoufakis, and Wikeleaks whistleblower Julian Asange
     Europe is Kaput – Long Live Europe, 06/01/2016
     www.youtube.com/watch?v=MORRo-B1xCY
5   TED talk by the journalist Carol Cadwallader confronting the heads of social media platforms in relation to the (unethical) practice of harvesting personal data for

influencing election outcomes in democracies around the world: she asks are free and fair elections a thing of the past?
Facebook's role in Brexit – and the Threat to Democracy, 10/06/2019
www.youtube.com/watch?v=OQSMr-3GGvQ

Notes

1 www.uhr.se/en/start/laws-and-regulations/Laws-and-regulations/The-Higher-Education-Ordinance/Annex-2/ [2018.11.09]
2 www.uhr.se/en/start/laws-and-regulations/Laws-and-regulations/The-Higher-Education-Ordinance/Annex-2/ [2018-11-29]

References

Arendt, Hannah. (2001). Ideology and terror: A novel form of government. In Arendt, Hannah (ed.), *The origins of totalitarianism*. New York: Houghton Mifflin Harcourt, pp. 460–479.
Arendt, Hannah. (1961). The crisis in education. In Arendt, Hannah (ed.), *Between past and future*. New York: Penguin Books, pp. 170–193.
Armando, Luís Grandin & Apple, Michael. (2002). Thin versus thick democracy in education: Porto Alegre and the creation of alternatives to neo-liberalism. *International Studies in Sociology of Education*, 12(2), 99–114.
Bakker, Cok, & Montessori, Nicolina Montesano. (2016). *Complexity in education: From horror to passion*. Rotterdam, Netherlands, Boston, MA, Taipei, Taiwan: Sense Publishers.
Ball, Stephen J. (1995). Intellectuals or technicians? The urgent role of theory in educational studies. *The British Journal of Educational Studies*, 43(3), 255–271.
Ball, Stephen J. (2016). Neoliberal education? Confronting the slouching beast. *Policy Futures in Education* 14(8), 1046–1059.
Ball, Stephen J. (2008). *The education debate*. Bristol, UK: The Policy Press.
Ball, Stephen J. (2003). The teacher's soul and the terrors of performativity. *Journal of Education Policy*, 18(2), 215–228.
Ball, Stephen J., Maguire, Meg & Braun, Annette. (2012). *How schools do policy: Policy enactments in secondary schools*. London: Routledge.
Benhabib, Seyla. (2004). *The rights of others: Aliens, residents, and citizens*. Cambridge, UK: Cambridge University Press.
Biesta, Gert. (2010). *Good education in an age of measurement: Ethics, politics, democracy*. Boulder, CO: Paradigm Publishers.
Biesta, Gert. (2011). *Improving learning through the lifecourse: Learning lives*. New York: Routledge.
Biesta, Gert. (2013). *The beautiful risk of education*. Boulder, CO: Paradigm.
Biesta, Gert. (2012). The educational significance of the experience of resistance: Schooling and the dialogue between child and world. *Other Education. The Journal of educational alternatives*, 1(1), 92–103.
Bingham, Charles W. & Sidorkin, Alexander M. (2004). *No education without relation*. New York: P. Lang.
Browning, C. R. (2018). The suffocation of democracy. *New York Review of Books*, 25 October, 65 (16), 14–17.
Carr, Paul. (2008). Educators and education for democracy: Moving beyond "thin" democracy. Interamerican Journal of Education for Democracy, 1(2), 146–165.
Cochran-Smith, Marilyn, & Lytle, Susan L. (1998). Teacher research: The question that persists. *International Journal of Leadership in Education*, 1(1), 19–36.
Colnerud, Gunnel, & Granström, Kjell. (2002). *Respekt för läraryrket. Om lärares yrkesspråk och yrkesetik* [Respect for the teaching profession. On teachers' professional language and ethics] (updated edn.). Stockholm, Sweden: HLS förl.

Coolahan, John. (2001). Teacher education in Ireland and Western Europe. *Irish Educational Studies*, 20(1), 335–368.

Council of Europe (2019). Competences for life in democracy. Retrieved from www.coe.int/en/web/education/competences-and-qualifications

Debord, Guy. (2012). *Society of the spectacle*. London: Rebel Press.

Dahlstedt, Magnus, & Olson, Maria. (2013). *Utbildning, demokrati, medborgarskap* [Education, democracy, and citizenship] (1st edn.). Malmö, Sweden: Gleerups.

Dewey, John. (1916). Democracy and education [Elektronisk resurs]. Retrieved from https://en.wikisource.org/wiki/Democracy_and_Education

Edling, Silvia. (2014). Between stereotypes and task complexity. Exploring stereotypes of teachers and education in media as a question of structural violence. *Journal of Curriculum Studies*. Retrieved from: www.tandfonline.com/doi/abs/10.1080/00220272.2014.956796

Edling, Silvia. (2016). *Demokratidilemman i läraruppdraget. Att arbeta för lika villkor* [Democracy dilemmas in the teacher mission. To strive for equity]. Stockholm, Sweden: Liber.

Edling, Silvia. (2012/2018). *Vilja andra väl är inte alltid smärtfritt. Att motverka kränkning och diskriminring i förskola och skola*[Wanting others' wellbeing is not always painless. To oppose violence and discrimination in preschool and school]. Lund, Sweden:Studentlitteratur.

Edling, S. & Liljestrand, J. (2019). Let's talk about teacher education!: Analysing the media debates in 2016–2017 on teacher education using Sweden as a case. *Asia-Pacific Journal of Teacher Education* (Online). Retrieved from www.tandfonline.com/doi/full/10.1080/1359866X.2019.1631255. doi:10.1080/1359866X.2019.1631255

Edling, Silvia, & Mooney Simmie, Geraldine. (2017). Democracy and emancipation in teacher education: A summative content analysis of teachers' democratic assignment expressed in policies for teacher education in Sweden and Ireland between 2000–2010. *Citizenship, Social & Economic Education*, 1–15. Retrieved from http://journals.sagepub.com/eprint/jFcYzHFHvbI2DYyFIAs2/full

Ekerwald, Hedvig & Säfström, CarlAnders. (2012). *Levd demokrati? Skola mobbning i ungdomars liv*. Stockholm, Sweden: Liber.

Englund, Tomas. (1997). *Undervisning som meningserbjudande*. In Uljens, Micael (ed.), *Didaktik*. Lund, Sweden: Studentlitteratur, Chapter 7.

Fransson, Göran & Grannäs, Jan. (2011). Dilemmatic spaces in teachers work: Towards a conceptual framework for dilemmas in teachers work. Paper presented at the American Educational Research Association, New Orleans, LA.

Frelin, Anneli. (2010). *Teachers' relational practices and professionality*. Uppsala, Sweden: Uppsala universitet, Institutionen för didaktik.

Freire, Paulo. (1970). *Pedagogy of the oppressed*. London: Penguin Education Politics.

Furman, Gail & Shields, Carolyn. (2005). How can educational leaders promote and support social justice and democratic community in schools? In William, Firestone & Carolyn, Riehl (eds.), *New agendas for research in educational leadership*. New York & London: Teachers College Press, pp. 119–137.

Gunter, Helen. (2001). Critical approaches to leadership in education. *Journal of Educational Enquiry*, 2(2), 94–108.

Hallsén, Stina. (2013). *Lärarutbildning i skolans tjänst? En policyanalys av statliga argument för förändring* [Teacher education in the service of schools? A policy analysis about state arguments for change]. Uppsala, Sweden: Uppsala University.

Hess, Diane. (2009). *Controversy in the classroom*. New York: Routledge.

Honig, Bonnie. (1994). Difference, dilemmas, and the politics of home. *Social Research*, 61(3), 563–597.

Honig, Bonnie. (2009). *Emergency politics: paradox, law, democracy*. Princeton, NJ: Princeton University Press.

Johansson Heinö, Andreas. (2009). *Hur mycket mångfald tål demokratin? Demokratiska dilemman i ett mångkulturellt Sverige* [How much plurality can democracy endure? Democratic dilemmas in a multicultural Sweden]. Göteborg Studies in Politics, 116. Malmö, Sweden: Gleerups.

Kelchtermans, Geert. (1993). Getting the story, understanding the lives: From career stories to teachers' professional development. *Teaching and Teacher Education*, 9(5–6), 443–456.

Klette, Kirsti. (2007). Trends in research on teaching and learning in schools. *European Educational Research Journal*, 6(2), 147–160.

Labaree, David F. (2000). On the nature of teaching and teacher education: Difficult practices that look easy. *Journal of Teacher Education*, 51(3), 228–233.

Labaree, David F. (2004). *The trouble with ed schools*. New Haven, CT: Yale University Press.

Linné, A. (1996). *Moralen, barnet eller vetenskapen? En studie av tradition och förändring i lärarutbildningen*. Stockholm, Sweden: HLS Förlag.

Ljunggren, Carsten. (2012). Theme introduction: Citizenship education under liberal democracy. A contextualization of the comments on the IEA/ICCS 2009 study. *Utbildning & Demokrati: Tidsskrift för Didaktik och Utbildningspolitik*, 21(1), 1–16.

Lundgren, U. P. (1989). *Att organisera omvärlden: En introduktion till läroplansteori* [To organize the world around us: An introduction to curriculum theory]. Stockholm, Sweden: Utbildningsförlaget.

McLaren, Peter. (2016). *Pedagogy of insurrection*. New York, Bern, Frankfurt, Berlin, Brussels, Vienna, Oxford & Warsaw: Peter Lang Publishers.

McLaren, Peter & Petar, Jandrić. (2019, in press). *Post-digital dialogues, liberation theology and information technology*. London: Bloomsbury.

Marcel, J.-F. (2013). Critical approach to the contribution made by education research to the social construction of the value of teaching work. *Policy Futures in Education*, 1(3), 225–240.

Mooney Simmie, Geraldine. (2014). The neo-liberal turn in understanding teachers' and school leaders' work practices in curriculum innovation and change: A critical discourse analysis of a newly proposed reform policy in lower secondary education in the Republic of Ireland. *Citizenship, Society and Economics Education*, 13(3), 185–198.

Mooney Simmie, Geraldine. (2012). The pied piper of neo liberalism calls the tune in the Republic of Ireland: An Analysis of education policy text from 2000–2012. *Journal for Critical Educational Policy Studies*, 10(2), 485–514. Retrieved from www.jceps.com/archives/725

Mooney Simmie, Geraldine. (2020). The power, politics and future of mentoring. In Irby, Beverly J., Searby, Linda, Boswell, Jennifer N., Kochan, Fran & Garza, Rubén. *The Wiley international handbook of mentoring, paradigms, practices, programs, and possibilities*. Hoboken, NJ: John Wiley, pp. 453–469.

Mooney Simmie, Geraldine & Edling, Silvia. (2016). Ideological governing forms in education and teacher education: a comparative study between highly secular Sweden and highly non-secular Republic of Ireland. *Nordic Journal of Studies in Educational Policy*, 2(1), 1–12.

Mooney Simmie, Geraldine & Edling, Silvia. (2018). Teachers' democratic assignment: A critical discourse analysis of teacher education policies in Ireland and Sweden. *Discourse Studies in the Cultural Politics of Education*, 40(6), 832–846.

Mooney Simmie, Geraldine& Lang, Manfred. (2018). Deliberative teacher education beyond boundaries: discursive practices for eliciting gender awareness. *Teachers and Teaching Theory and Practice*, 24(2), 135–150.

Mooney Simmie, Geraldine & Lang, Manfred. (2020). *School-based deliberative partnership as a platform for teacher professionalisation and curriculum innovation*. London: Routledge.

Mooney Simmie, Geraldine& Lang, Manfred. (2012). *What's worth aiming for in educational innovation and change?*Münster, Germany:Waxmann.

Mooney Simmie, Geraldine & Moles, Joanne. (2011). Critical thinking, caring, and professional agency: An emerging framework for productive mentoring. *Mentoring & Tutoring Partnership in Learning*, 19(4), 465–482.

Mooney Simmie, Geraldine, Moles, Joanne & O'Grady, Emmanuel. (2019). Good teaching as a messy narrative of change within a policy ensemble of networks, superstructures and flows. *Critical Studies in Education*, 60(1), 55–72.

Mouffe, Chantal. (2000). *The democratic paradox*. London & New York: Verso.

Nussbaum, Martha C. (2010). *Not for profit why democracy needs the humanities*. Princeton, NJ: Princeton University Press.

Ó'Buachalla, Séamas. (1988). *Education policy in twentieth century Ireland*. Dublin, Ireland: Wolfhound Press.
O'Sullivan, Denis. (2005). *Cultural politics and Irish education since the 1950s. Policy Paradigms and Power*. Dublin, Ireland: Institute of Public Administration.
Pillow, Wanda. (2003). Confession, catharsis, or cure? Rethinking the uses of reflexivity as methodological power in qualitative research. *International Journal of Qualitative Studies in Education*, 16(2), 175–196.
Priestley, Mark & Biesta, Gert. (2013a). *Introduction: The new curriculum*. London, New Dehli, New York & Sidney: Bloomsbury.
Priestley, Mark & Biesta, Gert. (eds.). (2013b). *Reinventing the curriculum. New trends in curriculum policy and practice*. London: Bloomsbury Academic.
Ross, Alistair. (2000). *Curriculum construction and critique*. London & New York: Falmer Press.
Säfström, Carl Anders& Månson, Niclas. (2010). Ordningens pris. *Utbildning och demokrati*, 19(3), 5–10.
Sahlberg, P. (2012). *Report on the international review panel on the structure of initial teacher education provision in Ireland. Review conducted on behalf of the Department of Education and Skills*. Dublin, Ireland: Higher Education Authority.
Sahlberg, P. (2018). *The structure of teacher education in Ireland: Review of progress in implementing reform*. Dublin, Ireland: Higher Education Authority.
Santoro, Doris A. (2017). Cassandra in the classroom: Teaching and moral madness. *Studies in Philosophy of Education*, 36, 49–60.
Schön, Donald A. (1983). *The reflective practitioner: How professionals think in action*. New York: Basic Books.
Sellar, Sam & Lingard, Bob. (2013). The OECD and global governance in education. *Journal of Education Policy*, 28(5), 710–725.
Skerritt, Craig. (2018). Discourse and teacher-identity in business-like education. *Policy Futures in Education*, 17(2), 1–19.
Skerritt, Craig. (2019). Irish migrant teachers' experiences and perceptions of autonomy and accountability in the English education system. *Research Papers in Education*, 34(5), 569–596.
Snyder, Timothy. (2017). *On tyranny twenty lessons from the twentieth century*. New York:Tim Duggan Books, Penguin.
Snyder, Timothy. (2018). *The Road to unfreedom*. London: Penguin Random House.
Stanley, Edward & Stronach, Ian. (2013). Raising and doubling 'standards' in professional discourse: a critical bid. *Journal of Educational Policy*, 28(3), 291–305.
Svanberg, Ingvar & Westerlund, David. (2008). *Religion i Sverige* [Religion in Sweden]. Stockholm, Sweden: Dialogos Förlag.
Swedish Council for Higher Education. (2015). Annex 2. Retrieved from www.uhr.se/en/start/la ws-and-regulations/Laws-and-regulations/The-Higher-Education-Ordinance/Annex-2
Swedish National Board of Education. (2014). *Allmänna råd för arbetet mot diskriminering och kränkande behandling* [General advice against discrimination and violating treatment]. Stockholm, Sweden: Fritzes.
Tan, Emmanuel. (2014). Human capital theory: A holistic criticism. *Review of Educational Research*, 84(3), 411–445.
Teaching Council. (2017). *Initial teacher education: Criteria and guidelines for programme providers*. Revised Edition, March 2017. Maynooth, Ireland: The Teaching Council.
UNESCO. (2015). Retrieved from file:///C:/Users/siaedg/Downloads/244834eng.pdf
Weedon, Chris. (1999). *Feminism, theory and the politics of difference*. Malden, IL: Blackwell Publishers.
Wiklund, M. (2012). Konstruktioner av den goda läraren i Dagens Nyheter på 1990-talet: En fråga. In T., Englund (ed.), *Föreställningar om den goda läraren*. Göteborg, Sweden: Daidalos, pp. 199–213.

Wiklund, M. (2006). *Kunskapens fanbärare. Den goda läraren som diskursiv konstruktion på enmediearena* [The flag bearer of knowledge. The good teacher as a discursive construction at a media arena]. Örebro, Sweden: University of Örebro.

Yates, Lyn & Collin, C. (2010). The absence of knowledge in Australian curriculum reforms. *European Journal of Education*, 45(1), 89–101.

Zipin, L. & Brennan, M. (2003). The suppression of ethical dispositions through managerial governmentality: A habitus crisis in Australian higher education. *International Journal of Leadership in Education*, 6(4), 351–370.

2 Historical background[1]

Introduction

Many countries in the world now claim to be and to support democratic systems (Kirsch & Welzel, 2019), where **democracy** in broad terms can be described as a folk rule (Held, 1997). At the same time there are evidence showing that democracy is in recession due to political and cultural changes in various societies (Fukuyama, 2020; The Economist, 2018). Indeed, democracy's position in society is far from given. It is not given today and was not given in Athens 500 BC when the idea was first born. Aristotle, for example, was deeply concerned when democracy grew in popularity in ancient Greece since it meant that elite free men had to give up some of their power to poor free men who were considered too illiterate and unintelligent to take part in governing the realm (Dahl, 2002; Held, 1997, pp. 37–38).

If a word with such a broad use and significance in various societies as for instance democracy, is not clearly defined it risks becoming an **empty signifier**, i.e. dried of meaning (e.g. Eagleton, 1991, pp. 6–7). Thus, democracy is not something obvious and its meaning can be difficult to pin down when people ranging from right to left and from the top to bottom are all claiming to be in favour of democracy. The word democracy is practically used by everyone today from far right to the far left, like: social democrats, democrats (in the US), Swedish democrats, New Democrats (Sweden), and a new Social Democratic party in Ireland. If democracy is everything, it risks at the same time being nothing (e.g. Held, 1997, p. 17; Säfström & Bieta, 2001). For this reason, it is important to shed light on and problematize the **meaning** of the democratic concept, e.g. how it is defined, interpreted, and understood, in relation to various purposes and desires.

It is difficult to say anything substantial about the present without a glance to past events since the many threads of what takes place today are intimately interwoven with webs of historical events (Karlsson, 2003; Pinar, 2004; Rüsen, 2006). The chapter strives by no means to capture all the facts about the past, but aims at providing an overview of questions, which we find important to highlight when grappling with dilemmas regarding democracy and (teacher) education today (see Table 2.1).

The chapter can broadly be said to be divided into four parts that intersect, namely a political dimension, a historical dimension, a research dimension and a current dimension. Within the political dimensions, ideological governing forms of education are discussed, arguing that neither politics nor education have ever been ripped from values and hence value systems. The concept of emancipation is explored in relation to forces striving to stifle it. The historical part sheds light on how democracy as a governing form has taken shape as a response to wars and their brutalities against those who are considered as

Table 2.1 An overview of dilemmas discussed in Chapter 2

Dilemmas
Conserve (past) versus change (future)
Purity versus complexity
Plurality versus similarity
Majority versus minority
Values versus neutrality
Freedom versus constraint
Order versus disorder

different. In order to explore the role of research we turn to Descartes and his four principles and broaden the notion of science and education by turning to four different philosophical stand-points. The chapter ends by linking our reasoning to present day trends. The dilemmas in Table 2.1 thread throughout the various sections of the chapter.

Politics: The battle of ideological governing forms (of education)

The image of education as a battlefield where some wills aim to dominate others has been a historically reoccurring one in discussions about education (e.g. Collier, Hidalgo, & Maciuceanu, 2006; Gallie, 1964). This section deals with discursive struggles, not the least within the field of research that have been called **paradigm wars**, an awareness that science does not proceed in a linear fashion but takes form in clashes between contradictory world views, creating frictions (Kuhn, 1996) between those who argue that education is neutral, stripped of values and those maintaining that education is always imbued with values. Ideology can be categorized as one among many different political governing forms in which nation states control education. Other control modes are through legal measures like various forms of *legally grounded policies* that teachers' are obliged to follow, *economical divisions and organizations* and *state control*, i.e. testing in forms of national examinations and regular inspections (Lindensjö & Lundgren, 2000; Lundgren, 1989, see also Chapter 3).

Ideological battles for what knowledge and values should dominate educational systems to form a good citizen capable of participating in society and as a productive member of the workforce, have accompanied notions of public schooling since 1850s (Englund, 1986). **Ideology** encapsulates certain systems of ideas, values, norms, taste, beliefs, and ways of behaving that are regarded as ideal or desirable contrary to undesirable (in education) by people in society. Ideology has in the past been made equal with formal and political belief systems such as the conservatives, liberals, and socialists and more extreme forms such as fascism, Nazism and Stalinism (Augoustinos, 1998, Chapter 10). Ideology is however not just purely political but can be in relation to other areas in life, for instance religion, economy, morality, and ecology. It is seldom homogenous but complex, consisting of different aspects that are in constant need of negotiation (Eagleton, 1991, pp.152, 45–46).

After the Second World War there were many who declared the 'Death of Ideology', due to its extreme forms such as Nazism and Communism. It was instead replaced by science which was believed to be **neutral,** objective and as such free from values. However, this notion of neutrality is questioned for masking the unavoidable presence of ideologies and power relations which often function in a controlling manner. Indeed, ideology as a system of ideas or beliefs that form our material realities exist in every society – even those claiming to be neutral – and permeate all levels ranging from the private to the institutional. The **organic** features of ideology influence the practical consciousness of everyday life (Augoustinos, 1998, Chapter 10). Consider this dialogue for instance:

BOB: This institution is without a doubt an esteemed institution based on science and absolute neutrality.
LYNN: Interesting! Don't you have any ideas underpinning your institution?
BOB: Of course but they stem from science.
LYNN: Ok. But can you elaborate some more about what these ideas are and how they affect people's life conditions?

Accordingly, since the content of education, all around the world is always established in relation to certain cherished values and norms, no education can be said to be free from an ideology even though some might claim that education is neutral and objective (see for instance, Bartolomé, 2008; Dewey, 1916; Hopmann, 1997, 2007).

Although ideology influences people's thoughts and materialization of society, it is important to stress that ideologies are **illusion** in the sense that they are not the sum of reality itself. An unawareness of this can be described as a **naïve consciousness**, that is to say a systematic misrecognition of social reality that involves a perception of how a society is interconnected without an awareness of a distance between perception and reality as well as its limits. As such, the notion of ideology therefore continually needs to be brought to attention and problematized (Zizek, 1989, p. 28). One such naïve consciousness is that: 'Sweden/Ireland is a democratic country and people in Sweden/Ireland are just and good hearted compared to other countries'. Accordingly, the statement overlooks the fact that a country consists of people, ideologies, practices and values that at times collide and break with democracy as an ideology even though a country on a governmental level is said to be democratic.

In sum, every system that is based on some idea on how it should be governed taps into some type of ideology. In the section below examples of grand ideologies are presented and discussed in relation to democracy and emancipation involving questions such as how plurality, universality, sameness, majority, minority, order, disorder, freedom and limitations should be approached in society.

Various forms of ideologies and their relation to the nation and its 'people'

There are numerous forms of ideological governing forms in the world from a historical and contemporary perspective of which democracy is mainly one. In Table 2.2 we present a slim selection and provide brief descriptions of what characterizes them as well as who's got the power to rule.

What characterizes the most common of the ideological governing forms that have dominated over time is that it is one person or a small group of people in society who have held the power to rule over everyone else in an empire or in a **nation state**. The development of the nation state was influenced by **nationalism**, that is to say ideas that the best political government takes form when a nation is isolated from another and governed in accordance to the nation's rules and regulations (e.g. Bartolini, 2005; Gellner, 1981).[2]

Nationalism creates a feeling of 'homogenous we' through a shared language, culture, history and laws that function as a national glue and are dependent upon the loyalty of its

Table 2.2 An overview of a selected number of ideological governing forms together with a brief description of each and who is/are in power (see Arrow, Bowles, & Durlauf, 2000; Dah 2002; Linz, 2000)

Forms of government	Brief description	Who has the power
Anarchism	stateless non-hierarchical societies created on voluntary basis.	No one/the strongest
Authoritarian	a) constrained pluralism in political institutions and legal acts, b) playing on people's feelings in order to appear as a protector against evil in society, c) political mobilization of any kind is not allowed, d) the formal power to act is vague, e) a certain freedom of the people is allowed if they leave the government in peace.	Centralized authoritarian state often one person rule
Totalitarian	is an extreme form of authoritarianism and focuses on absolute control of all dimensions of the social life – even people's thoughts and feelings.	Centralized authoritarian state often one person rule
Dictatorship	a dictatorship is a form of *authoritarian* or *totalitarian* governing.	Centralized authoritarian state often one person rule
Oligarchy	It is based on an idea that a small group of people based on for instance family ties, wealth, noble backgrounds, education etc. have the right to govern the people. The power is often inherited.	Oligarchy literally means "rule of the few"
Theocracy	A country governed by a religious elite.	Religious elite
Meritocracy	Groups in a society are selected to govern a society based on their knowledge and various skills in an area.	The group who are selected and those who establish the criteria.
Absolute monarchy	In this case the monarch is the head of a state and the main governing authority.	Centralized state (similar to dictatorship) governed by one
Constitutional or parliamentary Monarchy	The monarchy is subjugated to a parliament who dictates its powers through a formal constitution or/and law	A king or queen has limited powers
Democracy Direct/ Representative	Democracy is form of government based on an idea that people in a society should be part in governing the society not just a few. There are many forms of democracy. For example, it can be direct, where people take part in voting in every situation or representative where they choose who are to govern.	Democracy literally means 'folk rule'. People in a country are given the right to influence in different ways.

citizens in return for a sense of safety and a belonging. Nationalism is a relationship between the ideas of what it means to live in a nation and what it means to be a citizen in that nation. Nationalism can be both broadly and narrowly approached. Whereas nationalism in a broad sense involves a certain acceptance of plurality, nationalism in a narrow sense focus upon homogeneity and sameness in ways that make it more difficult to promote peace between nations as well as handling plurality within the borders of a nation state (Gellner, 1981; Harris, 2009; O'Leary, 1997). **Pluralism** is here grasped in terms that there exist various groups in society that differ such as women, men, ethnic groups, disabled people, homosexuals, heterosexuals and so forth, but also in terms that each and every individual is radically different from one another (Mouffe, 2000, pp. 18–20, see also Edling, 2016, 2018).

Practically all ideological governing forms existing in the world today oppose the idea that a nation should be governed with the help of the people living within its borders and also of paying regard to the intrinsic plurality present in the notion of 'people' (see Table 2.1). While a pleasant dictator might be kind enough to listen to his/her subjects, the structure and belief system of the government is solely based on that person's perceptions and good will. Regarding dominating ideological governing forms it is the ideas of a small group with power, **minority rule** that permeate the lives of the **majority**.

Majority and minority are like two sides of the same coin and cannot exist without each other, which means that a majority is created in relation to a minority. Whereas a minority with power has dominated the majority, minorities without power have historically been persecuted, devalued, cast out and at times even killed. A person or a group of persons who do not fit into the majority's feeling of belonging and homogeneity are regarded as a stranger (s). Those who diverge from a dominating world-view have generally been regarded as dangerous since they alter the order of things and have therefore not had the same conditions as those belonging to a majority (Benhabib, 2004; Moses & Saenz, 2012; Nirenberg, 1998).

The desire for **purity**, keeping things (same) free from messiness and pollution (difference) of any kind, is one of the major driving forces in social history and also one central cause for mass violations and persecutions. Purity in this sense is about keeping homogeneous groups based on for instance religion, race and culture clean from those who are considered different (Bauman, 1995). This is understood as an early primal instinct for survival of the species, the need for imitation as a form of learning coupled with innate rivalry which can extend to dangerous levels and can be termed 'mimetic rivalries', that is to say rivalry that involves seeking to isolate and scapegoat the person from the in-group and harm to the point of persecution and even murder (McLaren & Jandrić, 2019). This is happening in the world now – can you see where?

Purity is a central ideology in **ethnopluralism** which can be found in some radical right groups. Ethnopluralism is a system of ideas claiming that people may be of equal worth, but a society needs to be protected from ethnic differences since this leads to extinction of a culture in a nation. Two or more ethnic groups cannot mix, since culture and ethnicity are regarded as fixed, monolithic and homogenous. Irish people should live with purely Irish people, Swedes with purely Swedes and so forth. It differs from classical racism since it is not hierarchical, at the same time it creates a lot of harm to (groups of) people who violate this idea and live amongst 'pure cultures' while being different (Rydgren, 2018, pp. 3–4).

Historically, people deemed as different have been brutally persecuted. There are many examples of minorities who, through time, for different reasons have been diminished, hurt, and/or killed: Roma people, Sami people, Indians, Jews, prostitutes, strong women, Christians, Muslims, Atheists and so forth. Who is to be considered part of a minority varies from time to time and from context to context. For example, after the French Revolution people who believed in God were punished while there is still the death penalty in many countries for those who do not believe in God (e.g. Kuru, 2009). We can often find nationalism and religion inextricably linked in persecutions and struggles. The *Good Friday Agreement* of 1998 in Northern Ireland, with American intervention, brokered a substantial and lasting peace agreement after a thirty-year conflict in Northern Ireland between nationalists, unionists, Catholics and Protestants and involved new structures and diplomatic understandings between Northern Ireland, Britain and Ireland. After twenty-one years, this peace agreement continues to be fragile and there is concern that the issue of the border (backstop) might threaten this peace in whichever way Brexit is finally agreed with Europe.

Historically, the idea that people should participate in ruling a country is only captured by advocators for democracy, meaning 'folk rule'. This does not mean that democracy is perfect, but that it is the best form of governance for those who think that a country should invite its people to govern it rather than simply allow a few powerful people to rule as they see fit (e.g. Dahl, 2002). This does not automatically mean that a country that claims to be democratic provides the necessary conditions for promoting democracy in everyday action – far from it. A country that merely sees democracy as a majority vote can use democracy to establish an ideological governing form based on, for example, authoritarianism or totalitarianism that persecutes those who are in any way different and especially those who critically question or contradict the government. For this to happen all that is needed is for the majority in a country to find the message of authoritarian leaders appealing (e.g. Williams, 2018). It is therefore important to be aware that the strife to dominate others and struggles for emancipation have been constant companions in human history.

It was therefore not until after the Second World War that the hierarchical structures of society and the nation state and the lack of critical thinking in schools really came to be questioned in ways that led to drastic changes in the ideological governing forms of education (Englund, 1989). Central in political debates in many countries after the war ended was the will to prevent the horrors from the past happening again by exchanging radical nationalism and Christianity that both emphasized strong obedience and were seen as major causes of the war happening (Benhabib, 2004).

The *Bretton Woods Agreement* struck in 1944 in a New Hampshire village between Europe, America and forty allied nations in the western world arose from the mass destruction of the Second World War, and resulted in debts from countries wiped clean and the introduction of a new global financial system (Varoufakis, 2016). The construct of the **social welfare state** that emerged established publicly funded solutions for the welfare of society (e.g. public services and infrastructure, such as public health systems, public schooling systems, public libraries, public transport) and for people who for whatever reason found themselves in poverty and/or vulnerable, e.g. the elderly or unemployed. In this system, for example, state unemployment benefits and state pensions rights were introduced.

The (never-ending) strive for emancipation and domination

During the 19th century a **process of democratization** took form in many western countries as a consequence of the Enlightenment and its demands on emancipation of people historically suppressed by various forces. The German philosopher Immanuel Kant, active during the 18th century, stressed the radical idea, at the time, that all human beings independent of social background, were equipped with a God-given reason and that they should have the right to use it rather than blindly obey a superiority:

> Enlightenment is man's release from his self-incurred tutelage. Tutelage is man's inability to make use of his understanding without direction from another/ … /Sapere aude! 'Have courage to use your own reason!' – that is the motto of enlightenment.
> (Kant, 1784)[3]

Forces of emancipation were mixed up with many other events taking place in the 17th centuries. For example, the Industrial Revolution radically changed the precondition of mankind and creating a huge sense of self confidence in man's ability to invent, develop and control his own environment (Schivelbusch, 2014).

The **Westphalian peace agreement** in 1648 put a definitive end to the Thirty Years War by securing religious freedom in many small states within the larger German-Roman realm and has been said to constitute the start of nation states in Europe (Agrell, 2017; Arons, 1983, van Creveld, 1991). The process of developing nation states took form by creating a sense of national identity and belonging amongst citizens inhabiting a nation contrary to realms (empires) kept together by emperors and kings who inherited the throne and demanded loyalty from the people by dent of position, often by force. The forging of one united history, one language, common traditions and ways of thinking became important to glue together a multitude of different people living within the same nation and as such create a sense of "we" versus "them" (Hobsbawm, 1990).

In 1789, the **French Revolution** broke out using slogans inspired from the Enlightenment, namely: Liberté (freedom), Egalité (equality), and Fraternité (brotherhood), which shook the foundations of Europe. The event contributed to paving the way for new ideological governing forms and universal suffrages (Petersson, 1994).

However, the process looked very different from country to country. In Sweden and other Scandinavian countries, the growth of the nation state took shape as an emancipation from the power of the Church and King. It took until January 2000 before the Swedish church definitively came to be separated from the state (Ekman & Todosjevic, 2003). Other countries like Ireland directed its emancipatory struggle against Britain and penal laws which forbid Catholicism and the use of the Gaelic language (e.g. Edling & Mooney Simmie, 2017). While Ireland achieved freedom from Britain's colonial rule and was founded on a proclamation of independence as a Republic (1916), the nation that emerged took shape within a spirit of cultural nationalism and strong church–state authoritarian relations and this influence remains to date in schooling and higher education (Edling & Mooney Simmie, 2017; Mooney Simmie & Edling, 2016, 2018; O'Buachalla, 1988).

The educational systems that took shape during the 19th century became the (public) business of the nation state and an important mechanism and governance tool to shape citizens to act in ways that put the nation's interests first (obligations) and as a reward the state granted citizens political and social protections (rights). Hence, it is not a coincidence that schools were institutionalized at the same time as the nation state was created (e.g. Englund, 2005; Lundgren, 1998).

Although the process of securing a school for all children independent of background was essential for the newly born nation states and can be considered to be part of a democratization of societies, the content of education was far from democratic. Analysis of school curricula during this period shows that the primary focus was upon fostering obedient Christians, patriots, and a work mentality necessary to feed the growing industries. The citizens should know their bible and be compliant when the nation needed them (Edling, 2018; Ekman & Todosojevic, 2003; Mooney Simmie & Edling, 2017). At the same time the intellectual ideas of emancipation were kept alive.

Philosophies of emancipation: examples that have influenced understandings of education

The American philosopher, psychologist and pedagogue **John Dewey** (1859–1952) lived at a time when **emancipatory** forces, the powers of industrialization, growth of natural science, nationalism as well as emancipation amongst others were flourishing. His research was based on the philosophy of **pragmatism** that posits that the quality of a theory, idea or meaning is intimately interlaced with the consequences of action as well as their usefulness to achieve social aims, hence creating an important link between research and theory and practice (Bacon, 2012). Dewey problematized the very foundation of thinking embedded within many societies at that time stressing a rigid categorization of the world based on the logic of essentialism, narrow categorizations, and hierarchy which he argued were unethical since they were unable to capture the flow of life and the consequences of action taking place there. Essential in his writings is the need to not suffocate and stagnate education, but allow the organic character of education and the people in it to constantly grow and change. Thus, emancipation or liberation from authorial and totalitarian ideologies in politics and the logic of science were central in his understanding of democracy (Dewey, 1916, Chapter XIX).

Dewey was far from the only thinker during the 19th and 20th century stressing the need to create a society (and education) that took into account questions of plurality, people's lived experiences, and social justice. The period was a vast melting pot of movements, revolts, and struggles for various groups of people in society. For example, in, the 19th century **Karl Marx** and **Friedrich Engels** (2009) stressed the need to liberate the working class from the oppression of the middle and upper classes, while women like **Mary Wollstonecraft** (1793) argued that women should be given the same rights as men. At the end of the 19th century, several movements such as the women's movement (with the suffragettes), religious movements, and working-class movements took form, claiming equality which eventually led to universal suffrage for both men and women independent of social class and gender.

Similarly, the **Frankfurt School**, which was established by a group of people in Frankfurt, Germany found the governing ideologies at the time, such as capitalism, fascism, and communism to be deficient in managing social controversies and risks taking place in people's day-to-day lives (Jay, 1996 [1973]) Critical theorists argue that education and schooling systems without critical literacy and dilemmatic spaces to question taken-for-granted assumptions and ideological governing forms are merely instruments for reproducing class privilege and existing social and power relations for the advantage of a circle of privilege (Kincheloe, 2004). The philosopher and sociologist **Jürgen Habermas** (1972), a central figure within the Frankfurt school, maintained that communication is an important emancipatory tool to reattach to people's lived experiences and provide spaces influenced by rational forms of deliberations (pp. 197–198, see also Dryzek, 2000, Englund, 1986)

Besides the Frankfurt School the Brazilian theorist and pedagogue **Paulo Freire** (1972) influenced the debate about democracy, emancipation and education. In his book, *The Pedagogy of the Oppressed*, he shed light on widespread illiteracy problems existing in Brazil at the time. According to Freire, education is not merely, or perhaps even foremost, about shaping children's and young people's characters in a preferred direction by giving them solutions in restricted environments, but rather about setting their thoughts, critical questioning, problem solving, problem-posing and engagement in movement and in discursive struggles of conscientization (e.g. Breunig, 2010; Freire, 1972; Giroux, 1988; Keesing-Styles, 2003; McLaren, 1998, 2016; Giroux & McLaren, 1989).

The French professor of philosophy **Jacques Rancière** questioned the common assumption that people start from a position of inferiority or inequality. As such he shifted attention from critical theory's liberation of the oppressed to the idea that all humans already are equal, and that this equality is the very precondition for democratic life (Bingham, Biesta & Rancière, 2010). Whereas the idea that all humans are equal is essential to pay regard to in accordance to Rancière, equality de facto can only be confirmed in practice when people's engagement for equality is materialized and influences people's experienced life conditions (see also Säfström, 2011). The force of emancipation from this way of arguing is positioned in an in-between space between an existing social order (polis) and the cogency in interrupting this social order. The dynamic interplay or dialectical struggle between order and claims for change like the balance between esteemed values and destructive values is eternal (Säfström, 2010, p. 607) and is forever generating dilemmas (Schnebel, 2016).

In sum, educational practice, independent of where in the world it is produced, is never neutral but is always shaped by values and norms that influence people's lives. As such, education is always political, formed and shaped on a political platform, and therefore it is important to always include the critical dimension, and critical pedagogy, to question, resist and challenge unequal power-structures created by governing value and norm systems (Keesing-Styles, 2003; Youdell, 2011; see also Edling & Mooney Simmie, 2017; Mooney Simmie, 2019; Mooney Simmie & Edling, 2016, 2018).

Historical wars: rebirth of democracy as responses against various forms of oppression

Hence, there is an assumption in many contemporary societies that democracy is the best form of government, since it strives to include the voices of all people in a society (*folk rule*) and as such carries the possibility for stimulating more equal and free communities than those favouring the dominance and power of a few. As such, democracy has come to be seen as a hope, to avoid past wars, genocide, oppression and violence in general (Beetham, 2008, Dahl & Lindblom, 1992/2017). From this way of reasoning: "[democratic citizenship] involves more than only doing good work in the local community but requires an ongoing orientation towards the wider political values of justice, equality and freedom" (Biesta, 2010, p. 2) in ways that take into account the intrinsic relationship between sameness and difference as well as a desire for peace.

There are numerous publications within peace research stressing the importance of democratic societies in the strife for **peace**(-ful) relationships (see for instance Barkaw & Laffey, 2001; Gledlitsh, 1992). Indeed, democracy as an idée or ideology has very much functioned as an antidote to military conflicts, like war, and to environmental destruction, unequal structures, crimes against human rights and so forth (e.g. Carr, 2008; Dahlstedt & Olson, 2013). Questions about democracy and education are therefore closely connected with strivings for peace and peace studies in the world:

> Positive peace stress the development of societies and relations which are close to concept such as democracy and development, social justice, and reconciliation.
> (Aggestam & Höglund, 2017, p. 25)

Since the middle of 1980s an increased attention has been directed towards how the relationship between states are influenced by the specific characteristics of each state. A central factor that has been highlighted in order to explain the risk for an intergovernmental war is the governance of the state. Countries with democratic political institutions have lower probability to be part in an armed conflict than countries

with non-democratic institutions/ ... /The thesis about the democratic peace is one of the most empirically grounded studies within the field of international relations.
(Fjelde, 2012, p. 90, *our translation from Swedish*)

This should not be interpreted in causal terms or as the delivery of automatic peace when democracy as a government is introduced (on the contrary), merely that democracy as a form carries the structural possibility for negotiating peace (ibid., pp. 91–92).

Hence every time democracy as an ideology has been seen as a mirage of a better society, it has been in form a force or resistance against various variants of oppression created due to narrow, hierarchical and otherwise violent social systems. Following the reasoning of political theorists Robert A. Dahl (2002), a professor of political science at Yale University, the strength of democracy is the possibility it carries for promoting justice and equity (p. 131, see also, Edling, 2016).

At the same time the democratic ideal has therefore a long history of being oppressed by forms of majority and authoritarian rule. Browning (2018), writing about the slow suffocation of democracy currently under way in the world, compares this with the Second World War. While he observes many similarities he notes that the symbolic violence to democracy under way nowadays is of a different type. Instead of extermination camps what we nowadays have are globalised systems of fake news and populism, technological (social media) platforms operating without ethical limits that conspire to afford unlimited spaces to new acceptable modes of authoritarianism that cause oppression of the most vulnerable in society, e.g. newcomer people, homeless. We will show in Chapter 3, how for example, the Organisation for Economic Cooperation and Development (OECD) using its rationale for economic success is shaping narrow teacher accountability and appraisal through new soft modes of constant comparison at international, national and local levels.

Democracy as fixed and/or a process

John Dewey (2004 [1938]), who has been described as one of the most influential researchers and thinkers to understand the relationship between democracy and education, described, two years before the start of the Second World War, how democratic aspirations appeared to erode due to a widespread distrust against the possibilities of a democracy coming to terms with social disorder. Dewey's analysis at the time was that democracy had lost its connection to people's lived lives and it was imperative that history played a key role in meaning-making in the present and thinking for the future:

> the issues and problems of present social life are in such intimate and direct connection with the past that students cannot be prepared to understand either these problems or the best way to deal with them without delving into their roots in the past. In other words, the sound principle that the objectives of learning are in the future and its immediate materials are in present experience is stretched, as it were, backward. It can expand into the future only as it also enlarged to take in the past.
>
> (Dewey, 1938, p. 77)

One year after Dewey's article was written the Second World War broke out. The democratic ideology was in many places exchanged for totalitarian ones like Nazism and Fascism where a reflexive blind spot of cherishing the nation state led to *the right to do anything towards humans as long it was for the overall common good of the nation state* (Benhabib,

2004, p. 55, see also Edling, 2016). The importance for educators/teacher educators of reflexive interrogation is considered in greater detail in Chapter 6.

Democracy is currently intimately interlinked with and interdependent of the nation state. Consequently, democracy and the nation are not necessarily enemies, and being proud of one's country is not automatically equal with being a racist. The problem is when a narrow form of nationalism strives to eliminate all kinds of plurality and when controversies are silenced by the demand of being blindly loyal (obedient) (Bar-on, 2018, p. 26; Edling, 2016).

At the same time, the possibility of protecting the borders of democracy is not feasible if all plurality is to be seen as good and legitimate, since the existence of democracy lies in the strife for equality and liberty for all. The meaning of these concepts, however, is not given, but needs to be continuously articulated and negotiated in ways described by Mouffe (2005) as **conflictual consensus** (a strife to work together for certain values, within an awareness that contradictory views exist and need to exist). It is important to take a stand against those who reject the fundamental institutions of democracy (if the questions democracy stands for are deemed as important), but resistance is done on political terms instead of moral terms (ibid., pp. 120–121). Democracy, from this way of reasoning is never merely given, a fixed starting-point, or fixed order (Biesta, 2010) but an ideal, a possibility or hope for a better future to live with plurality in a less harmful way than within alternative governing forms (Dewey, 1888; Dahl, 2002).

Accordingly, the idea that **plurality** is at the heart of democracy has been advocated from several researchers from different standpoints (Held, 1997, chapter 6). Consequently, it is argued that the very reason for preferring democracy over other forms of governments is that it creates spaces and structures for handling plurality, i.e. "the fact that individuals within society have different conceptions of the good life, different values, and different ideas about what matters to them" (Biesta, 2010, p. 24). Simultaneously, and paradoxically, the most dominant approach towards grasping the meaning of democratic communities is to see them as 'communities of sameness' and communities for consensus, a liberal value-based order which people are expected to adopt.

The non-avoidable presence of plurality and the will to eliminate it

In the Third Reich order, just like other totalitarian countries today is mainly about eliminating pluralism. The state should be the one thinking in the place of its citizens and plurality is to be combated by all means at hand. Those who are different or think differently than the government like Jews, political dissidents, slaves, homosexuals, Romani, Jehovah's witnesses, black people, disabled people are some examples of groups considered as inferior and non-human and in need of extinction (Bar-on, 2018). Between 55 and 60 million people, as civilians, were killed during the Second World War compared to nine million soldiers in the First World War. Cities, important buildings, industries, and ports were in many instances left in ruins or in a poor state. The human misery did not end *per se* with the war. A huge amount of children were left alone without their parents, many people lacked homes and shelter, money and food (Gilbert, 1989/2014).

Even though there is a huge amount of research stressing that a diminishing of plurality risks increasing harm towards dissidents, the tensions between plurality and similarity keep reoccurring in teacher education. For instance:

> During a course about the Swedish democratic value system a student teacher got upset about the strong focus on plurality, where plurality mainly was understood as

ethnicity and gender. He felt that a cherishing of plurality was permeating the entire education program rather than strengthen what is particularly Swedish. If he mentioned any of this critic to the teachers he felt that all they responded was that plurality is central in Sweden today, written in the Swedish state legislation. He stressed that: "it feels like I'm suffocated by a politically correct culture."

A student within a course about the Swedish democratic value system failed an exam and wrote an angry mail to the teacher.

"I feel sincerely blessed to have failed a course about democracy. A lot of Swedish people think this today but don't dare to speak about it and I'm sure the philosophy of democracy will disappear soon along with its stupid stress upon plurality." The student re-wrote the exam and passed it after a while. The teacher, however, felt violated and uncertain what to do. She received several aggressive e-mails and showed them to the head of the department who answered that as long as the student pass the course there is nothing to be done.

In Ireland, students in their final year of a four-year undergraduate degree program in teacher education (over 200 students) learn at lectures about new understandings of teachers as professionals. One nine-country report on learning to teach conducted by University College Cork and commissioned by The Teaching Council speaks to teachers' practices described by four roles: moral and caring person, generous expert, instructional manager and civil and cultural person (Conway et al., 2009). When teachers were invited to identify which of these roles they identified most with only a tiny minority selected the role of *civic and cultural person* (pp. 16–17).

It is particularly telling that policymakers and public policy documents in general in Ireland, fail to use the language of politics in ways that connect it to either the micro-politics of schooling and/or with capabilities to critically read the wider moral, social and political issues of the day. Conway et al. (2009) understand

> the cultural, civic and political role of teachers in creating the society of the future through their mediation of knowledge and influence on learner identities has implications for teacher education ... [where the] global flow of ideas and people is leading to new forms of cultural identity and diversity and is a significant pedagogical and political challenge for education systems around the world – including Ireland's.
>
> (p. 16)

Three core issues for the teacher's role as a *cultural and civic* person are grasped: 'self-understanding by teachers, teachers' capacity to challenge misconceptions about cultural-ethnic groups, and the role of the teacher in the new accommodation between cultural and civic nationalisms' (p.16). The teacher is understood as someone who is interrogating themselves and their practices and 'accommodating' issues of 'cultural identity and diversity' (p.16) and not someone charged with capabilities to critically read the world and/or to generate dilemmatic spaces for an emancipatory practice and/or for a dynamic plural view of democracy (Arnot & Dillabough, 1999; Biesta, 2010; Freire, 1972; Giroux, 1988) – in this case, Ireland as a democratic nation state, with membership of the European Union, and whatever that might mean for an education and teacher education system.

Student teachers who engaged with this question pointed out that the role of *civic and cultural person* was more of an add-on to their primary roles as moral and caring persons and instructional managers. Gendered differences were in evidence as only some students showed any interest, most notably male students in a class of predominantly female students. Moreover, students expressed the role in ways that had little or nothing to do with wider critical questions of education and democracy. Instead narrow understandings of securing the existing social order are captured in the following comments:

> I would also feel that being a civic and cultural person to be very important because here we are moving away from just our own subject and teaching students to be good all round functional members of society. When it comes to the teacher's role as a civic person, it means that the teachers look at education that provides the students with tools for their future role in citizenship. That can be both in political matters as in global issues such as the environment or sustainability.
> (Male student teacher, Ireland)

> The inclusion of this by the Teaching Council proves that this is now a requirement for teachers to educate the pupils in relation to politics, democracy, society etc. For me as a teacher it is important that I familiarise myself with these four dimensions as they will be necessary skills to help me in my future career.
> (Male student teacher, Ireland)

One student expressed his *civic and cultural* role through positioning himself as unbiased and neutral, an essentialist positioning which we will discuss later in the chapter:

> teaching as a civic and cultural being is one where the teacher needs to leave their opinions and experiences at the door (of the classroom). This is in order to engage students effectively in the learning process ... teachers need to know their students and their academic abilities individually rather than relying on racial or ethnic stereotypes or prior experience with other students of similar backgrounds. This means that teachers need to create environments in the classroom where all cultural backgrounds are respected.
> (Male student teacher, Ireland)

However, a small number of student teachers noticed tensions and dilemmas of stereotyping both in the practice settings of their schools and in the teacher education course at the university:

> being a civic and cultural being; this refers to teachers (and schools) conveying and supporting the wider social and political organization of society. If you cannot be open minded and treat all pupils regardless of any differentiating factor. Unfortunately in my own experience I went to an all boys' school that had a very strong religious ethos. This led to pupils of other religions being left at the back of classes during certain activities and classes such as religion so they felt excluded and alienated.
> (Male student teacher, Ireland)

> I find it interesting when sitting in lectures and tutorials, that there is no diversity in the teaching profession. Even all our lecturers and tutors are of white ethnicity. Therefore, we tend to see culture as something other people have, rather than something in which we are deeply (embedded).
> (Female student teacher, Ireland)

In sum, the section above describes how democracy in Sweden, and far less so in Ireland is regarded as a solution to various forms of violence and where the cherishing and protecting of everyone's equal value and hence plurality becomes central in this strife. However, for people who long for a state with a specific order, cleaned from the messiness of plurality in world-views, arguments, looks and other forms of expression democracy and its ethical dimension is not something desirable. Consequently, it is important to remember that democracy never just is, but constantly comes into being in people's everyday lives. Democracy requires people who are willing to engage for common concerns peacefully, and higher education (teacher education) carries the potential to be such sites (Andrews et al., 2018). As such, democracy contains an in-built dilemma/paradox since it on the one hand advocates for plurality while on the other hand it restricts those who criticize the existence of plurality.

Free speech and political correctness

One example is between **the right to free speech** and **political correctness** (freedom/order) that stems from a political assignment to protect people who historically have been discriminated against. The term political correctness (PC) is often brought forward by movements and groups by the far right, meaning that the elite protects plurality so much in the name of democracy that it obstructs the ordinary people's possibilities to articulate and express the truth about the world (see Hare & Weinstein, 2012; Hume, 2016 cited in Edling & Liljestrand, 2019a; Rydgren, 2018).

Fifty-six Swedish student teachers' understandings of democracy were analysed in 2017 (e.g. Edling & Liljestrand, 2019a) and one dimension concerned the notion of free speech. Several student teachers mentioned that they understood democracy as to be about free speech and that they found the demand for being politically correct or 'political correctness' problematic since it impedes free speech. Thoughts of unlimited free speech are mentioned as a central part in some of the student teachers' writing about their democratic assignment:

> Another part of democracy which is undoubtedly of great value is the freedom to be who you are and express your opinions without having to worry about the consequences.
> (Swedish student teacher, autumn 2017, cited in Edling & Liljestrand, 2019b)

> The politically correct culture is often good, but it cannot be allowed to overstep the freedom of expression that people enjoy.
> (Swedish student teacher, autumn 2017, cited in Edling & Liljestrand, 2019b)

If political correctness is used to silence people who want to discuss controversial issues it is highly problematic, but without a (political) protection for those who are vulnerable in a plural sense all kind of violence against them risks becoming accepted. Freedom in democratic countries cherishing liberty renders people more free than in authoritarian countries, but it is always freedom with boundaries. People seem to forget that, for example, free speech is free to a limit:

Article 11 corresponds to Article 10 of the European Convention on Human Rights, which reads as follows:

1   Everyone has the right to freedom of expression. This right shall include freedom to hold opinions and to receive and impart information and ideas without interference

by public authority and regardless of frontiers. This article shall not prevent States from requiring the licensing of broadcasting, television or cinema enterprises.

2   The exercise of these freedoms, since it carries with it duties and responsibilities, may be subject to such formalities, conditions, restrictions or penalties as are prescribed by law and are necessary in a democratic society, in the interests of national security, territorial integrity or public safety, for the prevention of disorder or crime, for the protection of health or morals, for the protection of the reputation or rights of others, for preventing the disclosure of information received in confidence, or for maintaining the authority and impartiality of the judiciary.[4]

While the notion of free speech stresses a desire for absolute freedom without restriction there are also examples of teacher educators and student teachers longing for order – at times turning their minds back in time and the illusion of an ordered past.

Order and disorder

There is at times a longing for a better past, which seemed more structured and ordered than the present.

> A Swedish teacher educator in her sixties stressed during a lunch break that she really missed the order existing in education during 1960s and 1970s when the pupils and students did not contradict the teachers, worked hard and had discipline. According to this teacher many students of today are lazy and unwilling to do the work required and often claim to be violated when they are told things they dislike. This Swedish teacher educator is far from alone in these thoughts. It is interesting to notice that student teachers express similar opinions. The past seems ordered while the present gives the impression of lacking order.
>
> (experiences from Teacher Education)

At the same time a teacher educator described the following:

> One of my relatives died when he went to elementary school during the 19th century. The school teacher beat him to death without facing any legal consequences. Indeed, there wasn't any juridical protection that restricted teachers' harsh up-bringing of the children.

No period in historical time is free from problems and whether ideas from the past are to be used today depends upon the challenges we face today and upon what we find is desirable. At the same time there are also those regarding the past as something we leave behind for a better future hence in ways that stop all dialogue:

> On several occasions, in courses student teachers in Sweden have posed the question as to why they have to read books older than ten years and pay regard to thinkers from the 19th century when they are to teach in the present. Instead, teacher education should provide the latest and best (most efficient) methods for counteracting current challenges that occur in schools and pre-schools.
>
> (experiences from Teacher Education)

38 *Historical background*

Figure 2.1 Soldiers marching in Third Reich.

Although ideologies of authoritarianism and totalitarianism can take form gradually and imperceptibly they are always guided by a conviction that the function of the nation state is to control all levels in society and guide people's thinking (Heater, 2004, chapter 4).[5] During the 1940s many people found the order and efficiency that this ideology appeared to represent as most appealing (Browning, 1998, see Figure 2.1).

However, the longing for order is not just something unique to the 1940s:

> Friction between order and disorder is present in numerous discussions with teacher educators who at times find it much easier to follow clear guidelines than give space to spontaneous discussions, creativity, and difference breaking into education and disturbing the planned path forward.
>
> (experiences from Teacher Education)

There are also examples of teacher educators expressing exasperation over the demands on control and order while having to juggle all the various demands placed on their shoulders:

> At several occasions teacher educators at various universities in Sweden have stressed a frustration over the fact that the administrative burdens are increasing while the various responsibilities they have in relation to education are increasing too. During a staff meeting a heated debate erupted where a male teacher educator stood up and pointed out with emphasis that: "We who work as teachers within teacher education need to learn student teachers today about how relations and group processes impact on learning environments, various ways of understanding learning, conditions for learning, how

education has come to look as it looks today, how to be scientific and well-grounded in all their judgments, write in a correct and scientific manner, understand the educational policy, understand that they need tools to interpret the policy, understand that besides knowledge they need to learn what values that are accepted in a democracy and also about questions concerning discrimination and violation, make the students understand how these questions are interrelated – just to mention a few examples. If we don't live up to the high standards required the UKÄ [Swedish state control system] will take away our exam rights to student teacher programs. At the same time the new system to report grades through internet takes a lot of time from us, we are supposed to work with zoom but there are often problems with the sound, we are to be giving students more and better feed-back after their exams and so forth. Please let us know how to handle all this before we collapse?".

(experiences from Teacher Education)

Similar value struggles are also present in research between those who argue that positivism is the sole foundation for research and those claiming that other perspectives rooted in social sciences need to be allowed space too.

Research: Evidence-based research and the historical heritage

The free **market economy** influenced by New Public Management (NPM) and neoliberalism has at times brought a new language to schooling and higher education that tends to rub off in practice (Tan, 2014). Pre-school and school institutions are at times described less as public institutions for the common good and more as private profit companies where students and children are customers, teachers sellers of an item of merchandise, and where education is seen as entrepreneurship, concurrence, freedom of choice and where input–output, efficiency are presented as desirable aims (Apple, 2013; Nicoll et al., 2013). Examples of dilemmas that we encounter within teacher education in relation to this are for instance teachers and student teachers telling us that:

(1) Sara a student teacher visited an upper secondary school in Sweden during one of her practices and was confused over the teachers reasoning when it comes to inform about bullying. The teachers told her that: "We know that we have problems with different kind of violence/bullying and we put down a lot of effort to counteract it and we can really see that it has become better in many ways. However, we do not dare to write anything about this on our webpage since it can scare off students and their parents from coming here. On our webpage it sounds as if we do not have any problems at all, which the school inspection can frown upon if they do an investigation of our school."

(experiences from Teacher Education)

(2) A teacher educator, we can refer to as Marcus, experienced a massive critique from the student teachers within the pre-school teacher program in a course he was teaching in. Marcus was really worried how he should do with the exams he was marking in relation to the course. "To be franc I really do not think many of the student teachers reach the aims necessary to pass the course, but I'm so afraid they may create a witch hunt against me. They might complain to the educational leaders at the university, or worse go to media and complain

over how lousy teacher education is. They actually threatened that they would. I'm really thinking of lowering the level of my grading."

(experiences from Teacher Education)

(3) Student teachers were asked to discuss the example (see below) taken from a documentary film in Sweden regarding "free schools". The discussions during a seminar stirred up many emotions: a TV-reporter claiming to be parent to a child with social disabilities was talking to a principle while tape recording the conversation in secret. The principle kindly let the parents know that the school unfortunately was fully booked now and wished the parents good luck elsewhere. Shortly after another camouflaged TV-reporter claiming to be a parent to a high achieving girl wanted to know if the school had vacant places and received the answer: yes.

(experiences from Teacher Education)

Nowadays, the **will to create certainty** and order through increasing control, introducing measurable aims, and discerning the right answer to the question "what works" have increased drastically in education and teacher education and in society at large. The messiness, nuance and complexity of education, teaching and teacher education is often explained as to be caused by woolly non-scientific perceptions and folk-psychology dominating the field and the solution to come to terms with this wooliness is to turn to evidence grounded on positivism and post-positivism (e.g. Hattie, 2008, 2009, 2012; Levinsson, 2013, see Edling, 2016). The belief that the role of research is to present the best solutions is presented here by some Swedish student teachers:

One questions student teachers often express is why they are presented with various perspectives in teacher education rather than instead being told what to do.
For example, a student teacher in Sweden wrote in an anonymous evaluation that she really thinks the quality of teacher education is low since it is mainly based on various angles and theoretical perspectives making it too complex rather than to pick out the simple methods for teaching based on research. The consequence of this according to the student teacher is that s/he will leave education without the proper knowledge for how to be a good teacher.

(experiences from Teacher Education)

Those who argue that education should be grounded on evidence claim that it can contribute to generalizability, measurability, and regularity in ways that may render education more efficient:

Thus, in my lecture I set a high standard: research should provide decisive and conclusive evidence that if teachers do X rather than Y in their professional practice, there will be a significant and enduring improvement in outcome/ … /Without high probabilities of an improved outcome, and demonstration of enduring effects, supported by confirming replications, the outcome is probably trivial or merely Hawthorne effect and cannot reasonably be used as decisive grounds for urging a teacher to change from X to Y.

(Hargreaves, 1997, p. 413)

1 That social practices are activities which need to be justified as effective and efficient means of producing desirable outputs.
2 That means and ends are contingently related. What constitutes an appropriate means for bringing about the ends-in-view needs to be determined on the basis of empirical evidence.
3 That the determination of means requires a clear and precise pre-specification of ends as tangible and measurable outputs or targets, which constitute the quality standards against which the performance of social practitioners is to be judged.

(Elliott, 2001, s. 560)

Evidence-based research is founded on the logic of **positivism** (e.g. Biesta, 2007). The term was coined by the French socialist Henri de Saint-Simone during the 18th century, but it is Auguste Compte's and later Emile Durkheim's definitions of the concept that have been used most frequently within the field of Science. Positivism is not a homogenous philosophy, but contains various traditions that differ from each other like classic positivism, methodological positivism and logical positivism (e.g. Bredo, 2012; Riley, 2007). Although there are small differences between them positivism as such has certain features in a general sense (Bredo, 2012; Cohen & Manion, 1994, see Chapter 1). Positivism is closely related to **empiricism**, that is to say a scientific conviction that the only way to gain knowledge about the world is through our senses and through systematic (scientific) experimentation. The logic of positivism, and its deductive reasoning, can be linked to the French philosopher, mathematician, priest, scientist, and lawyer René Descartes (1596–1650), who in turn was inspired by ancient Greeks like Plato.

The story about four principles

According to Descartes the **essence of knowledge** and science needs to be clearly defined in order to prevent world destruction or total chaos. He made several experimental attempts during his lifetime with the intention to locate this essence, the core knowledge, in people's customs and way of living. However, travels in this journey made him deeply concerned and disappointed, seeing that people's actions were changeable and there turned out to be a worrying amount of differences amongst people that made the essence impossible to fixate.

The discovery made Descartes worried, since he maintained that without a core it is impossible to establish a science, and without science all that is left is chaos. Fields of inductive reasoning found in philosophy, theology, rhetoric and history did not give him much comfort either, since they expressed a multitude of opinions that at times collided with each other and showed different logical strands (Descartes, 1998). He also worried that curiosity, which was a driving force in many subjects of reasoning character awakens passion and stills the voice and purity of reason (Descartes, 1952, regel IV, s. 5). Drawing from his experiences, he concluded that none of these (arts and humanities based) subjects could constitute a foundation for science (Descartes, 1998). Descartes' worry/anxiety or the Cartesian worry/anxiety is still alive today in the world, society, education and teacher education and stems from a fear of losing control and prediction nurtured by a will for absolute certainty and purity.

Concerned, Descartes tried to solve and still the **Cartesian anxiety** he felt over the presence of plurality in the world when it came to people's customs, traditions, actions and thoughts, which so brutally escaped his attempt to be purified and fixated. In order to clean up the messiness in the human world he created four principles. Descartes principles are as follows: (a) the principle of dichotomy, (b) the principle of everything's essence, (c) the principle about measurability, categorization, and visibility, and (d) the principle of the elimination of doubt (e.g. Edling, 2016; Fuller, 2009; Nordström, 2008).

His four principles have played a crucial role for a lot of areas in society such as science, politics, education and popular debates and it definitively deserves attention since it has contributed in building and structuring a rational deductive science beyond loose beliefs, dogmas and religious convictions. With the help of these principles, lots of useful knowledge has been generated over the years that has supported human needs (Pinker, 2018). However, and simultaneously, these four principles have also caused major human sufferings, due to their negative sentiment to human plurality, which deserves serious interrogation in the contemporary field of education.

Descartes found the **principle of everything's essence** through the conclusion that the sole thing that guarantees stability in the instability that exists in subjective feelings is the power in one's own thoughts. The phrase 'cogito ergo sum' i.e. 'I think therefore I am' became the stable core he so desperately had searched for and made the other principles in his model feasible. It became the firm truth that did not yield when strong winds blew. The I (the spirit) is strong and reliable since it can be disconnected from the impurities of the body (material). This particular way of reasoning was central for him in the quest for science and the motto implies that if the I (spirit) grasps something clearly, beyond doubt, this truth needs to be perused in every detail. Knotted within this logic was the idea that everything on earth is interlinked and can be studied with the same method. In order to be able to reach this conclusion Descartes had to define universal grounds valid for all humans and humanity writ large (e.g. Descartes, 1952, 1998).

The principle of dualism[6] became the means to secure the logic of the thought's purity (essence) without any kind of pollution from the body. If thought is really to be seen as good without the sneaky interference of the devil it had to be a mirror of God. God for Descartes symbolizes perfection, unity, simplicity, order, reason, security and so forth. God gave humans the ability to think and with the help of thought strive for perfection which entailed the opposite to forces like disorder, pollution, fuzziness, doubt etc. which were the makings of the Devil Lucifer. In this way, evil is defined as negations to the good, which is the feature of dualism as for instance: God–Devil, Light–Darkness, Love–Evil, Order–Disorder, Security–Insecurity, Similarity–Difference, Perfection–Chaos, and Clarity–Ambiguity. Accordingly, if God gave people the ability to find order in disorder this ability cannot be evil (Descartes, 1998). *The use of thought* is therefore the essence that makes us humans and is given existential value. At the same time the principle activates a system of values in an either–or fashion. You are either good if you think in accordance with the model of goodness that I define with God's help or you are evil. If you are the same as me you are good but if you different from me you are evil.

The principle of elimination has to do with a scientific and hence systematic elimination of doubt created because differences, messiness and division of opinion have not yet been sorted out. While God is considered as to be the symbol of certainty, the presence of doubt is the presence of God's opposite, the Devil and therefore needs to be erased. In order for this to happen, the individual has to become emancipated from authorities who simply tell you how it is. Rather than blindly obeying authorities the scientist needs to start from his doubt and subsume that all previous knowledge is wrong. The first is that man is able to come to a divine point where evil doubt dissolves, to a point where a certainty of how things really are can be reached. For this to happen everything that lacks essence needs to be erased such as people's experiences, opinions, feelings, history, traditions and customs – since these interfere with the order that is sought (Descartes, 1952, 1998).

Following the rationalistic and deductive reasoning of Descartes, no one can top God, and the purpose of science is not to go beyond God's divine powers and creation, but rather to locate God's true intentions and re-make them as correctly as possible through empirical and systematic studies of reality. To secure this ambition it is of utmost importance that the researcher follow certain fixed rules and that truth is only that which can be seen, measured, mapped and categorized. This is labelled the principle of visibility, categorization and measurability. Drawing on Plato, subtle (unclear/invisible) and contradictory events in the world are there to confuse the purity of reason and therefore need to be ignored. In other words, the subtle, the nuanced and the implicit, in much the same way as difference and ambiguity, are powers of evil and as such awaken nagging doubt/anxiety that has to be falsified and terminated with the help of the visible, united and measurable. This is the sole route to the clarity and truth that is the rationalistic role and mission of science to find (Descartes, 1952, 1998). Descartes' reasoning has had a major impact on the foundations of Natural Science; however, besides essentialism central in Descartes' belief system, other philosophies, i.e. ways of viewing education have taken form over the years.

Philosophical struggles: perennialism, essentialism, progressivism and reconstructivism

When studying education historically, struggles of various philosophical stances appear. Here we consider four philosophical starting-points as follows: **perennialism, essentialism, progressivism** and **reconstructivism** (Englund, 1986; Mooney Simmie & Edling, 2019). Contemporary social demands on education to find best practice in education is not simply a question of empirical observations, but also and foremost a question of philosophical outlooks expressed by various policy actors and educators where various philosophical perspectives find different things desirable.

Perennialism and essentialism can be categorized as narrow philosophical conceptions of democracy and education in that they exclude the need to scrutinize the choice of content, human complexities and contextual experiences. Within ideas stemming from perennialism, the focus of education is to transmit the canon of western knowledge and culture to a younger generation without questioning the content and has historically been the most dominating one. Contrary to perennialism, essentialism as an idea is born within the rational logic of science and underlines the importance of grounding educational practice on empirical observations proven to work. This philosophy has been particularly strong during the 20th century but is nowadays revived in many countries (Mooney Simmie & Edling, 2016, 2018). The philosophy of essentialism supports the focus to apply the best method(s) to transmit content to students necessary for a view of a dominant market economy (Tan, 2014). Democracy, within essentialism, is primarily about formal issues and does not incorporate the content of people's everyday life into the meaning of the term (Arnot & Dillabough, 1999). Both perennialism and essentialism are based on dualism, which means that subject content knowledge is regarded as neutral rather than value-laden, students are viewed as passive (receivers of knowledge) rather than active, and teachers are viewed as objective transmitters of knowledge and securers of social order rather than as subjective beings (see Chapter 5 for a focus on knowledge). This way of structuring the world is highly accurate today and was also something which Dewey noticed during his life time and which he found problematic. While either–or is appealing in thought, practice tends to require more nuanced approaches:

> Mankind like to think in terms of extreme opposites. It is given to formulate its theories in *Either–ors*, between which it recognizes no intermediate possibilities. When forced to recognize that the extremes cannot be acted upon, it is still inclined to hold that they are all right in theory but when it comes to practical matters circumstances compel us to compromise.
>
> (Dewey 2004 [1938], p. 17)

The philosophy of progressivism stresses, in a similar way to essentialism, the importance to transmit knowledge efficiently, yet the playfields on which they rest differ radically. Drawing on pragmatism and the ideas of John Dewey, progressivism moves from a dualistic way of seeing the world to a dialectical approach. Democracy from this way of reasoning is not given and merely about procedures, but also about paying regard to the small practical events in day-to-day lives and their consequences for people's life conditions. Without paying regard to context, interactions, people's differences and their life conditions it becomes difficult to create situations where democratic negotiations can take form (Dewey, 1916). As such, Dewey added a moral and social justice dimension to democracy and education that incorporated the content and outcomes of practice and the notion that practice never stands still – it is in a constant state of flow and of dynamic change.

Viewing education through the lenses of progressivism, fostering of democratic citizens becomes a vital task for education by taking into account the flow of practice. Rather than simply seeing students as passive receivers of knowledge her/his meaning-making and previous experiences become equally important to acknowledge. This does not mean a pendula movement from being passive to allowing the student to dictate the content of education, but mainly that if knowledge is to be *meaningful* to someone then their *meaning-making processes* need to be taken into account. Teachers are here asked to be as objective as possible, but within an awareness that this is not entirely possible. In order to do a good job they cannot mainly follow external experts, but have to start thinking for themselves based on previous knowledge. During their work day they are encouraged to acknowledge what takes place in practice through systematic interpretations and judgements drawing on previous knowledge (e.g. Englund, 1986, 1997).

Just like progressivism, reconstructivism is also founded on a dialectical foundation. However, whereas progressivism is primarily concerned with individual growth and development, reconstructivism stresses the necessity for stimulating prerequisites for social and political change. Teaching from a reconstructivist stance is therefore about creating possibilities for encouraging an emancipatory citizenship where people are capable of partaking in and critically constructing and shaping a vibrant democratic society in a desired direction (Englund, 1986).

Present: Why do we need to care in the 21st century about Descartes' anxiety?

Professor Iris Marion Young (1949–2006), a political theorist and feminist focused on the nature of justice and social difference, argued that there is a tendency to get tired of questions that have occupied the thoughts of people, including scientists, and hence dismiss them as old-fashioned just because they have had their place in the sun. Nevertheless, just because these same questions and issues have been brought up again and again does not mean that they suddenly have to be regarded as out-of-date if the challenges they seek to address still remain and cause turbulence:

Unfortunately fashion seems to guide contemporary intellectual and political life as much as it rules hairstyle or shoe heels. Too many people think that ideas should be rejected on the grounds that they do not have intellectual substance. Others think that political claims to justice should be rejected because people are tired of hearing about the same old grievances, rather than asking whether the social conditions that seemed to validate the grievances uttered twenty years ago have changed.

(Young, 1997, p. 3)

One such challenge that threads through the chapters of this book are the concepts of dualism/dichotomy, essentialism, and hierarchy in relation to questions of plurality central in modern democracies. There has been a significant research base problematizing the logic of dualism when it comes to grappling with various social justice issues, violence, and difference over the years.

Within the field of Natural Sciences as well as outside it, researchers have systematically come to challenge the notion of dualism, dichotomy and essence as building blocks for science since these very same notions can be seen as the very cause of many injustices between various groups of people in society (see for instance Harding & Hintikka, 1983; Lloyd, 1983, Walkerdine, 1989).

It is even possible to ask the blunt question: why does a preschool teacher, teacher, student teacher, and teacher educator still have to read about a man and his anxiety that existed 500 years ago? A simple answer to this question is that the principles of Rationalism he created still hold many people's thoughts and reasoning and the education policy cycle today is in a tight grip and therefore needs to be once more faced and questioned. The rationalistic model from the Enlightenment is strongly anchored in many cultural, social, political, religious, legal and psychological theories and studies; it is therefore vital to return to why it is problematic when social justice dimensions of democracy as well as an acknowledgement of plurality are to be taken seriously (Weedon, 1999, Chapter 1, see also Edling, 2016).

Moreover, it appears frequently in the logic of the media (Edling, 2014) and as such has a strong impact factor. It is not just Descartes who has an anxiety that the insecure, chaotic, relative, plural and subjective will devour the good strife for perfection, purity, similarity, order and the safe – many people in today's world and in the field of education, teacher education and research share this anxiety. Cartesian anxiety is visible in every discussion that enfolds a dualistic either–or way of thinking, which makes it imperative to acknowledge (Bernstein, 1983). Examples of this way of arguing are as follow:

- there is disorder in school which is bad – a good school/teacher has order
- the school lacks a solid ground for what works – the school needs to build on what works
- democracy is either about (objective) rules and procedures – or about (subjective) relations, values, perceptions and so forth
- in the bad school we can find bullying – in the good school there is no bullying
- a bad teacher is subjective and hence relative – a good teacher builds on objective facts
- a bad (pre) school uses woolly norm criticism – a good school uses knowledge
- either the method to criticise norms works – or the solution is to have more guards on the (pre)school yard
- a bad (pre) school is based on postmodernism – a good school is based on cognitive science

- either firm rules help to prevent bullying – or teachers' judgement helps to prevent bullying
- education should either be based on the child's experiences – or on subject content
- you are either an unclear leader – or you are a clear leader who points with your whole hand
- it is either the individual's behaviour that should be changed and adjusted to the norm – or it is the group that needs to adjust to the individual (see Edling, 2016).

A student teacher who visits a school or pre-school for her/his practice may very well notice that the school and pre-school have both merits and deficits depending on what the focus is.

> One such example is when Sebastian visited an upper secondary high school in the middle of Sweden, which, during a period had marvellous results in the students' development in math. At the same time, Sebastian noticed that the school was suffering from a harsh social climate that resulted in a lot of student complaints and sick leave amongst teachers. Only one of the class within the natural science program seemed to have a good peer climate according to his observations and dialogue with the students, which he found strange since they all shared the same teacher. Sebastian was really surprised to have seen these patterns, and asked one of the joint seminars at the university how to understand and handle this phenomenon.
>
> (experiences from Teacher Education)

Current debates about the need to base education on positivist grounded evidence, has its roots in Cartesian anxiety and the four rationalistic principles described above. However, there is currently plenty of new evidence from studies drawing on positivism, such as brain and cognitive research that implicitly question the rigidity of the four principles. For instance, brain research shows that all brains are unique, that brains change dependent on context/stimulation and nutrition (Caine & Caine, 1991; Caine et al., 2005), that it is not scientifically possible to differ between male and female brains (Davis & Sumara, 2006), and that people are capable of focusing on more than one thing at a time. The playing field that Descartes created fulfils a lot of purposes, but far from all. As such it becomes important to move beyond dualism (Bernstein, 1983), which does not mean moving from objectivism to subjectivism but to *handle existing and pressurising social problems as well and objectively as possible.*

> The example with the student teacher in Sweden, let us call her Anna, who raised her hand during a seminar about democracy and the democratic value foundation and pointed out that she finds the course literature to be based on quasi science, produced outside the logic of Natural Science, can also be regarded as a result of this anxiety. Thus, the perception is far from dead but takes concrete forms, which impacts on education. The situation that occurred in that context did not have a simple solution. Anna actually stated that the program she is forced to go through in order to become a teacher is not based on science and therefore not something she takes seriously. She explicitly devalued both the group responsible for the course as well as other students present in the seminar who had exams in subjects governed by other logics than Natural Science, which brings to the fore ethical aspects in need of being addressed. The event could have been handled in a multitude of ways. How would you handle it and why?
>
> (experiences from Teacher Education)

Conclusion

A central starting-point in the book is that no education is free from values and belief systems, referred to as ideology and that reigning ideologies exist in tension with other ideologies. Education as such can never be a neutral entity but is interwoven with the current state governing, rendering it important to constantly scrutinize. From a historical perspective democracy as an ideology has come into being as emancipation from various forms of authoritarian regimes that oppress dissidents.

Democracy has thus been seen as a counterforce to wars and genocide. It is a vulnerable system that tends to be caught between various dilemmas like purity/complexity, plurality/similarity, majority/minority, values/neutrality, order/disorder, freedom/constraint and conserve/change. These value struggles also exist within research where those applying a narrow focus on Descartes' rationalism strive to eliminate uncertainty and plurality in their research findings, contrary to those arguing that research also needs to keep human complexity and imperfectness alive. We have during the years gathered numerous observations from dialogue with other teachers and through experience that are positioned in the centre of these tensions creating different dilemmas that plead for attention. In this chapter we have gathered some of these that can be discussed.

Questions

1   What kind of spontaneous idea(s) did this chapter evoke in you? Can you put words on it/these using literature and concepts from the chapter as a point of departure?
2   Why might we need to turn to historical and cultural contexts to better grasp dilemmas in the present and to open new spaces for the future?
3   What do you think about Descartes' reduction of complexity and plurality in relation to (teacher) education?
4   Can you see patterns of oppression of people who are different that took form before the eruptions of the World Wars occurring in present-day life?
5   What kind of philosophical struggles or ideas can you see in current educational policy and the educational contexts you have taken part in?
6   In relation to what you have read in this chapter regarding the dangers of overlooking values and the assumption of neutrality in (teacher) education how would you handle it as a teacher?
7   What kind of dilemmas in relation to the topic discussed would you like to add, and why?

Supplementary readings: podcasts related to education and democracy

1   Professor Christopher R. Browning author of the *Slow Suffocation of Democracy* from the New York Review of Books in December 2018 here speaks about what of the features of a Republic
    Browning 2012 Symposium on the Rules of a Republican Form of Government, 25/01/2014
    www.bing.com/videos/search?q=youtube+Browning+democracy&view=detail&mid=7C4357B3ADCE52515F857C4357B3ADCE52515F85&FORM=VIRE
2   Slovenian philosopher argues that while before people were blinded by religion, today they are subjugated by technocracy and capitalism
    Slavoj Zizek: Down with Ideology! 18/01/2019

www.youtube.com/watch?v=Zm5tpQp6sT4
3   Francis Fukuyama, Alexander Dugin and Ivan Krastevc
    Is there one human nature or do different cultures create their own versions of human nature?
    Competing Ideologies, 11/02/2015
    90-minute conversation about democracy, liberalism, human nature and what is happening in the conflict between Russia and Ukraine.
    www.youtube.com/watch?v=wIiKiDnMSFw
4   TEDxTeen talk by Professor Benjamin B. Ferencz Prosecutor at Nuremberg Trials
    The Greatest Trial The World has Ever Seen, 28/08/2017
    Talks about lessons from the Second World War the world has yet to learn.
    www.bing.com/videos/search?q=u+tube+Benjamin+Ferencz&ru=%2fsearch%3fq%3d u%2btube%2bBenjamin%2bFerencz%26src%3dIE-SearchBox%26FORM%3dIE11SR% 26pc%3dEUPP_&view=detail&mid=9DF687821C0155495BD39DF687821C0155495 BD3&&mmscn=vwrc&FORM=VDRVRV

Notes

1 Parts of this chapter is freely translated from Swedish to English based on Edling, Silvia. (2016). *Demokratidilemman i läraruppdraget. Att arbeta för lika villkor [Democracy dilemmas in the teacher mission. To strive for equity]*. Stockholm.
2 There exists a sense today that the Nation State is dissolving due to global economies (Ohmae, 1995).
3 https://pdfs.semanticscholar.org/dc3e/6ea5f77724114ac39252dbeabe6ab1909aca.pdf [19.09.17]
4 https://fra.europa.eu/en/charterpedia/article/11-freedom-expression-and-information [19.08.05]
5 The seduction in following external orders should not be underestimated. In countries which, for long had been governed by totalitarian dictatorship people felt lost when more liberal ideologies took over.
6 The logic of dualism has existed ever since the ancient Greek [or even before that] (Lloyd, 1983) but it has been revived through Descartes' foundation for science based on the abyss between body (material) and soul (the spirit) (de Beauvoir, 1973).

References

Aggestam, Karin & Höglund, Kristine. (2017). *Om studiet av krig och fred*. In *Om krig och fred. En introduction till freds- och konfliktsstudier*. [About studies of war and peace: An introduction to peace and conflict studies.] Lund, Sweden: Studentlitteratur.
Agrell, Wilhem. (2017). *Historiska och samtida krig*. [Historical and current wars]. Lund, Sweden: Studentlitteratur.
Apple, M. W. (2013). *Can education change society?* New York: Routledge.
Arnot, Madeline & Dillabough, Jo-Anne. (1999). Feminist politics and democratic values in education. *Curriculum Inquiry*, 29(2), 159–189.
Arons, Raymond. (1983). *Clausewitz: Philosopher of war*. London: Routledge.
Arrow, Kenneth, Bowles, Samuel & Durlauf, Steven. (2000). *Meritocracy and economic inequality*. Princeton, NJ: Princeton University Press.
Augoustinos, Martha. (1998). Social representation and ideology: towards the study of ideological representations. In Uwe Flick (ed.), *The psychology of the social*. Cambridge, UK: Cambridge University Press, pp. 156–169.
Bacon, Michael. (2012). *Pragmatism. An introduction*. Cambridge, UK: Polity Press.
Bar-on, Tamir. (2018). The radical right and nationalism. In Jens Rydgren (ed.), *The Oxford handbook of the radical right*. Oxford: Oxford University Press, pp. 17–43.

Barkaw, Tarak & Laffey, Mark. (2001). *Democracy, liberalism, and war: Rethinking the democratic peace debate*. Boulder, IL & London: Lynne Rienner Publishers.

Bartolini, Stefano. (2005). *Restructuring Europe: Centre formation, system building, and political structuring between the nation state and the European Union*. Oxford & New York: Oxford University Press.

Bartolomé, Lilia I. (2008). *Ideologies in education: Unmasking the trap of teacher neutrality*. New York: Peter Lang.

Bauman, Zygmunt. (1995). Dream of purity. *Theoria: A Journal of Social and Political Theory*, 86 (Dimensions of Democracy), 49–60.

Beetham, D. (2008). *Democracy and human rights*. Cambridge, UK: Polity Press.

Benhabib, S. (2004). *The rights of others: Aliens, residents, and citizens*. Cambridge, New York: Cambridge University Press.

Biesta, G. (2010). *What is education for? Good education in an age of measurement: ethics, politics, democracy*. Boulder, IL: Paradigm Publishers.

Biesta, G. (2007). Why "What works" won't work: Evidence-based practice and the democratic deficit in educational research. *Educational Theory*, 57(1), 1–22.

Bernstein, R. J. (1983). *Beyond objectivism and relativism: Science, hermeneutics, and praxis*. Philadelphia, PA: University of Pennsylvania Press.

Bingham, C. W., Biesta, G. & Rancière, J. (2010). *Jacques Rancière: Education, truth, emancipation*. London & New York: Continuum.

Bredo, E. (2012). Philosophies of educational research. In Judith L. Green, Gregory Camilli & Patricia B. Elmore (eds.), *Handbook of complementary methods in education research* (3rd edn.) (Online). New York: Routledge. doi:10.4324/9780203874769

Breunig, M. (2010). Teaching for and about critical pedagogy in the post-secondary classroom. *Studies in Social Justice*, 3(2), 247–262.

Browning, Christopher. (1998). *Helt vanliga män: Reservpolisbataljon 101 och den slutliga lösningen i Polen*. Stockholm, Sweden: Norstedt.

Browning, C. R. (2018). The suffocation of democracy. *New York review of books*, 65(16), 14–17.

Caine, R. N. & Caine, G. (1991). *Making connections: Teaching and the human brain*. Alexandria, VA: Association for Supervision and Curriculum Development.

Caine, R. N., Caine, G., McLintic, C. & Klimek, K. (2005). *Brain / mind learning principles in action. The fieldbook for making connections, teaching, and the human brain*. Thousand Oaks, CA: Corwin Press.

Carr, P. (2008). Educators and education for democracy: Moving beyond "thin" democracy. *Interamerican Journal of Education for Democracy*, 1(2), 146–165.

Cohen, L. & Manion, L. (1994). *Research methods in education. Fourth edition*. New York: Routledge.

Collier, D., Hidalgo, F. D. & Maciuceanu, A. O. (2006). Essentially contested concepts: Debates and applications. *Journal of Political Ideologies*, 11(3), 211–246.

Conway, Paul F., Murphy, Rosaleen, Rath, Anne & Hall, Kathy. (2009). *Learning to teach and its implications for the continuum of the teacher education: A nine-country cross-national study. Report commissioned by Teaching Council*. Maynooth, Ireland: The Teaching Council and Cork, Ireland, University College Cork.

Dahl, A. R. (2002). *Democracy and its critics*. New Haven & London: Yale University Press.

Dahl, A. R. & Lindblom, E. C. (2017 [1992]). *Politics, economics, and welfare*. London & New York: Routledge.

Dahlstedt, M. & Olson, M. (2013). *Utbildning, demokrati, medborgarskap* [Education, democracy, and citizenship] (1st edn.). Malmö: Gleerups.

Davis, B. & Sumara, D. (2006). *Complexity and education: Inquiries into learning, teaching, and research*. Mahway, NJ & London: Lawrence Erlbaum Associates.

de Beauvoir, Simone. (1973). *The second sex*. New York: Vintage Books.

Descartes, R. (1952). *Rules for the direction of mind*. Chicago, IL: Encyclopædia Britannica.

Descartes, R. (1998). *Valda skrifter*. Stockholm. Sweden: Natur och Kultur.
Dewey, J. (1916). Democracy and education [Elektronisk resurs]. Retrieved from https://en.wiki source.org/wiki/Democracy_and_Education
Dewey, J. (2004 [1938]). *Experience and education*. Stockholm. Sweden: Natur och Kultur.
Dewey, J. (1938). *Experience and education*. The Kappa Delta Pi Lecture Series. London & New York: Collier Books Macmillan Publishing Company.
Dewey, J. (1888). *The ethics of democracy*. University of Michigan, Philosophical Papers, Second Series, Number 1. Ann Arbor, MI: Andrews & Company Publishers.
Dorinda, Carter J. Andrews, Richmond, Gail, Warren, Chezare A., Petchaur, Emery & Floden, Robert. (2018). A call to action for teacher preparation programs: Supporting critical conversations and democratic action in safe learning environments. *Journal of Teacher Education*, 69(3), 205–208.
Dryzek, J. S. (2000). *Deliberative democracy and beyond: Liberals, critics, contestations*. Oxford: Oxford University Press.
Eagleton, Terry. (1991). *Ideology: An introduction*. London & New York: Verso.
Edling, S. (2014). Between stereotypes and task complexity: Exploring stereotypes of teachers and education in media as a question of structural violence. *Journal of Curriculum Studies*. Retrieved from www.tandfonline.com/doi/abs/10.1080/00220272.2014.956796
Edling, S. (2016). *Demokratidilemman i läraruppdraget. Att arbeta för lika villkor* [Democracy dilemmas in the teacher mission. To strive for equity]. Stockholm, Sweden: Liber.
Edling, S. (2012/2018). *Vilja andra väl är inte alltid smärtfritt. Att motverka kränkning och diskriminring i förskola och skola*. [Wanting others' wellbeing is not always painless. To oppose violence and discrimination in preschool and school]. Lund, Sweden: Studentlitteratur AB.
Edling, S. & Liljestrtand, Johan. (2019b). "Democracy for me is saying what I want": The teaching profession on free speech, democratic mission and the notion of political correctness in a Swedish context. In Raiker, Andrea, et al. (eds.), *Teacher education and the development of democratic citizenship in Europe*. London: Routledge, pp. 399–415.
Edling, S. & Liljestrand, Johan. (2019a). Let's talk about teacher education!: Analysing the media debates in 2016–2017 on teacher education using Sweden as a case. *Asia-Pacific Journal of Teacher Education* (Online). Retrieved from www.tandfonline.com/doi/full/10.1080/1359866X.2019.1631255. doi:10.1080/1359866X.2019.1631255
Edling, S. & Mooney Simmie, G. (2017). Democracy and emancipation in teacher education: A summative content analysis of teachers' democratic assignment expressed in policies for Teacher Education in Sweden and Ireland between 2000–2010. *Citizenship, Social & Economic Education* (Online), 1–15. doi:10.1177/2047173417743760
Elliott, J. (2001). Making evidence-based practice educational. *British Educational Research Journal*, 27(5), 555–574.
Englund, T. (1986). *Curriculum as a political problem: Changing educational conceptions, with special reference to citizenship education*. Dissertation. Uppsala, Lund, Sweden: Studentlitteratur.
Englund, T. (2005). *Läroplanens och skolkunskapens politiska dimension*. Stockholm, Sweden: Daidalos.
Englund, T. (1997). Towards a dynamic analysis of the content of schooling: narrow and broad didactics in Sweden. *Journal of Curriculum Studies*, 29(3), 267–288.
Fjelde, H. (2012). Orsaker till krig och väpnade konflikter [Reasons for war and armed conflicts]. In K. Aggestam & K. Höglund (eds.), *Om krig och fred: En introduktion till freds- och konfliktstudier* [About war and peace: An introduction to peace and studies of conflicts]. Lund, Sweden: Studentlitteratur, pp. 83–96.
Freire, P. (1972). *Pedagogik för förtryckta*. Stockholm, Sweden: Gummersson.
Fukuyama, Francis. (2020). 30 years of world politics: What has changed? *Journal of Democracy*, 31(1) 11–21.
Fuller, S. (2009). *The Sociology of intellectual life: The career of the mind in and around the academy*. London: SAGE Publications.
Gallie, W. B. (1964). Essentially contested concepts. In W. B. Gallie (ed.), *Philosophy and the historical understanding*. London: Chatto & Windus, pp. 157–191.

Gellner, Ernest. (1981). Nationalism. *Theory and Society*, 10(6), 753–776.
Gilbert, Martin. (1989/2014). *Second World War. A complete history*. Electronic version. New York: Rosetta eBooks.
Giroux, H. A. (1988). *Teachers as intellectuals toward a critical pedagogy of learning*. Westport, CT: Bergin & Garvey.
Giroux, H. A. & McLaren, P. L. (eds.) (1986). *Critical pedagogy, the state, and cultural struggle*. Albany, NY: State University of New York Press.
Gleditsch, Petter, Nils. (1992). Democracy and peace. *Journal of Peace Research*, 29(4), 369–376.
Habermas, J. (1972). *Knowledge and human interests*. London: Heinemann Educational.
Hare, Ivan & Weinstein, James. (2012). *Extreme speech and democracy*. Oxford: Oxford University Press.
Harding, S. G. & Hintikka, M. B. (1983). *Discovering reality: feminist perspectives on epistemology, metaphysics, methodology, and philosophy of science*. Dordrecht, Netherlands, Boston, MA: Springer.
Hargreaves, D. (1997). In defence of research for evidence-based teaching: A rejoinder to Martyn Hammersley. *British Educational Research Journal*, 23(4), 405–419.
Harris, Erika. (2009). *Nationalism: Theories and cases*. Edinburgh, UK: Edinburgh University Press.
Hattie, J. (2009). *Visible learning: A synthesis of over 800 meta-analyses relating to achievement*. London & New York: Routledge.
Hattie, J. (2008). *Visible learning: A synthesis of over 800 meta-analyses relating to achievement*. London & New York: Routledge.
Hattie, J.(2012). *Visible learning for teachers: Maximizing impact on learning*. London & New York: Routledge.
Held, David. (1997). *Demokratimodeller. Från klassisk demokrati till demokratisk autonomi*. [Democracy models. From classical to democratic autonomy]. Göteborg, Sweden: Daidalos.
Heater, Derek. (2004). *A history of education for citizenship*. London & New York: Routledge, Famler.
Hobsbawm, Eric. (1990). *Nations and Nationalism since 1780: Programme, myth, reality*. Cambridge, UK: Cambridge University Press.
Hopmann, Stefan. (2007). Restrained teaching: the common core of Didaktik. *European Educational Research Journal*, 6(2), 109–124.
Hopmann, Stefan. (1997). Wolfgang Klafki och den tyska didaktiken. In M. Uljens (ed.), *Didaktik: teori, reflektion och praktik*. Lund, Sweden: Studentlitteratur, pp. 198–214.
Hume, Mick. (2016). *Trigger warning: Is the fear of being offensive killing free speech?*London: HarperCollins Publishers.
Jay, M. (1996 [1973]) *The dialectical imagination: A history of the Frankfurt School and the Institute of Social Research 1923–1950*. Berkeley, CA, Los Angeles, CA & London: University of California Press.
Karlsson, Klas-Göran. (2003). The holocaust as a problem of historical culture: Theoretical and analytical challenges. In Klas-Göran Karlsson & Ulf Zander (eds.), *Echoes of the holocaust: Historical cultures in contemporary Europe*. Lund, Sweden: Nordic Academic Press, pp. 9–57.
Kant, Immanuel. (1784). What is enlightenment? [Was ist Aufklärung?]. Retrieved from https://pdfs.semanticscholar.org/dc3e/6ea5f77724114ac39252dbeabe6ab1909aca.pdf [19. 09. 17].
Keesing-Styles, L. (2003). The relationship between critical pedagogy and assessment in teacher education. *Radical Pedagogy*, 5(1), 1–20.
Kincheloe, J. (2004). The knowledges of teacher education developing a critical complex epistemology. *Teacher Education Quarterly*, Winter, 49–66.
Kirsch, Helen & Welzel, Christian. (2019). Democracy misunderstood: Authoritarian notions of democracy around the globe. *Social Forces*, 98(1), 59–92.
Kuhn, Thomas. S. (1996). *The structure of scientific revolutions*. Chicago, IL: University of Chicago Press.
Kuru, Ahmed. (2009). *Secularism and state policies toward religion: The United States, France, and Turkey*. Cambridge, UK: Cambridge University Press.
Levinsson, M. (2013). *Evidens och existens. Evidensbaserad undervisning i ljuset av lärares erfarenheter*. Göteborg, Sweden: Göteborgs Universitetet.
Lindensjö, Bo & Lundgren, Ulf P. (2000). *Utbildningsreformer och politisk styrning* [Educational reform and political governing]. Stockholm, Sweden: HLS förl.

Linz, Juan J. (2000). *Totalitarian and authoritarian regimes.* Boulder, CO & London: Lynne Rienner Publishers.

Lloyd, G. (1983). Reason, gender and morality in the history of philosophy. *Social Research,* 50(3), 490–513.

Lundgren, Ulf P. (1998). The making of curriculum making: Reflections on educational research and the use of educational research. In S. Hopmann & B. B. Gundem (eds.), *Didaktik and/or curriculum: An international dialogue.* New York: Peter Lang, pp. 149–162.

McLaren, P.(2016). *Pedagogy of insurrection.* New York:Peter Lang.

McLaren, P. (1998). Revolutionary pedagogy in post-revolutionary times: Rethinking the political, economy of critical education. *Educational theory,* 48(4), 431–462.

McLaren, P. & Jandrić, Petar. (2019, in press). *Post-digital dialogues, liberation theology and information technology.* London: Bloomsbury.

Marx, C. & Engels, F. (2009). *Kommunistiska manifestet.* Stockholm, Sweden:Nixon.

Mooney Simmie, G. & Edling, S. (2016). Ideological governing forms in education and teacher education: a comparative study between highly secular Sweden and highly non-secular Republic of Ireland. *Nordic Journal of Studies in Educational Policy,* 2016(1), 1–12.

Mooney Simmie, G. & Edling, S. (2019). Teachers' democratic assignment: A critical discourse analysis of teacher education policies in Ireland and Sweden. *Discourse Studies in the Cultural Politics of Education,* 40(6) 832–846.

Moses, Michele & Saenz, Lauren. (2012). When the majority rules: Ballot initiatives, race-conscious education policy and the public good. Review of educational research, American Educational Research Association. *Education, democracy and the public good,* 36, 113–138.

Mouffe, Chantal. (2005). *On the political.* London & New York: Routledge.

Mouffe, Chantal. (2000). *The democratic paradox.* London & New York: Verso.

Nelson, B. (2002, September 23). Schools must teach values. *The Age.* Retrieved from www.theage.com.au/articles/2002/09/22/1032055034022.html

Nicoll, K., Fejes, Andreas, Olson, Maria, Dahlstedt, Magnus & Biesta, Gert J. J. (2013). Opening discourses of citizenship education: a theorization with Foucault. *Journal of Education Policy,* 28 (6), 828–846.

Nirenberg, David. (1998). *Communities of violence: Persecution of minorities in the Middle Ages.* Princeton, NJ: Princeton University Press.

Nordström, S. (2008). *Illusionernas harmoni. Samhällsplanerandets tankestil och dess kraftfullaste topos: diskrepansförnekandet.* Karlstad, Sweden: Karlstad University.

Ó'Buachalla, Séamas. (1988). *Education policy in twentieth century Ireland.* Dublin, Ireland: Wolfhound Press.

O'Leary, Brendan. (1997). On the nature of nationalism: An appraisal of Ernest Gellner's writings on nationalism. *British Journal of Political Science,* 27(2), 191–222.

Pettersson, Olof. (1994). *Hur styrs Europa? Den politiska maktutövningen i Europas stater.* Göteborg, Sweden: Publica, Fritzes Förlag AB.

Pinar, William. (2004). *What is curriculum theory?*Mahwah, NJ: Lawrence Erlbaum.

Pinker, S. (2018). *Enlightenment now: The case for reason, science, humanism, and progress.* New York: Penguin Audio Books.

Riley, Dylan. J. (2007). The Paradx of positivism. *Social Science History,* 31(1), 115–126.

Rüsen, Jörn. (2006). Historical consciousness: Narrative structure, moral function, and ontogenetic development. In Peter Seixas (eds.), *Theorizing historical consciousness.* Toronto, Canada: University of Toronto Press, pp. 63–85.

Rydgren, Jens. (2018). The radical right. An introduction. In Jens Rydgren (ed.), *The Oxford handbook of the radical right.* Oxford: Oxford University Press, pp. 1–16.

Säfström, C. A. (2011). Rethinking emancipation, rethinking education. *Studies in Philosophy of Education,* 30(2), 199–209.

Säfström, C. A. (2010). The immigrant has no proper name: the disease of consensual democracy within the myth of schooling. *Educational Philosophy and Theory,* 42(5–6), 605–617.

Säfström, C. A.& Biesta, G.(2001). Learning democracy in a world of difference. *The School Field*, 12(5/6), 5–20.

Schivelbusch, Wolfgang. (2014). *The railway journey: The industrialization of time and space in the nineteenth century*. Oakland, CA: University of California Press.

Schnebel, K. (2016). Dilemma over the issue of inequality: A strategy against political apathy (Politikverdrossenheit). *Citizenship, Social, and Economic Education*, 15(3), 262–270.

Tan, Emmanuel. (2014). Human capital theory: A holistic criticism. *Review of Educational Research*, 84(3), 411–445.

The Economist (2018). Democracy continues its disturbing retreat. Retrieved from www.economist.com/graphic-detail/2018/01/31/democracy-continues-its-disturbing-retreat

Van Creveld, Martin. (1991). *The transformation of war. The most radical reinterpretation of armed conflict since Clausewitz*. New York: The free press.

Varoufakis, Yanis. (2016). *And the weak suffer what they must? Europe's crisis and America's economic future*. New York: Nation Books.

Walkerdine, Valerie. (1989). Femininity as performance. *Oxford Review of Education*, 15(3), 267–279.

Weedon, C. (1999). *Feminism, theory and the politics of difference*. Malden, Netherlands: Blackwell Publishers.

Williams, Michelle Hale. (2018). The political impact of radical right. In Jens Rydgren (ed.), *The Oxford handbook of the radical right*. Oxford, UK: Oxford University Press, pp. 305–326.

Wollstonecraft, M. (1793). *A vindication of the rights of woman: with strictures on political and moral subjects*. Dublin, Ireland: J. Moore.

Youdell, D. (2011). *School trouble identity, power and politics in education*. London; Routledge.

Young, I. M. (1997). *Intersecting voices: Dilemmas of gender, political philosophy, and policy*. Princeton, NJ: Princeton University Press.

Zizek, Slavoj. (1989). *The Sublime object of ideology*. London & New York: Verso.

3 The policy cycle

Introduction

This chapter examines the **policy cycle** in education, that is to say the cyclical nature of policy making and policy into practice and the multiple ways **reforms** nowadays shape and continually reshape new risk-managed understandings of teacher education and democracy. Biesta's (2013) assertion is that

> Education always involves a risk ... The risk is there, because, as W.B. Yeats has put it, education is not about filling a bucket but is about lighting a fire. The risk is there because it is not an interaction between robots but an encounter between human beings. Yes, we educate because we want results ... but that does not mean an educational technology ... a perfect match between 'input' and 'output' is possible or desirable. And the reason for this lies in the simple fact that if we take the risk out of education, there is a real chance that we take out education altogether.
>
> (p. 1)

Throughout this chapter, and indeed throughout the book, we will be arguing that taking the risk out of teacher education leaves the distinct probability that education itself will be removed. By reforms we mean changes that are required of practice settings by governments, more often than not mandated in public (political) policies by legislation, by the state and state agencies (and professional bodies). The tendency to regulate education through policies is not problematic in itself, seeing that education is a public matter and an important political question. Indeed, the purpose of the chapter is not to argue that policies need to be abolished but rather to problematize the way current policy in education is both framed and used in contemporary times and how it sets the frames for teachers' and (student) teachers' everyday conditions in education – not least for questions concerning democracy.

New modes of network governance and superstructures have spawned policy flows and assemblages in education (Ball, 2016; Youdell, 2011). Policies are nowadays understood as already diversity proofed for social justice issues, equity and inclusion. Using this new construct of governance means that policymakers, such as state inspectors and state agencies can increasingly distance themselves from direct (moral) responsibility for provision of inputs/resources and instead focus on making new policies and quality assurance methods, testing whether desired outcomes have been achieved. Some researchers and teacher educators in policy studies ask who are the policy actors with the most influence, whose voices are pushed to the margins and overall whose interests are served by new global reforms.

How is the relationship expressed between global, national and local interests? How is the relationship expressed between Biesta's three stated purposes of education (see Chapter 1) – grasped by us as handling dilemmas for the teacher: the push for **qualification** and skill-set needed by the fast changing needs of the economy, the requirement for **socialization** into a culture and heritage and **emancipatory** spaces for subjectification of the young person emerging as a unique subject and for affordances for a dynamic plural view of democracy?

In this chapter we will highlight dilemmas/tensions which we consider from the perspectives of the rhetoric of policy and the lived reality and experience of practitioners. To begin with the chapter deals with the interplay between the global, national and local levels in education – why certain discourses achieve epistemic dominance (in relation to questions of knowledge, knowers and values) and why others experience push-back or are written out of the policy agenda. In relation to the tensions between the global, national and local levels, dilemmas related to education as public and/or public good are explored as well as questions concerning the desire for certainty that tends to be materialized in the increased construction of Acts (juridification) in order to overcome uncertainty. The chapter also highlights tensions between policy understood as 'Policy as Implemented' and/or 'Policy as Enacted in practice settings', which in turn focuses on dilemmas linked to the relationship between official policy imperatives and the dynamic, contextualized and nuanced nature of practice. The dilemmas created in the tension of these values distinguish between mainstream discourses, where it is understood that policy is implemented in straightforward rational ways and the sophisticated processes at play in processes of policy enactment – the teacher engaged in complex, creative and critical processes of translation, interpretation where affordances for particularity, plurality and context are taken into account. Finally, we examine tensions between the contemporary use of a new language of 'learning', concentrating on individual and national competitiveness to define all aspects of policy and/or education understood as a multi-disciplinary field including history and philosophy. In these dilemmas we see that strong external demands for new modes of public accountability (given responsibilities), a fixation on metrics, understaffing and weak financial supports risks pushing teachers/educators felt responsibilities for student-centred education to the margins (e.g. Edling & Frelin, 2013). The tensions in question can also be connected to ideas about the existence of pure objectivity that stand in opposition to subjectivity.

We will structure the chapter as follows. First, we examine the rapid changes taking place today in the education policy cycle due to the epistemic dominance of global policy actors, especially multinational companies and economic agencies, such as the World Bank, European Commission and OECD (European Commission, 2018; Sellar & Lingard, 2013). Second, we interrogate the policy cycle and the distinction that Ball, Maguire & Braun (2012) make between policy implementation and policy enactment for an alternative understanding of teacher education as emancipatory practices that play a significant public interest role in securing a vibrant and decent democracy. Third, we show how a market-led discourse with its black box of standards, components and competences presents a narrow view of an ideal teacher and how this is supported by a new language of learning (Edling & Mooney Simmie, 2017; Skerritt, 2018). Finally, we consider some implications of (re)framing the student teacher as a compliant functionary inside the contemporary social order and without the critical capabilities, transformative possibility, agency, activism and potentiality of working toward and (re)shaping that social order in the direction of an equitable and decent democracy.

Table 3.1 An overview of dilemmas discussed in Chapter 3

Dilemmas
Global versus national versus local
Public versus the private
Certain versus uncertain
Policy as implemented versus policy as enacted
Language of 'Learning' versus other aspects of education
State Control through Fixation on Metrics versus Student-Centred Education (control versus freedom)
Objectivity versus subjectivity

Various policy cycles

Since the start of public forms of schooling in the 1800s, coinciding with the formation of nation states and the start of the industrial revolution, education policy has been shaped by the changing needs of the economy and political philosophies and has always changed to reflect 'crises in the economy' (Arendt, 1961). In relation to this, four different and intersecting tools to analyse political governing can be used in order to understand the policy cycle and hence the relationship between state and education over time, namely: **legal-**, **ideological-**, **economic-** and **governing through control**. Legal governing has to do with the way the state creates acts that are mandatory to follow and which define responsibilities and set the limit for action. The acts are always tinted by a governing ideology that defines desired values, visions and outcomes. Democracy is one example of an ideology that is regulated through acts. Education is also governed by economy and the way the economy is structured to shape education to harmonize with law and ideology. Finally, in dialogue with the former, the state governs through control, i.e. by for instance doing visits to schools, creating national test scores, and intervening in conflict situations (Edling & Liljestrand, 2019; Lindensjö & Lundgren, 2000; Lundgren, 1989; Mooney Simmie & Edling, 2016). The governing forms are here used as tools to grapple with the policy cycle of education.

Besides these governing forms, **globalization** and **technologization** have become expedient policy solutions for a new ideal human and a new social order since the aftermath of a global recession. By globalization we mean the way key political and economic decisions are taken on a world stage in preference to a national stage. The global recession has added to fears in the west of losing national economic competitiveness. This fear has resulted in massive changes in education, including securing new teacher education policies based on scientific certainty and buttressed by legislation, layers of bureaucracy and more authoritarianism, testing and evaluation than heretofore (Ball, 2003; Cochran-Smith et al., 2017; McLaren, 2016).

The rhetoric of public policy documents in teacher education suggests there is an ideal quality teacher and ideal school leader and that all teachers and school leaders can be compared, and can compare themselves, to this ideal type using data analytics – a view of education that suggests that what counts can also be counted – leading to a new fixation on metrics (Lynch, 2015; Muller, 2018).

Mainstream views of the **policy cycle** suggest that reforms travel from the state and state agencies to the field of practice through straightforward linear rational processes of policy implementation. Instead, Ball, Maguire and Braun (2012) using research evidence from twelve case study schools in London, argue for an alternative theorization of policy enactment. **Policy as enactment** places the spotlights on teachers and teacher educators working in their practice settings are understood as engaging in highly sophisticated and complex relational and intellectual processes that take culture, contexts, diversity, particularity and plurality into account and have affordances for spaces for teachers' democratic assignment in relation to emancipation and democracy. By policy enactment we mean that official policies become embedded in real-world settings through complex, creative and critical processes of translation, interpretation and (re)contextualization. This supports arguments in the book that dilemmatic spaces need to be recognized in teacher education for emancipation and democracy.

This places the attention on various ways of understanding **norms**. A norm comes into expression as a social rule that dictates what is an acceptable mode of being and acting with other people. If people do not adapt to norms they tend to be excluded, implicitly or explicitly attacked in different ways by people abiding to this norm. Norms can come into expression on macro, meso, and micro levels. **Norms on a macro level** are those that are expressed in various political acts, which define what is acceptable and not acceptable in accordance with those who govern. **Norms on a meso level** provide an awareness that norms on a macro level have to be interpreted in various institutions and organizations in ways that influence their meaning and direction for action. For example the notion of value foundation needs to be interpreted by schools and preschools in order to bring the act into educational practice, but during the process of interpretation the emphasis and understanding of what this work means tend to shift. Finally, there are also **norms on a micro level** through the way various people bring their world-views created in social settings outside education into the space of education, hence influencing their perceptions and actions (Edling, 2016). While policy implementation mainly focus on the seemingly objective norms expressed in state acts, policy enactment also emphasizes the intrinsic and complex ways policy comes to be approached in the various social levels and in relations always coloured by the subjective.

This is an important distinction because an understanding of policy as implemented sets up the teacher as a technician (Ball, 1995) and a compliant functionary of the system, whereas policy as enacted positions the teacher as an intellectual engaged in a complex epistemology of education (Kincheloe, 2004). Inherent dangers of symbolic violence and injustice can be found in this mainstream view of **policy as implemented** as there is no requirement for mediation with the wider world and no consideration given to power relations. By this way of thinking teachers/teacher educators are expected to step up, take responsibility and do whatever is (often legally) required/mandated of them. A global governance turn toward practice and profit provides the rationale for reconceptualization of the ideal educator and teacher as a self-regulating entrepreneur, using a toolkit of methods and techniques to act as a producer of evidence-based outcomes for all students, irrespective of background, context, race, gender or class (see Figure 3.1).

In classroom teaching this involves stating, diagnosing, fixing, measuring and reporting learning outcomes of students that are considered to be fixed and predetermined. Dylan William, an educational researcher in a research cluster called *Inside the Black Box* in Kings College London in his podcast (see Supplementary readings), speaks of his understanding of good teachers. Using the metaphor of a pilot controlling an aeroplane he compares the work of the teacher to that of a pilot who knows exactly in advance where he/she starts his/her flight from, how he/she charts the journey taking all significant coordinates into account, what airport he/she wants to land the aeroplane in, in which city and at which

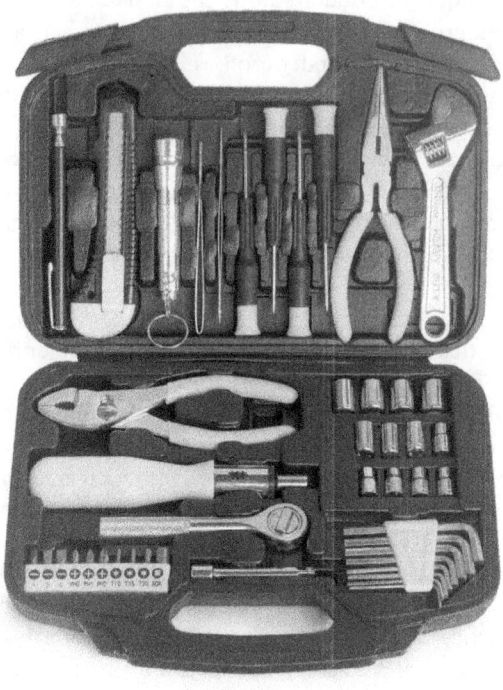

Figure 3.1 Quality teaching understood as a well-defined toolkit of pedagogies.

Figure 3.2 William compares the teacher's role with a pilot landing an aeroplane.

pre-specified runway (see Figure 3.2). This presents the task of the teacher as an instructor who is engaging in a technical and pre-specified task of scientific planning and certainty. It exemplifies a policy imperative of Darwinian strength that we will write about later in Chapter 6.

Tensions between global, national and local policy spaces

In the 20th century it was customary to understand the policy cycle as primarily reflecting national interests and involving a minority of key national players, not all with the same power and privilege to influence the policy debate (O'Buachalla, 1988). There were also international influences on policies, as governments collectively responded to the changing polity, such as reforms for every young person to complete compulsory education and diversified pathways through new comprehensive school systems. Comparative policy impulses between countries were always in existence, from the mid-nineteenth century onwards, often using giant annual exhibitions. This comparative impulse was to become far more pronounced as the push toward comparative statistics in psychology in education for an understanding of pedagogy as a science took hold in the 1960s (Arendt, 1961).

However, what is different nowadays in the current crisis in education, which in many ways can be interpreted as a crisis in democracy (the subject of this book), is that a new economic purpose of education for competitive individualism underpinned by **Human Capital Theory** (HCT) (for qualification, credential, knowledge, skill, training, coaching and instruction) has gained dominance over other purposes (e.g. subjectification, socialization, emancipation and democracy) which have all become subordinated to a lower positioning. Human Capital Theory was established by economists and policymakers coming from a neoliberal school of thought and quickly became a preferred way of understanding and predicting human behaviour using data analytics (Harvey, 2007). Tan's (2014) holistic critique shows how HCT uses the pre-eminence of the economy, underpinned by rational choice theory and methodological individualism to take precedence over 'the social, cultural, intellectual, and aesthetic benefits of education' which assume a subsidiary position. In this way the wider moral and socio-political aspects of democracy have become debased and subjugated as secondary spin-offs, what Tan (2014) calls "**positive externalities**" (p. 413), by which he means that they can and might proffer positive outcomes but if and when they do they will do this only as a spin-off rather than the primary rationale. In this way, politics once considered the art of the possible has become narrowly constructed using a reductionist view of scientific planning and **New Quality Management** that implies former understood spaces and affordances for creativity, arts, autonomy, aesthetics, the feminine, imagination, the local have been subsumed into an essentialist view (Lynch et al., 2012; Lindblad, Pettersson, and Popkewitz, 2018; Snyder, 2018).

Public policies, such as education policies, are continually made, remade and implemented in **cyclical cycles** of policymaking, remaking, forming and reforming that require ongoing connections with policy actors from civil society, research, higher education institutes, government agencies, non-government agencies, trade unions, parent/guardian representatives, business interests, church bodies, schools and colleges etc. **Policy actors** include policymakers, government ministers, politicians, researchers, teacher educators, church interests, school administrators, managers, teachers, students, parents, trade union officials and business interests. Social partnerships staged by government agencies are involved in consultation in the public forum. However, not all policy actors carry the same weight in negotiations and differential power and social relations operate in a deeply uneven playing field (Apple, 2012; O'Buachalla, 1988).

In contemporary times, this policy landscape has become an uneven policy landscape of multinational corporations and supranational agencies, e.g. the EC, World Bank, OECD, their CEOs and *New Quality Managers* (Lynch et al., 2012). These are supported by a number of non-government agencies and a variety of neoconservative policy actors and professionals. Because of the primacy of the economy, reforms defined as a **Global Education Reform Movement** (GERM) dominate over pressing national and local interests, as the law, science, finance and every available means is used to push through modes of schooling for competitive individualism and national competitive advantage (Ball, 2003; Mooney Simmie, 2012, 2014, 2015, 2019; Tan, 2014). Arguing otherwise carries a price as Ben Ferencz reminds us in his podcast (see supplementary readings) that lessons from the Second World War have yet to be learned and that people can be ostracized and murdered if found critically questioning or threatening in any way one of the following: the economy, religion and/or the nation state.

In Europe and across the OECD, GERM introduces a change in ideology and ideological governing forms (see Chapter 2) which greatly diminish the role of the state in upholding public interest values and providing public services such as education, health, housing. We are living at a time in Europe where the former **Social Welfare State** based on the public good and care for the vulnerable in society is changed to a new privatized view of a **Social Investment State**. In this latter view the ideal human is considered as an entrepreneurial individual who practices resilience, invests in themselves and who never looks toward the state for support. This ideal human is grasped using a masculinist discourse of Darwinian strength for a competitive individual whose social relations while necessary are often portrayed as functional and limited to exchange-value (see Chapter 6).

This make-over of the ideal human is supported by a vast technology of data analytics, bits and bytes for developing an ideal healthy, perpetually young, active and fit body and mind (McLaren & Jandrić, 2019). To enact this neoliberal model the state relies on schools and teacher education institutions to comply with this policy experiment, new authoritarian systems of schooling for a **disciplinary order**, rather than a democratic social order and practice (Ball, 2003, Mooney Simmie, 2012, 2019; Säfström, 2011). From this perspective we arrive at an actuarial model of teaching and teacher education where schooling is solely about providing a private good, a personalized investment in a career trajectory, adding value and increasing future earning power, and all the while increasing productivity for national economic growth.

Private good and/or public good

Tensions between education as a **private good** and/or a **public good** are worth pausing at for a minute, seeing that the relationship between the two sets the scope for the responsibilities for the state. Education for a private good narrows down the responsibilities of the state to only focus on principles and forms leaving people's everyday relations, behaviours and ways of being to others and to the private domain. However, when education is regarded as a **public good** it implies that some private issues cannot be kept solely in the private sphere, since they impinge on what is deemed as good and desirable for society at large (Levin, 1987; McNeil, 2002).

The interrelationship between the public and private domain of education implies that teachers and school staff are obliged to pay attention to and interpret what takes place in the flow of practice in their everyday work (Edling, 2016). It can be about aspects associated with a broad understanding of democracy and hence the ways in which justice, ethics and equity come into play in people's day-to-day lives.

An example of a dilemma discussed at a teacher education institution in Sweden is a series of violent cases that took place at an elite boarding school in 2009, 2011 and 2013. One case regarded a student who was burned with an iron by older students during an initial ritual and who, together with his parents, filed a complaint to the police. The complaint obliged the Swedish School Inspectorate to interfere in the school's business by conducting an inquiry and taking measures based on this analysis. The Swedish School Inspectorate found that staff at the school did not put sufficient focus on the overall environment where reoccurring violations in everyday relations were normalized. While the school reacted when those breaking rules (Acts) were caught, they did not have any language to analyse the flow of relations. As such the elite boarding school did not live up to the Democratic Value Foundation which is emphasized as vital to pay regard to in the School Act and the Swedish school curriculum. Consequently, the school was shut down for a short time, creating a massive protest amongst parents, teachers and students who argued that it was not fair since it was only a few persons who broke the rules while the majority of the students were good. The staff also argued that the fights taking place after school were a private matter and hence a question amongst siblings (see Francia and Edling, 2016).

The example generated a discussion amongst student teachers where some argued that state interference feels like a police state, while others argued that it is good that the state interfered since pupils where suffering. The frictions between education as a public good and a private good are ongoing and can also be connected to a will to overcome the fuzziness and hence uncertainty of human relations by increasing Acts that can provide greater clarity and the right answers.

The phenomenon of juridification

Teacher failure to expediently arrive at desired successful outcomes can become all too readily construed as non-compliance with policy understood as legal mandate in a new wave of **juridification** (Arneback, 2012) and/or (political) interference (Mooney Simmie, 2019). The concept **juridification** is a process in westerns nations where an increasing number of areas in education come to be regulated by law, rendering a shift from ethics and teachers' professional judgements to the expertise of legal professionals. Accordingly the legal dimension of political governing increases within the field of education as a strife to strengthen control and certainty (Novak, 2018; Runesdotter, 2016), which also involves the field of human relations.

Thus, we understand juridification to include all educational policy requirements that are legally binding, and ideologically framed by policymakers, and for which teacher educators/teachers must publicly account for successes using evidence, such as, predetermined 'black boxes' of standards, competences, skills, components and dispositions for a risk-managed activity of quality instruction.

Currently, the right to exist without being subjected to physical and psychological violence grounded on the Convention of the Children's Right (CDR) is regulated by various steering instruments: (a) School Act [*Skollagen*], Chapter 1, 5 and 6 (2010: 800), (b) Discrimination Act [*Diskrimineringslagen*] (2008: 567), (c) The Swedish Work Environment

Act [*Arbetsmiljölagen*] (1977: 1160), (d) The Swedish Penal Code [*Brottsbalken*] (Ds 1999:36), (e) The Swedish Social Services Act [*Socialtjänstlagen*] (1980: 620), (f) Curriculum [*Läroplaner*] (Lpfö,11, Lgr-11, Lpf-11), and (g) local documents.

This implies that teachers are **given a responsibility** by the state in Sweden to actively work with aspects related to a broad conception of democracy. The responsibility is legally binding and municipalities are held accountable and are hence punished if the policy documents are not followed, which implies that preschools, schools and school staff (including teachers) are implicitly held accountable too. This tends to create fear and stress amongst teachers of being punished when they interfere in classrooms and schools (Arneback, 2012) and often they choose to report events taking place in schools to the police to watch their backs. The consequence of this is that teachers, rather than handling challenges through dialogue, file crime reports where the problem is handled through the logic of the court (Lunneblad & Johanson, 2018).

There are several examples when a teacher striving for order has ended up in court. For example, three boys at an elementary school in Sweden placed a sofa in the middle of a corridor that made it difficult for the staff and other pupils to pass. When the students did not listen to the nearest adult a teacher was summoned, who ordered them to put the sofa back and leave. Two of the boys obeyed, while the third one refused, which made the teacher finally lift him physically in order to remove him. The event led to the parents filing a complaint with the help of BEO (child and pupil ombudsman/representative) and accusing the school of violating their son who has a diagnosis that requires low affective strategies in conflicts. The case went to court and the municipality and the teacher was freed on two levels, but BEO decided to proceed to the High Court.[1] A similar example was discussed at a course about the democratic value foundation, where one student teacher stressed that these Acts should be abolished because they are obstacles to order and knowledge, another raised the question how teachers should act since whatever they do they tend to end up as failing, while a third teacher maintained that Acts are important in order to handle soft values like equal treatment since they otherwise tend to be ignored.

A public education without acts is difficult to achieve while at the same time a strong belief in the power of acts to reduce human complexity is problematic too. The acts are written by people who are legally skilled and it is not always easy for teachers to understand them since the language and logic are different than what takes place in education (Hult & Lindgren, 2016). Teachers are at times forced to face dilemmas between **given responsibilities** stemming from state policy and **felt responsibilities** that erupt in encounters with students (Edling & Frelin, 2013). In a dialogue with a teacher educator in Sweden, whom we can call Miranda the burden of not doing enough erupted:

> Some of the student teachers are really weak and I feel that the time I give them is not enough. They need someone who guides them in the beginning and who takes time listening to their question. I try, but there is so much else that I'm obliged to do. This situation drains energy from me now and then ... is it worth it? But then suddenly someone writes me a long email and thanks me for my help and suddenly it feels worthwhile, but it is difficult.

In Ireland, there has also been a ramping up of laws in the last decade that introduces a new language of policy compliance and (law) enforcement across all aspects of the curriculum, teacher education and more recently in policy reforms in relation to school leadership. This is a live issue in a doctoral study by Sheehan (2016) where he critically interrogates the changing shape of policy directives in primary school education and interviews primary school principals/administrators in the south-west of Ireland in relation to their understandings on moral leadership. The study reveals a time of intense fixation on metrics in primary school education and can be interpreted as a new wave of juridification when school principals/administrators feel under intense pressure to comply with policy directives as a top-down mode of policy implementation rather than engage in more sophisticated understandings of policy enactment and discursive spaces for dilemma management and/or capability to question authority and critically read the world. This is captured in a comment from a doctoral study on leadership:

> this case study suggests a highly conservative and compliant group of moral leaders who are focused on managerial effectiveness and fulfilling duties and statutory obligations while, at the same time, working with staff and others to avoid conflict and maintain positive relationships through forms of consensus, in their cultural and historical contexts.
>
> (Sheehan, 2016, p. 166)

It was noted in the study that the way of handling diversity does not involve seeking to generate tolerance of all viewpoints and the creation of democratic relations in the school settings:

> instead, the moral imperatives (for inclusion) appears in keeping with Catholic social teaching and the development of non-adversarial forms of communitarianism, as described by O'Sullivan (2005) and understood within the statistic that 92% of primary schools in Ireland are publicly funded and privately managed by Catholic trustees, with Catholic ethos protected in the Education Act (1988).
>
> (p.166)

School principals were conscious of their (moral) role in seeking to mind and retain gaps for altruistic care of the child as well as handing increasing levels of bureaucratic policy imperatives. However, their approach appeared to rely on practical maturity/experience rather than philosophical co-inquiry with critical friends, debate and/or connection to the literature. One school principal, let's call him Neil, suggested that

> maturity and experience allows you to take chances. The gaps can be breached and widened with a bit of common sense and knowing how things work. We are human and we need to be human. People have to be looked after, not statistics.
>
> (Sheehan, 2016, p. 140)

Another principal, let's call him Conor, suggested that he was 'very conscious of creating that space or that gap for the staff to work in. My creating that space is having a good environment around the school (Sheehan, 2016, p. 140). A female school principal, let's call her Aoife had difficulty with a scientific focus: 'I don't believe in reducing children's achievements to outcomes or SMART targets. I won't do SMART targets. everything now is based on results. It is appalling' (Sheehan, 2016, p. 141). Another male principal concurred and wanted to ask: 'Where are the children in all this talk of targets and scores? What space is there for the child?' (p. 141).

Female school principals in the study were particularly conscious of the problem of doing the job of school leadership and making sure they exuded Darwinian strength in the role (see Chapter 6). The following comment from the school principal, let's call her Anna, summarizes this dilemma:

> Being open and available can be abused and can be taken as a weakness, particularly from male members of staff when I put on the heels to give me a little bit of height. Being a female leader of a large school is not an easy task. The glass ceiling is still there. Members of the male staff also sometimes don't like to have to be answerable or accountable to a female leader. You have to learn to hold your ground and toughen yourself up a bit I find, if you are a woman on the job. There's no doubt about that.
> (Sheehan, 2016, p. 154)

What is at times forgotten is that seemingly clear and precise acts need to be interpreted in ways that require tools for interpretation, rendering it important not to isolate social relations from acts but rather start from broader social perspectives and questions that help widen the understanding of social challenges and ways to approach them (Edling, 2016).

New language of learning

Besides a legal turn and the enhancement of a legal language, a specific 'scientistic' turn is more intensely stressed today in the way teaching and teacher education are increasingly understood as a new **language of learning** – such as self-directed learning, lifelong learning, teaching and learning – in the field of education. Biesta (2012) calls this a new 'empty discourse of learning' (p. 35) as it fails to take into account **what** content is to be learned, **why** this content needs to be learned and **from whom** content is learned. Moreover, this new language of learning has nowadays colonized the field of education and we notice that it has started to replace the term 'education' itself with 'learning' in policy documents. For example, a European Commission policy document in 2018 defined education as 'nested systems of learning' (European Commission, 2018). A new language of learning greatly simplifies the complexity of good teaching and teacher educator development (Edling & Mooney Simmie, 2017; Mooney Simmie, Moles, & O'Grady, 2019; Skerritt, 2018). Education as learning starts to be viewed using an experimental lens that relies more on empiricism and the natural sciences for a (medicalized) clinical view, which has more in common with scientism than with good science, as the latter is always partial and incomplete (Hyslop-Margison & Naseem, 2007). While this kind of research is important, a narrow focus tends to increase polarizations that overlook complexity. For example:

On several occasions student teachers and teacher educators in Sweden and Ireland have argued that education needs to move from the field of abstract and useless theories to methods that work. A doctoral student from London whom we can call Christine was studying teacher education using a statistical lens, and she was worried because the empirical data she had gathered did not fit her methodological tool kit. According to Christine she did not know what to do because she was obliged to use the same methods and research questions as her supervisor and research group did. After a long discussion she decided to only use the data that could fit into the method while saving those aspects that did not fit into the tight framework for later.

What in former times was considered teacher's Continuous Professional Development (CPD) has become reframed as Teacher Professional Learning (TPL) and Teacher Educator Professional Learning (TEPL). The emphasis on public policy and research studies has moved from a humanistic and holistic discourse of relations and dialogue to an atomistic view of listings of characteristics and orientations of teacher learning. According to Crowe (2014), using the scientific method as a problem-solving approach to issues of pedagogy in teaching, and the pedagogy of teacher education and learning, is similar to 'studying the stars using a microscope'. Instead, Crowe and others argue for **complexity theory** which, while data driven, takes context, particularity and nuance into account and is not prepared to make simplistic correlations between teacher outcomes and student outcomes (Opfer & Peddar, 2011; Mooney Simmie et al., 2019). This latter viewpoint is increasingly important in a runaway world where teacher education is increasingly imbued with statutory laws and requirements for a technocratic and risk-managed albeit specialized activity.

One example of the narrowing of teacher learning can be seen in the national training of support service personnel in Ireland. Support service personnel are generally teachers seconded from their teaching posts to act as regional support personnel and trainers to teachers and schools for the initial phase of enactment of various policy reforms. In the past, it was customary for each presenter to be given slides at national level as a shared resource which presenters could draw from to make their presentations to teachers and school administrators at regional venues. Nowadays, presenters receive a set of 'locked' slides from state agencies which they are required to present in the same way at each venue and with no affordances for interpretation, nuance or context. Moreover, the rationale for this view of the policy cycle, with its highly contestable concepts, remains discursively overworked and under-theorized.

In the new **performative discourses** of 'quality' and 'quality assurance' commensurate with business-like education, the teacher, and by implication, the teacher educator are singled out as the most important factors for developing, problem-solving and reporting young people's success trajectory. This reshapes a new blame game directed toward educators by politicians, legislators and policymakers. Teaching and teacher education are viewed as exercises in problem-solving and there are little or no affordances for problem-posing, revealing the hidden curriculum, examining unexamined assumptions and ideological governance forms that underpin current education and teacher policies. In this regard, much of the mainstream research in teacher development and Gunter's (2001) designation of the 'critical' is cast aside using rationales that legitimate techno-managerial discourses of learning for teacher effectiveness and improvement.

Qualitative research studies in teacher education capture the stress, anxiety and potential for damage inherent in a rhetoric of policy implementation. Brady (2016, 2019a, 2019b) shows that new modes of teacher self-evaluation enacted in Ireland's policy reforms act as 'debased modes' for an era of performativity. Bourke, Lidstone and Ryan (2015) share the reductionist form public accountability takes in teacher education in Australia. Santoro (2017) re-names the problem as teacher demoralization and speaks to the ethical suppression of teachers' agency and voices by virtue of the effects of a hierarchical system of schooling and the (political) primacy of economic competitiveness.

Teacher educators are often forced to handle new intensive bureaucratic demands, such as filling in official forms and writing laborious reports, while their professional observations and judgements evoke a different type of responsibility in relation to students' immediate needs. Every unexpected event like a group of student teachers having difficulties cooperating, a student teacher feeling sad for failing an exam, a student teacher suffering from dyslexia, an arrogant student who dominates groups and so forth all become events that should be handled but are in danger of being overlooked due to other bureaucratic demands. Indeed, the balance between external demands and internal judgement is always challenging, but what is known is that too much external control, that signals a distrust in teachers' work, risks hampering teachers' professional judgement (e.g. Krantz & Fritzén, 2017; Stanley & Stronach, 2013; Swann et al., 2010) just as teachers acting on their own is equally problematic.

In this way the tyranny of a market-led policy discourse of education enacts a **quiet suffocation of democracy** (Browning, 2018). For example, a new deficit discourse is in evidence in the use of a new language of learning, used profusely in public policy documents. Biesta (2012) calls this an 'empty discourse of learning' (p. 35) and argues that for people to learn they have to learn some selected content, they need to learn it for a particular purpose and they need to learn it from somebody. Instead, a discourse of learning – and education nowadays portrayed as nested systems of learning (EC, 2018) – aligns itself unproblematically with a commodification of education as a competitive discourse for individual and national economic successes (Ball, 2003, 2016). We will now briefly explore the epistemic dominance of the OECD in education and democracy and the multiple soft and strategic ways it bends teacher education in an arc of performativity for the primacy of the economy.

Epistemic dominance of OECD

The teacher education policy has increasingly come under the epistemic dominance of organizations, such as the World Bank, the International Monetary Fund (IMF) and the Organisation for Economic Cooperating and Development (OECD) (Sellar & Lingard, 2013). We understand **epistemic dominance** as meaning everything to do with knowledge and whose ways of knowing are privileged and by implication whose voices and ways of knowing are silenced. This dominance works in soft ways, shaping teacher education using new modes of constant comparison and public accountability, e.g. test scores and results from OECD PISA and OECD TALIS (2013), while supported by new European treaties, such as the Lisbon Agreement, which regard the field of public education as a new lucrative market for privatization (Rönnberg, 2017).

Global reforms are not just tweaking what educators do, instead they are calling up new types of teachers and teacher educators acting as disinterested dispassionate researchers mandated to interrogate their selves (self-evaluation) and their practices (researcher-in-practice), without any mention of capability to mediate with and critically read the wider world (Freire, 1970; Gunter, 2001). Such deficit discourses have a profound effect on the ways teachers and teacher educators are required to teach for, about and through democracy. Students are expected to learn to become responsible and dutiful civic beings bound to an existing social order but without the necessary critical capabilities and critical consciousness to begin to shape the social order in more equitable democratic directions.

The **epistemic dominance** of OECD policies in the field of education tends to redefine the notion of the ideal teacher (Mooney Simmie, 2019) – through strategic use of a surveillance toolkit of public accountability and constant international, national and localized comparison, e.g. peer review, 360 degree review etc. The outcome aims to generate a competitive individual who is forever doing things to themselves to report to others how successful they are becoming (Edling & Mooney Simmie, 2016; Mooney Simmie, 2015; Sellar & Lingard 2013). For example, the *Teaching and Learning International Survey* (OECD TALIS 2013) redefines the ideal teacher as a learner who works within an improvement mind-set.

Renewed efforts by the OECD at direct causal linkages between teacher/educator learning outcomes and student learning outcomes continue unabated (Marcel, 2013). The logic is closely related to the philosophy of **behaviourism** that aims to stimulate people's behaviour in desired directions through various stimuli. While behaviourism can help to grapple with some aspects in education, the logic used in this way tends to ethically suppress teacher agency since external experts have the power to reward and/or punish teachers and thus impose "a hegemonic closure on meaning" (Watson, 2014, p. 22). This seeks to "regulate and circumscribe professional development for the purposes of increasing pupil attainment" (p. 24). OECD policy makes it clear that the strategy to push higher education into the markets and in the policy direction of improved rankings is to be fulfilled by a deliberative policy of cutting back finances to all activities other than desired ones.

The case of Ireland and Sweden: contextual understandings and spotlight on policy

The schooling system in both Ireland and Sweden is described as a state-aided system of education, where the state pays, for example, for teachers and maintenance of buildings and schools. In opposition to Sweden where the division between state and the state church is more or less absolute (Edling, 2018), Irish education is regarded as a publicly aided system as it is for the most part owned and managed by the institutional churches with a number of state-run schools. This can be explained by the strong interest of the churches in all education sectors – over 90% of primary schools and over 60% of secondary schools are under the patronage of the Catholic Church and there is a historical understanding of the denominational nature and purpose of Initial Teacher Education in higher education. While there has been some effort to open this to scrutiny, such as provision by the Department of Education and Skills (DES) of a recent policy on school patronage, it has only resulted in very small changes in provision and practice – for example, five schools have recently become designated multidenominational rather than Catholic schools (DES, 2016).

Both Sweden and Ireland are regarded as having democratic governments.

However, contrary to Sweden where democracy as an ideological governing form has come to play an important role in the Swedish education system since the Second World War, the issue of democracy and education has never played out strongly in Ireland, and in particular the notion of plurality and democracy has been largely absent and continues to remain absent from teacher education (Edling & Mooney Simmie, 2017; Mooney Simmie & Edling, 2016, 2018). Instead there are policies in Ireland that use terms, such as diversity and multiculturalism, but these are largely interpreted as being about **assimilation** and **respect** with the purpose of preserving the status quo rather than taking into account people's differences and working to change society to become more just and equitable. Whereas assimilation means abandoning one's own culture and ways of being in order to fully adapt to the existing culture (Brantefors, 2011), respect in this sense has to do with an ethic of human dignity. This can be seen in the typical provision of a one-off annual day of celebration in primary and secondary schools of young people from various cultural, racial and ethnic backgrounds. For the remainder of the year the (dominant) ethos of the school (patrons) is fully protected in legislation (Education Act, 1998). In Sweden, contrary to Ireland, the process of legal governance, referred to as juridification has increased schools' and pre-schools' focus on difference in such ways that teachers have difficulties managing various purposes of education in a space shared by many (see above).

When comparing how democracy is approached in Irish and Swedish policy for teacher education between 2000 and 2010, a shift from mainly progressive and reconstructivist curriculum towards an essentialist discourse can be found in both countries. This implies that whereas the policies in both Sweden and Ireland focused on describing the democratic and/or ethical assignment in teacher professionalism in broad terms and related to practice, more current policies mainly stress the knowledge assignment and simply state that democracy is important to learn about but lack a language for a democracy as a life (Mooney Simmie & Edling, 2018). The reduction of democracy can also be noticed in the amount of times democracy is mentioned in 2000 compared to 2010. The term democracy in Swedish policy for teacher education was mentioned seventeen times in 2000 but only twice in 2010 while it was mentioned twice in Ireland in 2000 and zero times in 2010 (Edling & Mooney Simmie, 2017). Similar changes as regards the narrowing down of democracy in education can also be noticed in the US and South America (Gandin & Apple, 2002; Cochran-Smith & Villegas, 2015; Gabbard & Atkinson, 2007).

We have over the year encountered a lot of creative, wise and engaged student teachers. However, when posing the question what the democratic assignment means for fifty-six student teachers in Sweden and 126 students in Ireland, the majority tended to define their democratic assignment in terms of following policy regulations. Their understanding of what this entailed was narrowly connected to obligations to protect the existing society. Few students expressed nuanced understandings of democracy as dynamic and needing affordances for dilemmatic spaces that were about becoming, emancipation and plurality rather than assumed and fixed in time and space. A male student teacher in Ireland commented that this was important for him as it was found in the Teaching Council's (2016b) definition to "respect spiritual and cultural values, diversity, social justice, freedom, democracy and the environment" and the four supports identified in this statement: A. building curriculum for life; B. Asking questions; C. Working in a diverse group and D. Practicing skills of civic action. A student teacher in Sweden considered that: "my thoughts about the democratic approach often agree with what we are expected to convey to the students" (Edling & Liljestand, 2018, p. 12 and another student teacher in Sweden noted that:

> the school has a very important function in today's society and it is therefore important that teachers follow the rules and documents that govern our teaching ... During our teaching practice I was conscious about working democratically [as indicated in the governance document] and taking the school's values into consideration.
> (Edling & Liljestand, 2018, p. 12)

In Ireland, it was felt by a male student teacher that the inclusion of this by the Teaching Council proves that this is now a requirement for teachers to educate the pupils in relation to politics, democracy, society etc. "For me as a teacher it is important that I familiarize myself with these four dimensions as they will be necessary skills to help me in my future career." And another male student teacher commented that:

> I would also feel that being a civic and cultural person to be very important because here we are moving away from just our own subject and teaching students to be good all round functional members of society. When it comes to the teachers' role as a civic person, it means that the teachers look at education that provides the students with tools for their future role in citizenship. That can be both in political matters as in global issues such as the environment or sustainability.

These examples direct attention to the importance of (teacher) education as a place where democracy has potential to be discussed and come into practice in a more nuanced and emancipatory manner. If democracy is to be deemed important how can it be approached in ways that make people engage beyond the scope of policy and laws and where the notion of being a good citizen is allowed to be problematized from various perspectives and for mediation with the wider world as well as in relation to everyday practice?

Concluding comments

In this chapter, we interrogated the way a deficit discourse in the education policy cycle has continued to be operationalized as a rationalistic model of policy implementation. This deficit discourse has changed, and utterly changed the face of democracy in teacher education in the last decade. A paradigm shift can be seen in policy efforts to reframe democracy and education inside a new social order committed to individual and national economic success at any cost. This dominant business-like discourse of education works alongside reportage of individual success in learning outcomes for a new 'scientistic' approach of data and evidence. This has profound implications for the policy cycle and teachers' democratic assignment in preparing the young for their place as agentic and activist citizens and actors, living in and continually reshaping and mediating their democratic worlds.

We have explained the policy reform ensemble introduced by the state, particularly in the last decade, under the influence and epistemic dominance of the OECD, which has radically changed democracy and generated crucial implications for teacher professionalism, the subject of our next chapter (see Chapter 4). In writing this chapter on the policy cycle we offered alternative theorizations, studies seeking to theorize the policy cycle differently, using the construct of policy enactment rather than policy implementation and reconsidering the language of teacher learning beyond a narrow risk-managed limitation of outcomes (Gore et al. 2017; Opfer & Peddar, 2011).

We argue that the role of educational researchers and teacher educators is significant if the contemporary purposes of teacher education and democracy are to be challenged and resisted and brought beyond the primacy of an economic stance (Tan, 2014) and the confinement of teachers positioned inside rather closed systems of 'learning' and policy compliance. If policy enactment processes are reduced to a problem-solving exercise of providing "turnkey solutions" (Tan, 2014, p. 234), without the necessary critical consciousness provided by the arts and humanities (Gunter, 2001; Nussbaum, 2010), and without teachers having authentic affordances for dilemmatic spaces. If this is the case then it will simply fail to "fully fulfil its social, critical and heuristic functions and provide a consistent contribution to the definition of the social value of teaching work" (Marcel, 2013, p. 226).

Questions

1 What kind of spontaneous idea(s) did this chapter evoke in you? Can you put words to it/these using literature and concepts from the chapter as a point of departure?
2 Why might we need to turn to tensions between policies and practices to better grasp dilemmas in the present and to open new spaces for the future?
3 What do you think about policy implementation as a reduction of complexity and plurality in relation to (teacher) education and democracy?
4 Can you see patterns of oppression for people who are different taking place in education policies that focus solely on the language of learning in present day life?

5   What kind of philosophical struggles or ideas can you see in current educational policy and the educational contexts you have taken part in?
6   In relation to what you have read in this chapter regarding the dangers of overlooking the complexity, creativity and criticality involved in teacher translation and interpretation of public policy enactment in (teacher) education how would you handle it as a teacher?
7   What kind of dilemmas in relation to the topic discussed would you like to add, and why?

Supplementary readings: podcasts in relation to the education policy cycle

1   Philosopher of education Gert Biesta talks about the language of learning
    Gert Biesta: What really matters in education (VIA Univ.College), 03/03/2015
    www.youtube.com/watch?v=CLcphZTGejc
2   Professor Henry Giroux speaks about the changing shape of current education policy
    Henry Giroux: Where is the Outrage? Critical Pedagogy in Dark Times, 22/10/2015
    www.youtube.com/watch?v=CAxj87RRtsc
3   Professor Dylan William explains how to embed assessment
    Dylan William: Formative assessment, 15/07/2016
    www.youtube.com/watch?v=sYdVe5O7KBE
4   Dr. Geraldine Mooney Simmie, Senior Lecturer, School of Education, University of Limerick, IRELAND talks about the policy cycle in education
    UL TALK Geraldine Mooney Simmie, 21/11/2016
    www.youtube.com/watch?v=nKgvpScuEtw

Note

1   https://skolvarlden.se/artiklar/larare-vann-ratten-efter-ingripande-anda-kraver-beo-skadestand [2019.08.23]

References

Apple, M. W. (2012). *Education and power.* 2nd edn. New York: Routledge.
Arendt, H. (1961). The crisis in education. In H. Arendt (ed.), *Between past and future.* New York: Penguin Books, pp. 170–193.
Arneback, Emma. (2012). *Med kränkningen som måttstock: om planerade bemötanden av främlingsfientliga uttryck i gymnasieskola.* Örebro, Sweden: Örebro.
Ball, S. J. (1995). Intellectual or technicians? The urgent role of theory in educational studies. *British Journal of Educational Studies*, 43(3), 255–271.
Ball, S. J. (2016). Neoliberal education? Confronting the slouching beast. *Policy Futures in Education*, 14(8), 1046–1059.
Ball, S. J. (2003). The teacher's soul and the terrors of performativity. *Journal of Education Policy*, 18(2), 215–228.
Ball, S. J., Maguire, Meg & Braun, Annette. (2012). *How schools do policy: Policy enactments in secondary schools.* London: Routledge.
Biesta, G. J. (2012). Giving teaching back to education: Responding to the disappearance of the teacher. *Phenomenology & Practice*, 6(2), 35–49.
Biesta, G. J. (2013). *The beautiful risk of education.* London: Routledge.

Bourke, T., Lidstone, J. & Ryan, M. (2015). Schooling teachers: Professionalism or disciplinary power? *Educational Philosophy and Theory: Incorporating ACCESS*, 47(1), 84–100.

Brady, A. M. (2019a). Anxiety of performativity and anxiety of performance: Self-evaluation as bad faith. *Oxford Review of Education*, 45(5) 605–618.

Brady, A. M. (2016). The regime of self-evaluation: Self-conception for teachers and schools. *British Journal of Educational Studies*, 64(4) 523–541.

Brady, A. M. (2019b). The teacher-student relationship: An existential approach. In Tom Feldges (ed.), *Philosophy and the study of education new perspectives on a complex relationship*. Abingdon, UK: Routledge, pp. 104–117.

Brantefors, Lotta. (2011). *Kulturell fostran. En didaktisk studie av talet om kulturella relationer i texter om skola och utbildning*. Uppsala: Acta Universitatis Upsaliensis, Uppsala Universitet.

Browning, C. R. (2018). The suffocation of democracy. *New York review of books*, 25 October, 65 (16), 14–17.

Cochran-Smith, M., Baker, M., Burton, S., Chang, W., Carney, M. C., Fernandez, M. B., Keefe, E. S., Miller, A. F. & Sanchez, J. G. (2017). The accountability era in US teacher education: Looking back, looking forward. *European Journal of Teacher Education*, 40(5), 572–588.

Cochran-Smith, M. & Villegas, A. M. (2015). Framing teacher preparation research: An overview of the field, part 1. *Journal of Teacher Education*, 66(1), 7–20.

Crowe, B. (2014). *Music and soul making*. Oxford: Scarecrow Press.

DES. (2016–2019). *Action Plan for Education 2016–2019. Department of Education and Skills. Strategy Statement*. Dublin, Ireland: Department of Education and Skills.

Edling, Silvia. (2012/2018). *Att vilja andra väl är inte alltid smärtfritt : Att motverka kränkningar och diskriminering i förskola och skola* [Wanting others' wellbeing is not always painless. To oppose violations and discrimination in preschool and school]. Lund, Sweden: Studentlitteratur AB.

Edling, Silvia. (2016). *Demokratidilemman i läraruppdraget. Att arbeta för lika villkor* [Democracy dilemmas in the teacher mission. To strive for equity]. Stockholm, Sweden: Liber.

Edling, Silvia & Frelin, Anneli. (2013). Doing good? Interpreting teachers' given and felt responsibilities for the pupil's well-being in an age of measurement. *Teachers and Teaching: Theory and Practice*, 19(4), 419–432.

Edling, Silvia & Liljestrand, Johan. (2019). "Democracy for me is saying what I want": The teaching profession on free speech, democratic mission and the notion of political correctness in a Swedish context. In Andrea Raiker, Matti Rautiainen & Blerim Saqipi (eds.), *Teacher education and the development of democratic citizenship in Europe*. London & New York: Routledge, Chapter 10.

Edling, Silvia & Liljestrand, Johan. (2018). Student teachers' task perceptions of democracy in their future profession – A critical discourse analysis of students' course texts. *Australian Journal of Teacher Education*, (Online), 43(7). doi:10.14221/ajte.2018v43n7.5

Edling, Silvia & Mooney Simmie, Geraldine. (2017). Democracy and emancipation in teacher education: A summative content analysis of teachers' democratic assignment expressed in policies for teacher education in Sweden and Ireland between 2000–2010. *Citizenship, Social & Economic Education*, 17(1), 20–34.

Education Act. (1998). Dublin, Ireland: The Stationary Office.

European Commission. (2018). *European ideas for better learning: The governance of school education systems*. Brussels, Belgium: European Commission.

Francia, G. & Edling, S. (2017). Children's rights and violence : A case analysis at a Swedish boarding school. *Childhood*, 24(1), 51–67.

Freire, Paulo. (1970). *Pedagogy of the oppressed*. London: Penguin Education Politics.

Gabbard, D. & Atkinson, T. (2007). Stossel in America: A case study of the neoliberal/neoconservative sssault on public schools and teachers. *Teacher Education Quarterly*, 34(2), 85–109.

Gore, J., Lloyd, A., Smith, M., Bowe, J., Ellis, H. & Lubans, D. 2017. Effects of professional development on the quality of teaching: Results from a randomised controlled trial of quality teaching rounds. *Teaching and Teacher Education*, 68, 99–113.

Gandin, L. A. & Apple, M. W. (2012). Can critical democracy last? Porto Alegre and the struggle over "thick" democracy in education. *Journal of Education Policy*, 27(5), 621–639.

Gunter, H. (2001). Critical approaches to leadership in education. *Journal of Educational Enquiry*, 2(2), 94–108.

Harvey, D. (2007). *A brief history of neoliberalism*. Oxford: Oxford University Press.

Hult, Agneta & Lindgren, Joakim. (2016). Med lagen som rättesnöre i lärares arbete mot kränkande behandling [With the acts as guidance in teachers' work against violating treatment]. *Utbildning & Demokrati– tidskrift för didaktik och utbildningspolitik*, 25(1), 73–93.

Hyslop-Margison, E. J. & Naseem, M. A. (2007). *Scientism and education empirical research as neo-liberal ideology*. Derdrecht, The Netherlands: Springer.

Kincheloe, J. (2004). The knowledges of teacher education: Developing a critical complex epistemology. *Teacher Education Quarterly*, Winter, 49–66.

Krantz, Joakim & Fritzén, Lena. (2017). From expert to novice? The influence of management by documents on teachers' knowledge base and norms. *Professions and professionalism*, 7(3), 2113.

Lindensjö, Bo & Lundgren, Ulf P. (2000). *Utbildningsreformer och politisk styrning* [Educational reform and political governing]. Stockholm, Sweden: HLS förl.

Lindblad, Sverker, Pettersson, Daniel & Popkewitz, S. Thomas. (2018). *Education by the numbers and the making of society*. London & New York: Routledge.

Lundgren, Ulf P. (1989). *Att organisera omvärlden: en introduktion till läroplansteori*. Stockholm, Sweden: Utbildningsförlaget.

Lunneblad, Johannes & Johanson, Thomas. (2018). Policing the school: In between dialogues and crime reports. *Power and Education*, 11(1), 1–15.

Lynch, K. (2015). Control by numbers: New managerialism and ranking in higher education, *Critical Studies in Education*, 56(2), 190–207.

Lynch, Kathleen, Grummell, Bernie & Devine, Dympna. (2012). *New managerialism in education commercialization, carelessness and gender*. New York: Palgrave Macmillan.

Marcel, J.-F. (2013). Critical approach to the contribution made by education research to the social construction of the value of teaching work. *Policy Futures in Education*, 1(3), 225–240.

McLaren, P. (2016). *Pedagogy of insurrection*. New York: Peter Lang Publishers.

McLaren, P. & Jandrić, P. (2019, in press). *Post-digital dialogues, liberation theology and information technology*. London: Bloomsbury.

McNeil, Linda. (2002). Private asset or public good: education and democracy at the crossroads: Editor's introduction. *American Educational Research Journal*, 39(2), 243–248.

Mooney Simmie, Geraldine. (2015). McLaren's pedagogy of insurrection and the global murder machine in education in "austerity Ireland". Book review: Pedagogy of insurrection, by Peter McLaren. *Journal for Critical Educational Policy Studies*, 13(3), 221–229.

Mooney Simmie, Geraldine. (2014). The neo-liberal turn in understanding teachers' and school leaders' work practices in curriculum innovation and change: A critical discourse analysis of a newly proposed reform policy in lower secondary education in the Republic of Ireland. *Citizenship, Society and Economics Education*, 13(3), 185–198.

Mooney Simmie, Geraldine. (2012). The pied piper of neo liberalism calls the tune in the republic of ireland: an analysis of education policy text from 2000–2012. *Journal for Critical Educational Policy Studies*, 10(2), 485–514. Retrieved from www.jceps.com/archives/725

Mooney Simmie, Geraldine. (2020). The power, politics and future of mentoring. In Beverly J. Irby, Linda Searby, Jennifer N. Boswell, Frances Kochan & Rubén Garza (eds.), *The Wiley international handbook of mentoring, paradigms, practices, programs, and possibilities*. Hoboken, NY: John Wiley, pp. 453–469.

Mooney Simmie, Geraldine & Edling, Silvia. (2016). Ideological governing forms in education and teacher education: A comparative study between highly secular Sweden and highly non-secular Republic of Ireland. *Nordic Journal of Studies in Educational Policy*, 2016(1), 1–12.

Mooney Simmie, Geraldine & Edling, Silvia. (2018). Teachers' democratic assignment: A critical discourse analysis of teacher education policies in Ireland and Sweden. *Discourse Studies in the Cultural Politics of Education*, 40(6), 832–846.

Mooney Simmie, Geraldine, Moles, Joanne & O'Grady, Emmanuel. (2019). Good teaching as a messy narrative of change within a policy ensemble of networks, superstructures and flows. *Critical Studies in Education*, 60(1), 55–72.

Muller, J. K. (2018). *The tyranny of metrics*. Princeton, NJ : Princeton University Press.

Novak, Judith. (2018). *Juridification of educational spheres. The case of Swedish school inspection*. Uppsala, Sweden: Uppsala University.

Nussbaum, M. C. (2010). *Not for profit why democracy needs the humanities*. Princeton, NJ: Princeton University Press.

Ó'Buachalla, Séamas. (1988). *Education policy in twentieth century Ireland*. Dublin, Ireland: Wolfhound Press.

OECD. (2013). TALIS results: An international perspective on teaching and learning. In OECD, *Teaching and Learning International Survey*. Brussels, Belgium: Organisation for Economic Cooperation and Development. Retrieved from doi:10.1787/9789264196261-en

Opfer, V. D. & Pedder, D. (2011). Conceptualising teacher professional learning. *Review of Educational Research*, 81(3), 376–407.

Sellar, S. & Lingard, B. (2013). The OECD and global governance in education. *Journal of Education Policy*, 28(5), 710–725.

Sheehan, Ciaran. (2016). *Contextual understanding and perspectives of primary school principals in the midwest of Ireland in relation to moral leadership in a global age of measurement*. PhD Dissertation. Limerick, Ireland: University of Limerick.

Runesdotter, Caroline. (2016). Avregleringens pris? Om juridifieringen av svensk skola ur skolaktörers perspektiv. *Utbildning och demokrati* [Tema: juridifiringen av skolan], 25(1), 95–111.

Säfström, C. A. (2011). Rethinking emancipation, rethinking education. *Studies in Philosophy and Education*, 30, 199–209.

Santoro, D. A. (2017). Cassandra in the classroom: Teaching and moral madness. *Studies in Philosophy of Education*, 36, 49–60.

Sellar, Sam & Lingard, Bob. (2013). The OECD and global governance in education. *Journal of Education Policy*, 28(5), 710–725.

Skerritt, C. (2018). Discourse and teacher-identity in business-like education. *Policy Futures in Education*, 17(2), 1–19.

Snyder, T. (2018). *The road to unfreedom*. London: Penguin Random House.

Stanley, Edward & Stronach, Ian. (2013). Raising and doubling 'standards' in professional discourse: A critical bid. *Journal of Educational Policy*, 28(3), 291–305.

Swann, Mandy, Mcintyre, Donald, Pell, Tony, Hargreaves, Linda & Cunningham, Mark. (2010). Teachers' conceptions of teacher professionalism in England in 2003 and 2006. *British Educational Research Journal*, 36(4), 549–571.

Tan, E. (2014). Human capital theory: A holistic criticism. *Review of Educational Research* 84(3), 411–445.

The Teaching Council. (2016a). *Code of professional conduct for teachers*. Updated 2nd edn. Maynooth, Ireland: The Teaching Council.

The Teaching Council. (2016b). *Cosán framework for teachers' learning*. Maynooth, Ireland: The Teaching Council.

The Teaching Council. (2011). *Policy on the continuum of teacher education*. Maynooth, Ireland: The Teaching Council.

Watson, C. (2014). Effective professional learning communities? The possibilities for teachers as agents of change in schools. *British Educational Research Journal*, 40(1), 18–29.

Youdell, D. (2011). *School trouble identity, power, and politics in education*. London: Routledge.

4 Teacher professionalism and democracy[1]

Introduction

Teacher education has ever since the 19th century carried an imperative role to provide future teachers with the skills, values and knowledge needed to teach students to live and act in a society with others (Carr et al., 2016; Edling & Mooney Simmie, 2017). In other words, the *task of teacher education is to teach student teachers to teach others* and this assignment is strongly connected with what kind of society is desired and thus what kind of citizens a society needs. As such, education is of huge political importance and involves us all and it is indeed of major interest for the state and those in power. Teacher education is the most state regulated program within higher education (Letiche, Lightfoot & Moriceau, 2016) (see Chapter 3).

In various places on planet earth the role of democracy within teacher education has been deemed as an important dimension in student teachers' professional development, and it has been discussed from various angles (see for instance Ball, 2000; Edling & Liljestrand, 2018; Gordon, 2006; Harber & Serf, 2006; Majhanovich & Malet, 2015; Zeichner, 2016). Furthermore, empirical research has shown that youth in 2002 and 2010 tend to support democratic values overall (Schulz, Ainley, Fraillon, Kerr, & Losito, 2010; Torney-Purta, 2002). However, the possibilities for democracy are dependent upon both the space created by educational policy for democratically inspired thinking and being, as well as through people's everyday actions. A politically designed space risks echoing empty and simply becoming a site for bureaucracy without continuous articulation of meaning and the engagement of people for private/common good (e.g. Zyngier, Delia & Murriello, 2015). Currently the space for teacher's democratic assignment is diminishing in many countries due to neoliberal and neoconservative policies and politics (Bagley & Beach, 2015; Edling & Mooney Simmie, 2017; Mooney Simmie & Edling, 2016).

In this chapter the spotlights are directed upon the teacher and the notion of teacher professionalism. Becoming a teacher is not something universally given but depends on the vision of a good life and a good society and it is therefore intimately interconnected with ideological struggles and opposing worldviews (see Chapter 2). Just as democracy, teacher professionalism can be approached in either broad or narrow ways. This is not to be understood in a dualistic sense, but is rather about where the range of teacher responsibility needs to be drawn.

The intention with the chapter is to highlight dilemmas that take form in the clash between a narrow and broad way of grasping teacher professionalism. A central question is whether teachers' work practices should be solely about knowledge and values transmission (see Chapter 5) and learning the precise technique of teaching or whether it also needs to involve other areas as well, such as relations and conditions and an awareness that humans and the flow of practice cannot be and perhaps even should not be fully tamed. There is at times a belief amongst student teachers and politicians that uncertainty, controversies, dilemmas and disorder can be erased by a method proven to be efficient in research, while teachers often stand face to face with dilemmas that take form independent of the methods and strategies deployed (see Table 4.1).

The chapter is divided into three parts. In order to understand teachers' professionalism and ways to approach democracy, three purposes of education are discussed in a general sense and in relation to a broad and narrow way of grasping democracy. The intention here is to provide an overview of why education is important and also to shed light on various approaches of perceiving democracy and how these worldviews affect teachers' work. The second part goes more into depth of multiple world-views of comprehending teacher professionalism in relation to theory and meta-studies as well as approaches to teacher judgements. Finally, the chapter ends with a brief conclusion.

Three politically defined assignments in education

It is possible to argue that teachers in a general sense have three different assignments in relation to one another: **knowledge assignment, socialization assignment**, and the **assignment for equal treatment** that have different content and emphasis in various times and contexts (Edling, 2012/2018). These assignments can be understood as three educational dimensions or purposes, namely: **qualification, socialization** and **subjectification** (Biesta, 2010). These purposes for education have not been static or been given equal emphasis in education, rather the focus and content of meaning have undergone major changes over time and from context to context (e.g. Cochran-Smith, 2011, 2004). They can be used as analytical devices for posing questions about where the weight in educational policy and practice lies today, if and how these three purposes intersect, and the content meaning they are given.

One general purpose of education is about providing students with qualifications necessary to handle a society's and vocational profession's needs and demands. The knowledge assignment linked to the teacher profession today demands both broad and deep qualifications. It includes knowledge about subjects, curriculum, educational policy, relations, ethics, theory, methods and so forth. Besides the knowledge, assignment teachers in some countries need to explicitly work with socialization. The socialization assignment has to do with forming characters that suit culturally and politically defined social orders. It is intimately linked to values and norms in that it defines what is desirable characteristics and what is not (Biesta, 2010). In many countries today one aspect of socialization is

Table 4.1 An overview of dilemmas discussed in Chapter 4

Dilemmas
Broad versus narrow
Technical versus intellectual
Outside-in-professionalism versus inside-out-professionalism
Theory versus practice
Order versus complexity
Control versus freedom
Majority versus minority
Values versus neutrality

interconnected with democracy and democratic values, i.e. about being tolerant, solidarity, being able to listen to others, discuss based on solid argument and so forth. The socialization assignment can be divided into: existential questions, moral character building, value influence, fostering citizens, fostering democratic citizens (e.g. Colnerud, 2004).

But socialization is not a button you can turn on and off seeing that people are socialized and people are socializing others even if they want to or not. Indeed, at times teachers unconsciously form students' characters that do not correspond to a politically defined socialization aim. The term **hidden curriculum** was coined by Philip Jackson (Jackson, 1990) in an investigation about classroom life where it turned out that, besides explicit aims with education, there were uncommunicated rules that governed classroom life and socialized the children to be patient, await their turn, and sit still – to mention some examples (ibid.). The hidden curriculum is also about undefined power structures that implicitly grade who are to be counted and who are not (Giroux & Penna, 1983). Research has been able to show that the borders between knowledge and socialization are not clear but concurrent and in mutual interdependence with each other.

Certainly, the teacher assignment as a whole is neither static, one dimensional, but dynamic, relational, changeable and complex (Bingham & Sidorkin, 2004; Edling, 2009; Endres, 2007; Frelin, 2010). **Complexity** is not the same thing as if something is **complicated**. If something is complicated, the pieces can be depicted and after some thinking the complication can be solved. Part of education is complicated but education as a whole is complex. When something is complex, it does not mean that it is complicated and that all that is required is to break it into its components parts – instead it means that various factors are woven together in such a way that makes it impossible to find one all-inclusive solution since every solution is a small pounce in a tangle that always is larger than the solution (Doll, 2012, p. 174).

This does not mean that teachers should stop solving problems, rather that the question 'please-tell-me-what-is-right-to-do-once-and-for-all' does not work, since the teacher first needs to interpret what the challenge is, and only thereafter has to start thinking about a strategy/method required in the specific context at hand. A convincing amount of research from various directions shows that education, in order to function properly, needs to be approached as a question of (social) relations rather than constructed out of fragments isolated from each other (e.g. Allodi, 2010; Bingham & Sidorkin, 2004; Frelin, 2013, Ramsden, 2003; Syal & Andersson, 2013).

This suggests that knowledge, socialization and equal treatment assignment are in relationship with each other. All knowledge that is taught is based on exclusion and inclusion and hence expresses choices of what is valued and not valued in human relations (see Chapter 5). Accordingly, knowledge, independent of how neutral it is packaged is value loaded and functions in a socializing manner (Cherryholmes, 1988; Englund & Quennerstedt, 2008; Säfström & Månsson, 2004). For example:

> A Swedish student teacher here referred to as Walter, learning to become a teacher in upper secondary high school, described an experience he had during his vocational training (VFU) where he encountered a social teacher who stressed that contrary to the ideologically grounded teacher education he based all his choices on meta studies. The teacher's ambition was to be neutral and objective and he encouraged Walter to be that too. Walter observed that the teacher systematically refused to allow relational complications, like fights, quarrels, and value opinions to enter the educational space. Walter was impressed by the order in the class. At the same time he noticed that it

was mainly two males who dominated the conversation and that the teacher used a (body) language that was diminishing towards the majority of the girls and at times used sexist jokes in front of the group, like 'Lisa have you had time to do your homework or did you party with boys this weekend?'. When Walter talked to the upper secondary high school students during the breaks some loved the social teacher for his structured lessons, while others were afraid of him. Walter felt confused, since teacher education stresses the importance of socialization and work against discrimination (equal treatment).

(experiences from Teacher Education)

An Irish student teacher, let's call him Kevin, expressed an understanding about his effort at generating a classroom where diversity was respected. He expressed this as leaving his prejudices at the door and becoming a neutral and objective (clinical) teacher. Other student teachers regarded a civic and cultural assignment as something that did not come under their radar, that it was not given a place in the grading rubric for school placement and that maybe it was something that might matter later as more experienced teachers. A student teacher, Michael, explained it as follows: 'Civic and cultural person was the least striking during my time on School Placement (SP). It was not something I was concerned with at the time. This is not what they're grading us on SP. We concentrate on trying to conduct a lesson so instructional manager and generous expert (are the most important)'. Another student teacher, Sandra, understood that schooling had little or nothing to do with active membership of a wider democratic society: 'Civic and cultural person: I don't feel that the way in which students contribute to society and to the community plays an essential role in learning I think the holistic development is more important, perhaps this comes after (that)'.

(experiences from Teacher Education)

Like Walter in Sweden above these Irish student teachers were displaying something of a hidden curriculum in their understandings of their teaching role(s). They perceived no great role for themselves in critically reading the world, or in doing anything that could be explicitly viewed as a democratic assignment – they were not acquainted with symbolic dangers in their practices and their need to engage with the hard reflexive work of interrogating their positionality (see Chapter 7).

This is a common story stressing the gap student teachers often experience between practice and theory as well as between order and disorder, objectivity/neutrality and values/subjectivity. Drawing from Walter's story, the teacher at the school seems to have interpreted order as being solely about the knowledge assignment, whereas real knowledge tends to be based on meta studies (we do not know how the teacher worked with knowledge content). Everything regarding relations was viewed as disturbances that needed to be eliminated. But relations do not stop existing just because we ignore them. Socialization that takes form in social relations has to do with forming people into a social order. It was expressed through the social teacher's choice of knowledge, whom he allowed space for and how he was referring to individuals in the group. From this way of reasoning it becomes important for teachers to be aware of the sometimes hidden content-meaning that **accompanies knowledge** (*följemening*) and says something substantial about what is valued and what is not (Östman, 1995; Östman & Almqvist, 2011). At least if these issues matter – and that is a value choice. Accordingly, if hidden content-meaning is not acknowledged the risk is that the teacher continues to socialize people in a direction that explicitly is not desirable.

However, it is not sufficient to talk about the school's assignment in terms of knowledge (qualification) and socialization. Teachers are also expected in many countries to step in and make changes in education when needed. While qualification and socialization is about standing in line and following something given, education can have a third purpose, namely *subjectification* (Biesta, 2010). Subjectification can be interpreted as allowing people's differences to break into the order in ways that can allow change or questioning of that order.

Subjectification can also be understood as **emancipation**, that is to say liberation from a dominating and oppressive order. When unique individuals' thoughts and feelings get space, it becomes possible to think about whether they feel well, if they have understood, if they have something new to add or if the conditions existing in a specific context are sustainable when it comes to perusing certain purposes and aims (Biesta, 2010). This is not about exchanging knowledge with unique people's subjective opinions, but rather to keep the juggling balls, knowledge, socialization and work for equity, in the air all at the same time and in communication with each other (Edling, 2012/2018; 2016). The complexity of this teaching task can be compared with a three-dimensional chess board – if one of the three boards moves, all three boards are affected. In other words, when we start to do something with knowledge in a classroom the way we do it and the content we choose automatically socialize the people in that room and set the conditions for learning.

The possibility for subjectification, as an interruption and reconfiguration of order is closely interconnected with democracy as an event (Biesta, et al., 2014). Democracy from an educational point of view can thus be grasped as to be **about democracy, in democracy** and **for democracy**. About democracy places the spotlight on the knowledge assignment and hence learning about democracy. Living in democracy highlights everyday practice with others, while for democracy accentuates the actual engagement and involvement with democracy (Mooney Simmie & Lang, 2020; Edling & Mooney Simmie, 2017; Letiche et al., 2016; Mooney Simmie & Edling, 2016, 2018). In order to capture the multiplicity of ways of approaching democracy the notion of a broad and narrow democracy is now considered.

Teaching for a narrow or a broad democracy?

Today, many countries call themselves democratic, yet how a democratic government approaches democracy in education and teacher education is not clear. Democracy is at times described in a fashion that can appear dualistic (either–or), namely *democracy as procedure* and *democracy as a form of life* (Dewey, 1916), *thick* and *thin democracy* (Armando & Apple, 2002; Barber, 1997, 2003; Carr, 2008; Green, 1999), and *deep* and *shallow democracy* (Furman & Shields, 2005; Strike, 1999). In this book we refer to them as narrow and broad approaches to democracy. However, the divisions should not be grasped in terms of either–or, rather as a question of where the scope for a society's responsibility should be drawn when it comes to democracy.

Should democracy *only* be about the form such as parliamentary elections, principles, procedures, student voting and so forth or should it *also* take into consideration other aspects linked to the flow of life, such as values, thoughts, perceptions and the consequences actions in general just like principles and procedures have on people's life condition. In modern democracy the ethical-social justice dimension is very central (Dahl, 2002), stressing the importance of acknowledging and valuing plurality (Mouffe, 2000). Yet, those who argue for a narrow way of viewing democracy generally start using the logic of Descartes: principles of dualism, principles about everything's essence, principles about measurability, visibility, categorization, and the principle of elimination (of doubt). These principles are grounded on an idea that human life is dangerous since it includes the subjective, the subtle (for the eye invisible) patterns that are not possible to categorize in a way that eliminates doubt once and for all.

Procedural questions such as election systems, majority rule, universal suffrage, the responsibilities of politicians, and so forth, can be understood as a means that a group of people, at a certain time in history, have decided to agree upon as suitable in order to uphold democracy. By democracy, we mean the idea that people should not be governed without their own consent, i.e. (popular rule) (Hadenius, 2001; Held, 1987). The procedural aspects of democracy come into expression in education when, for example, students raise their hands, vote or choose representatives for different school boards. These procedures are, however, not the same as aims and they do not carry any **intrinsic values** – although they at times are treated as if they are. On the contrary, Dewey (2004 [1938]) argues they constantly need to be placed in relation to practice and how they affect people's life condition (p. 154). Whereas intrinsic values mean that some phenomena in life have a value in themselves independent of what they do or contribute to, **instrumental values** have to do with the value people and things are given, dependent on what they produce, i.e. if they are useful (Abbarno, 2015).

Central in Dewey's description of democracy is the need to believe in people's will and potential to gain knowledge and their will to collective participation, which should not be confused with the idea that people are perfect. Democracy is always a possibility and no guarantee, but the possibility it opens up to enable a different coexistence than if we, from the beginning, assume that people are somehow stupid, need to be controlled, and that some people are smarter or more intelligent than others are. Furthermore, every *ism* that education has been based on, like essentialism or progressivism risks becoming counter-productive when it starts repeating itself without an "investigation of real needs, problems, and possibilities" (Dewey, 2004 [1938], pp. 154, 156, 165).

The bridge between democracy as procedure and democracy as a form of life requires a shift in the playing field from an either-or-thinking (dualism) to becoming aware of how various pieces are linked together in a chain or ecology that impacts on human life conditions (dialectical). If we ignore procedures or claims that they are instrumental and thus evil, the possibilities for creating spaces where democracy can enter become impeded, and at the same time, if procedures are made the sole goal for democracy, it risks overlooking the consequences of human action (Dewey, 1916, p. 127).

Democracy can be understood as a **social order** that influences institutions and organizations, and promotes a certain kind of thinking and acting (Dahlstedt & Olson, 2013, p. 19). Democracy as part of the social order can give the impression that democracy is a **fixed order**, i.e. something given that we step into or a passive object that we own, for example: 'they should be included *in* democracy', in Sweden 'we *have* democracy' or the 'school *is* democratic'.

Contrary to this idea, we argue that although democratic governments open up alternative possibilities to how the world can be viewed and can be supported by policy, constructing structures, spaces and organizations will also and always remain a possibility if not linked to the power in people's daily actions (e.g. Biesta, 2010; Honig, 1993; Rancière, 1995). Indeed, democracy is a **fragile construction** dependent on cooperation with others for a better social communality for all as well as engagement and active participation of citizens that exceeds being lawful and putting a vote in an urn during election-day that is based on the logic of majority rule (Zyngier et al., 2015).

In this sense questions about **majority** and **minority** risk creating dilemmas that teachers have to face.

> In Sweden the emancipatory dimension has become strictly regulated by law through the Discrimination Act and Other Violating Treatment in the School Act. This implies that teachers are obliged to pay regard to groups that historically have been subjected to discrimination as well as pay regard to how those diverging from the norm are treated. If they fail to do this the school/municipal is punished. During a seminar about Democratic Values, student teachers were told about Maya, a teachers' experience of a class who wanted to go to the forest for an excursion. Maya had planned this field-trip in September with the children to look at mushrooms, but Anton's mother phoned her asking whether the class could do something that her son Sebastian could partake in as well? Her son has a disability that makes it difficult for him to walk in the forest. The teacher felt really confused, feeling the obligation to pay regard to the mother's demands, seeing that disability is protected by the Discrimination Act. When the student teachers heard about this they became upset that the whole class was forced to give up their beloved mushroom excursion due to one person. 'Then the minority rules over the majority. That's not democracy!' one student exclaimed in agitation.
>
> (Experience from Teacher Education)

This puts the finger on the delicate tension between majority and minority present in modern democracy. A democracy that solely focuses on the majority vote tends to become an empty vessel for values that stand in opposition to the very existence of democracy itself (Mouffe, 2005), as well as risks becoming a force for minority oppression. At the same time democracy cannot be about minority rule either, since democracy is strongly connected to all people in a nation. Countries who call themselves democratic are caught in this dilemma and function as a reminder that '*Wanting other's well-being is not always painless*', since it demands people with power and in the majority to give up and redistribute power for the sake of others and for the minority. Constant negation between majority and minority is essential in a broad understanding of democracy (Edling, 2012/2018).

From this way of reasoning a broad understanding of democracy is more than simply transferring values and providing knowledge about democracy. A challenge for teachers is to handle the idea that there are certain liberal values possible to transfer to students, thus automatically making them into better democratic citizens, while at the same time being aware of what takes place in the flow of life where certain use of values, such as tolerance, might have the opposite effect on people's life conditions than intended (Edling, 2012). Hence, democracy from this way of reasoning never just exists but is a practice that breaks into the social order (comes into being) and colours it or influences it over and over again. When that force in the symbiotic relationship stops, democracy ceases to exist (Biesta, 2006; Dewey, 1916). Discrepancies between seeing democracy as an order and/or as a living entity made and remade through human interaction is also expressed by student teachers at a Swedish Teacher Education Institution:

> After a course about the Swedish democratic value foundation, 56 student teachers were asked to describe how knowledge in the course influenced their view in their teacher profession. The majority of students claimed that it is important to follow

the political guidelines and that they found the values important to uphold. However, only very few of the student teachers linked this reasoning to a more nuanced description of what this might entail, based on knowledge from the course and plausible complexities it might bring to their work. Thus they were aligning with the good value foundation without explaining the meaning of this as well as expressing a tendency to black and white reasoning, for example: "[t]hat human rights should be upheld and to make sure that the pupils we send out into the world have a positive intrinsic value … spread respect for everyone's common rights and environments." But, there were also students who began elaborating more in depth what their work might entail, for instance: "I don't think it's enough for educators to simply touch on the democratic processes in the hope of fostering citizens, but that it requires more dissemination of knowledge and at the same time a questioning perspective, a constant 'why?' that echoes in the students' minds every time they learn something new … I think that educators should take it even further, consciously raise awareness about structures and explain that everyone's equal value is an objective, something that we strive towards. [We need to] discuss visions of masculinity and femininity, look at it historically and problematize the delusion that we are an egalitarian country. First knowing, then knowledge. And finally, hopefully change."

(see Edling and Liljestrand, 2018)

It is important to stress that the different world-views expressed above are raising the importance about highlighting narrow and broad ways of grasping democracy as part of teachers' assignment and the consequences of various perceptions. This and similar examples are important to ponder, since it is more than just what meets the ear or the eye.

A broad democracy as part of an educational environment

According to research findings, a narrow approach to democracy is insufficient to handle the multifaceted challenges facing societies (e.g. Borman, Danzig, & Gracia, 2012). From an educational perspective, a broad approach to democracy means that teachers cannot merely teach children and young people about democratic procedures, they also need to direct their attention and their judgements to how they themselves and others relate to each other, people's expressed perceptions generating values and norms, the consequences for action they bring and so forth. Tensions between broad and narrow forms of education and democracy are not a question about either–or but rather the range of responsibilities and possibilities of a teacher, namely, should the teacher merely:

- teach **about** democracy in an objective hence neutral manner

   … or should teachers also …:

- develop students' consciousness about the fact that there are various ways of understanding democracy
- develop students' understanding about the relationship between different perceptions and how they are connected to thought and practice
- work with different political ideals in relation to social justice issues

- stimulate abilities to ethically investigate and critically observe the outcome of their actions and others' actions
- be observant as to how different choices in education impact on students' preconditions and possibilities

… and work with …

- their own practices and thoughts
- and the relationships between personnel and students
- the conditions present at the work place in general (e.g. Green, 1999)?

A broad understanding of democracy places the spotlight on the **educational environment**. Reviving John Dewey's (1916) notion of educational environment it is here argued that education is a social activity that always takes form in relation to something that sets the conditions for action: "[t]he environment consists of the sum total of conditions which are concerned in the execution of the activity characterized of a living being" (p. 22). Hence, environment indicates something more than simply the **surrounding** that encompasses a human being. Rather, it stresses the interdependence of various factors within a direct and indirect surrounding that impinge on people's activities that call for attention to **educational purpose**(s), **dynamic practice** and **conditions for action** (ibid.).

An environment can be grasped in terms of an **ecology**. Ecology means here ways in which a social environment constituted out of human relations is inevitably interlaced with a **biophysical environment**, implying that people and educational purposes are not only conditioned by other people but also by non-human artefacts like pollution, computers, papers, buildings, rooms etc. (Colwell, 1985; Dewey & Bentley, 1949) rendering all things that influence education important to pay attention to when planning education.

How does the school board work? Are there some who speak more than others? Are there those who have more power than others? Who and why? It is not just the formal gatherings that are included in a broad understanding of democracy, but also practices that take form in informal space. Who has the power to decide over others in the school yard and in the corridors? Who takes part in the games who sits alone? Which games dominate? Are there any similarities with social patterns in general? These, and similar, questions direct the focus onto culture: norms, values, ideas and practices (see also Thornberg, 2013) being created and recreated on a daily basis.

During a seminar with student teachers, the following example was used as a starting-point for discussion concerning challenges facing teachers when working with knowledge and values at the same time. What is your response when reading this example? At a school for adults (Komvux) in Helsingborg a teacher substitute ordered a student who questioned the existence of genocide to leave the room. The teacher substitute was thereafter summoned to the coordinator's office to explain himself. The conversation was secretly recorded by the teacher and thereafter sent to the media who published it:

> **Coordinator:** The student talked to me and said he felt misunderstood and violated and designated as being a genocide denier, says the coordinator in the recording. **Teacher:** What he said was genocide denying … **Coordinator**: In the back of your head you need to be aware of the fact that what we consider as history is what we have experienced. When we have students who've read other history books there is no need to put facts against facts. **Now the teacher felt betrayed** by the

school leaders. He felt as if he had protected the values in the Swedish school about gender equality, democracy and equal values.

(*Dagens Nyheter*, 26 February 2015,[2] cited in Edling, 2016).

What it is that is counted as an educational environment depends on current educational needs as well as judgements as to how to reach them (Dewey, 1916). Sixty years ago the workings of a photocopying machine was probably not an educational issue, while it most likely would cause disturbance for teachers and students today, therefore rendering it a place in the educational environment. Relational dependency in an environment can become most visible after the function no longer exists (Grannäs & Frelin, 2010), like for example when an IT-technician who was responsible for keeping computers running smoothly was fired from a school, forcing teachers to do the work themselves. In conclusion, different ways of grasping democracy influence the role and responsibilities of the professional teacher (in Edling, 2016).

Teacher professionalism and professionalization

The concepts **professionalization** and **professionalism** are not the same thing. Professionalization has to do with requirements for status/authority amongst a group of people within a specific profession while professionalism directs attention to how teachers should form education in a way that secures as good a quality as possible (Englund, 1996). Thus, professionalization places demands on **authority, professional autonomy, ethical principles** and a **common language** for professional practice.

Authority implies that a person within the profession is respected by the society for her or his qualified judgements and actions. The notion of authority is connected to professional autonomy, which means that the professional does not have to ask an external expert whether her or his actions are correct but is expected to have sufficient knowledge to come to a conclusion about what is the best thing to do in a certain situation. Important also when a profession becomes professionalized is also the use of a common language. In order to analyse and speak about work-related issues there need to be concepts, reasoning, frames of understanding that most of the group are familiar with. Finally, professionalization requires that there are ethical principles created by the group, outside the scope of policy (Colnerud & Granström, 2002; Frelin, 2010; Jönsson & Rubenstein, 2009).

A teacher, if governed by the logic of professionalization, is expected to form education based on the qualified knowledge and ethical values s/he has gained rather than simply obeying external expertise; this is not the case in all countries. There has been and probably will remain a tension between theory and practice in teacher education. That is to say a tension between forces stressing that student teachers should learn to become teachers through practical training including the use of universal methods, and those claiming that practical training requires that student teachers' reflective abilities are developed simultaneously (e.g. Zeichner, 2016).

Indeed, two general and dominating ways of approaching teacher professionalism is to see the teacher profession as *universal* or as *practice oriented (reflectional)*. The universal teacher puts her or his faith on measurability, the belief that it is possible to locate the essence of humans and groups of people, 'this is how students are' or 'this is how you teach English verbs properly', as well eliminating dilemmas based on ideas of dualism. Teachers' judgements based on interpretations are regarded as unsafe and hence unprofessional, since they risk being coloured by subjective sentiments rather than purely observed facts from external experts. This view was particularly strong during the 1960s and 1970s in many countries and supported by data from developmental psychology (Thiessen, 2000).

Contrary to this standpoint the practice oriented approach (Colnerud & Granström, 2002), also labelled **reflective practitioner** (Elbaz, 1983; Schön, 1986) has shown that a teacher who mainly is concerned with using **universal methods** does not stop making **judgements** in education. On the contrary, teachers tend to make a great deal of judgements based on common sense or subjective solutions despite good intentions of being neutral or objective, subsequently highlighting the importance to add a dimension where judgement is systematically practised at teacher education through theory (e.g. Ball & Cohen, 1999; Clark & Peterson, 1986; Elbaz, 1983; 1991). Central in research about the reflective practitioner is to develop a language where concepts and theoretical reasoning (naming) help the teacher interpret her or his surrounding and the consequences various understandings have (framed) (Schön, 1986). Whereas, Schön stressed the powers of theory lately, there are those arguing that reflective competences can also be regarded as having a strong concurrence between theory, evidence and practice in relation to certain educational purposes forming a professional knowledge-base (Thiessen, 2000).

The universal-oriented teacher versus the practice-oriented teacher can also be referred to as **inside-out-professionalism** versus and **outside-in-professionalism**. Inside-out-professionalism is based on a view where teachers themselves are expected to negotiate between external demands and internal needs. They are also expected to interpret a practice in constant movement and make judgements on these systematic interpretations, while outside-in-professionalism emphasizes that the judgement is located in the hands of experts outside education who beforehand decide what a teacher should or should not do in a given situation. How teacher professionalism is defined on a political level therefore greatly influences the possibilities a teacher has to handle complex educational situations. For instance, an over belief in outside-in-professionalism risks creating an illusion that education is possible to control externally in a way that tends to hurt people and functions counter productively (Stanley & Stronach, 2013, p. 293).

> Student teachers in Sweden often return to feeling exasperated over all theory connected to their education (course) and feel that teacher education does not give them the useful methods they need to handle their work. Per, a student teacher pointed out that he understands theory is important but he truly believes that what he needs is more tips and tricks drawing on research that works.
>
> While many student teachers and experienced teachers in Ireland nowadays focus more on research for 'what works' some experienced teachers draw from theoretical underpinnings to make sense of aspects of their teaching even if they don't overtly do this to interrupt routine practices or to problematise wider social justice issues. One experienced teacher, Liz, an English teacher in a community school with fourteen years experience explains how she used the writings of Paulo Freire to theorize student voice in her secondary school and build a critical literacy programme: "Paulo Freire's model of empowerment, because it is designed for …. listening to students voices and developing their voices …. I did a research project in my school last year (on this topic) …. it was for developing the critical literacy of second language learners using product based learning and activities and involved a literature review … how a teachers' role is to scaffold and support the students expression rather than imposing what is understood maybe as the 'correct' version."
>
> (see Lonergan, 2016, p. 228)

This tension between theory and practice is important to keep in mind. An education that becomes so theoretical that it distances itself from the work teachers are supposed to do is problematic. At the same time a teacher that blindly follows methods and orientates in a view of common sense and trial and error has difficulties handling multi-layered dimensions that are important for enhancing learning and handling issues linked to socialization and equal treatment (Edling, 2012/2018). At the same time it's important to bear in mind that a focus on an inside-out-professionalism requires **concentration** and hence **slow thinking** (system 2) contrary to mainly relying on **fast thinking** coloured by impulse and culture (e.g. Kahneman, 2013). It can therefore be persuasive to take fast expedient solutions rather than engage in discussions (e.g. Pinar, 2012) and the messiness of a complex praxis this is deeply intertwined with democracy as a living practice (Mooney Simmie, Moles & O'Grady, 2019, see Cochran-Smith in Supplementary readings).

Inside-out-professionalism just like outside-in-professionalism can be compared to what the Professor in Educational Sociology at the Institute of Education London (UK), Stephen Ball (1995) terms **teachers as technicians** and **teachers as intellectuals**. The technical point of departure requires that teachers act mechanically using manuals or methods from research stressing rationality, measurability and efficiency. In contrast to this, teachers as intellectuals are not merely supposed to act but also to reflect, to interrogate their reflexive positions (see Chapter 7) based on theories, values, taste, culture and empirical findings. The two ways of grasping teacher professionalism should not be seen as opposites in a dualistic fashion since the stress on the intellectual teacher (inside-out-professionalism) needs to also take into account evidence based and counter-intuitive knowledge forms (see Chapter 5).

To be **professionally present** (Frelin, 2013) implies being more susceptible for risks, dilemmas, controversies that erupt and also more inclined to handle them for the sake of others (Fransson & Grannäs, 2013; Honig, 2007; Liljestrand, 2011), and also be aware of the fact that teachers seldom will be able to act in ways where all demands are fulfilled. From a dualistic perspective this means that teachers can be seen as constant failures, since absolute perfection is impossible in a context where a multitude of aims, people and conditions exist all at the same time (Edling, 2014). Whereas the discussion above has focused on various ways of grasping teacher professionalism and their relation to a broad and narrow way of grasping democracy, it is also of interest to take a look at meta studies as regards views on the 'professional teacher'.

Meta studies and teacher professionality

There are various ways of approaching teacher professionality: cultural observations, policy, theory, meta studies, people's experiences and so forth. Different perspectives contribute with different aspects and it is important to keep the focus and what they might (and might not) contribute with alive. For example, whereas a meta study, in which a large amount of studies is gathered in one place, approaches education from a helicopter perspective (a distance), it cannot therefore provide ready answers on how to handle a unique situation or a unique individual. For that to happen other tools are needed, such as theories for instance. In this section, we turn to two meta studies as pieces of the puzzle we label education.

Basically, two meta studies are fleshed out here, namely Hattie's *Visible Learning* and Håkansson & Sundberg's *Excellent Education*. They are chosen since they are examples of two different kinds of meta studies. Johan Hattie (2012) who is a Professor in Pedagogy has been widely quoted for his research *Visible Learning*. The study is based on 800–900 meta analyses, 50,000 research articles, 240 million pupils and 150,000 effect sizes using quantitative tools for analysis. Håkansson & Sundberg (2012) maintain that they have selected twenty of the most important international research overviews about education and learning and twenty-three of the most important research overviews in Sweden between 1990 and 2010 (forty-three in total). The analysis is thus based on 12,000 pages and is quite unique from a Swedish perspective. However, contrary to Hattie, it is not a quantitative analysis of effect sizes (summary) and replicability (seeing the same results over and over as a strength), but a qualitative approach drawing on an inference chain from different sources. While Hattie mainly focuses on similarities in the studies, separated from their context, Sundberg and Håkansson try to keep similarities, differences, and complexities alive. In this section we ask three questions drawing on these meta studies: (1) What does the professional teacher need to know, (2) what is expected from students, and (3) what kind of personal traits do teachers need to nourish?

Both in *Visible Learning* and *Excellent Education* it is emphasized that teaching is not an outside-in-professionalism (although the word is not used explicitly) where teachers passively receive instructions how to do things, but requires active teachers, teachers who think.

The message in *Visible Learning* is not a prescription for success, another strife for security, no work sheets for professional development, no new educational method and no quick fix to turn to. It is a way of thinking (Hattie, 2012, p. 39, translated from Swedish by the author).

> robust and secure knowledge about education is not possible … but is found in the convergence between different types of sources.
> (Håkansson & Sundberg, 2012, p. 15, translated from Swedish)

> To be a teacher is something that in a high amount takes the entire person into consideration, with all the luggage as regards values, approaches, expectations, preferences, – and prejudices – that all people carry with them.
> (Håkanson & Sundberg, 2012, p. 168, translated from Swedish)

Similarly, Hattie, Håkansson and Sundberg stress that good education is not about singling out and polishing one factor to perfection, such as teachers' knowledge and actions. Rather, both studies show that the quality of education is constructed out of the way various pieces interconnect and support/strengthen a classroom climate, school climate and learning climate. This implies that besides the knowledge, skills and values of teachers it is important that school leaders support teachers' professional development, that people in general at a school take part in creating an environment where everyone feels safe, feels that they are allowed to make mistakes, and where learning is actively encouraged. Good education requires collegiality, that is to say that people in a school work together to peruse common goals. Hence, although teachers are important, the outcome of education depends on the environment inside and outside school as well as the engagement and perceptions of students (ibid.). If for example actors in a society such as parents, journalists and politicians in general systematically bash down on teachers and teacher education it damages the conditions of education (see also Edling, 2014).

Education is therefore very much a shared responsibility between all policy actors, society and the state and this requires a high trust–low control space for teachers to thrive. New public modes of accountability, driven by low trust policies of neoliberal reform, have enacted some damage on the teaching profession in recent years, and there have been renewed calls for new Democratic and Intelligent modes of accountability for teachers (see Cochran-Smith, 2019; Lynch et al. (2012) and Mooney Simmie (2017) in the Supplementary readings). The importance to approach education in a holistic fashion, i.e. as to be created out of many parts which stand in symbiotic relation to each other is stressed from other directions as well:

> The social climate, the quality and quantity of relationships established in the learning environment, is recognized as an essential factor in the educational process. This view is supported by a large body of evidence from research on classroom climate, self-efficacy, effective schools, inclusive education, special needs, classroom management, and wellbeing and health.
>
> (Allodi, 2010, p. 93)

This does not mean that teachers are not important. On the contrary. In accordance with Hattie and Håkansson and Sundberg, successful teachers need to master a multiplicity of skills and capabilities. When reading the two meta studies as regards explicit and implicit suggestions regarding what good teachers should handle, several similarities appeared which are listed in Table 4.2.

Table 4.2 should be seen as a rough overview of what is required of a good teacher – there is certainly more. Besides, whereas Hattie and Håkansson and Sundberg write about the themes mentioned above, there are also differences between the researchers. Håkansson and Sundberg stress more vigorously than Hattie the complexities in education as concern perspectives and the value loaded aspects of research and education, to mention just some examples.

In the process of enfolding research that seems to work, images of the good student are implicitly presented, especially in Hattie's research (Table 4.3). Håkansson and Sundberg do not mention anything about what a good student needs to think about – the attention is mainly on the teacher and environment in general.

Likewise, the stress on teachers' characteristics is not something that Håkansson and Sundberg write much about whereas Hattie emphasizes that teachers' characteristics are really important on almost every page. Examples of personal traits imperative in a good teacher according to Hattie are: skilful, active, passionate, respectful, intelligent, nice, engaged, safe, susceptible, straightforward, open to change, full of ideas, feeling responsible, loving the subject, dedicated, and ethical/caring.

Hattie does not explain further what he means by these personal traits, rather they are treated as if they are obvious, which is problematic since this opens up a vast range of interpretations. To quote Kahneman (2013): "[d]uring the last ten years we have learned many facts about happiness. But we have also learned that the word happiness does not have a simple meaning and should not be used as if it does" (p. 407).

This large-scale data analytic work has however captured the imagination of politicians and policymakers in the last ten years as nations of the world and supranational organizations try to cope quickly and expediently with the aftermath of a large-scale global economic crisis, shocks from OECD PISA comparative tests scores etc. This has resulted in a fixation on naming standards for teachers and a policy imperative to describe benchmarks for the ideal teacher (and ideal student) in terms of what can be measured. This has spawned a dehumanized and empirically driven way of viewing education and democracy that has become a dominant syntax that is difficult to wobble and resembles a narrow scientism (Mooney Simmie, 2020).

Table 4.2 A summary of themes found in *Visible Learning* and *Excellent Education* as concerns what a good teacher needs to know/handle

Themes	The good teacher
Subject knowledge	Teachers need to know their subject(s) broadly and in depth
	Teachers need to know how the subject has developed over time and which educational traditions have existed
Relational awareness (ecology) and problem-solving	Teachers need to have relational competence (relations between variables and relations between people)
	Teachers need to understand and handle complexity, i.e. see connections and solve problems
	Teachers need to be able to puzzle and critically reflect based on context, policy and research
	Teachers need to navigate and make analysis of the learning environment based on research and systematized experience
	Teachers need to depict education in pieces in order to see how they relate to each other
	Teachers need to have good relations with their students
Situated judgement	Teachers need to react in present situations (context sensitivity) with good judgement. Good judgement requires broad and deep knowledge in relation to various perspectives
Competence to teach	Teachers need to be able to keep focus, depict and systematize education (constructive alignment)
	Teachers need to be able to communicate the purposes and aims of education. They need to make education visible (see also feedback)
	Teachers need to have a deep approach to learning when they teach
	Teachers need to help students understand complexity
	Teachers need to oscillate between student-centred and teacher-centred learning
	Teachers need to know that students learn at different paces
	Teachers need to focus on students' perceptions in order to stimulate development/progression. The aim is to make students their own teachers
	Teachers need to offer students different strategies to learn
	Teachers need to challenge students in order for learning to happen
	Teachers need to give suitable feedback
Stimulate good conditions	Teachers need to have knowledge about the values and norms influencing education
	Teachers need to know about the conditions for learning and actively work to develop education in order to stimulate learning
	Teachers need to know how safe relations take form and develop
	Teachers need to pay regard to student's differences
	Teachers need to be aware of the fact that knowledge is always loaded with values and has a political and ideological side (battle about reality)
Plurality of perspectives: teacher seeing	Teachers need to be aware that their seeing (perspectives/prejudices) matters for what it is possible to do in education. What teachers cannot see they cannot acknowledge.
	Teachers' (and students') seeing is influenced by knowledge (theories are important)
	Teachers need to have a variety of perspectives to stimulate critical thinking
	Teachers need to be able to move between perspectives and educational repertoires
	Teachers need to be able to zoom out (distant perspective) and zoom in (close perspective) based on research and context
	Teachers need to know that research, learning and education are coloured by a plurality of perspectives that do not always easily match

Table 4.3 A summary of themes found in *Visible Learning* and *Excellent Education* concerning what a good student needs to know/handle

Themes	The good student
Openness, engagement, passion	The student needs to be open to new knowledge and understand what is expected of her/him
	The student needs to find her/his engagement and passion for learning
Student seeing	The pupil needs to be aware of her/his prejudices that rule her/him in order for learning to happen
Learning as rough, persistent and unilineal	The student needs to understand that progression is not linear: it goes up and it goes down.
	Sometimes they need to learn more than what is asked for
	The student needs to realize that learning is not always fun and easy
	The student needs to understand that it takes a lot of practice and repetition in order for learning to take place
Self-confidence	The student needs to become aware of her/his own confidence since bad confidence is an obstacle to learning
Social concern	The student needs to understand that s/he is part of a social context (climate) and therefore should show respect, consideration, susceptibility to others in the group – including the teacher

Meta studies approach education from a distance, like a helicopter hovering above the educational landscape and as such cannot say anything about what actually takes place on the ground, in a school, teacher education institution, or classroom – for that, other tools are needed such as theories.

The importance of judgement based on systematic interpretations of a practice in movement

An *inside-out-professionalism* requires that teachers make qualified interpretations of educational policy, everyday practice, educational environments, texts and so forth and make judgements based on these interpretations (Stanley & Stronach, 2013). An inside-out-professionalism places certain demands on teacher education and student teachers that can be related to **deep learning** rather than merely focusing on **shallow learning**. Whereas a shallow form of learning is based on memorizing facts of knowledge in a fragmented way, deep learning has to do with more than memorizing isolated facts. **Deep learning** stresses the need to also put various kinds of knowledge in relation to one another and in relation to context in order to stimulate meaning-making (Ramsden, 2003).

Meaning-making is never pure and neutral but is always coloured by people's repertoires, e.g. frames of understanding (see Chapter 7). People see what they value or/and already have knowledge about, implying that they do not necessarily see what they do not know and value. To start seeing what takes form in experience and systematize that seeing does not necessarily happen automatically but needs to be practised (e.g., Håkansson & Sundberg, 2012; Hattie, 2012; Oonk 2001).

There are many ways of *seeing* knowledge and learning. Amongst students as teachers and those in charge there are various *perceptions* that influence the structure of and practice in higher education. How *knowledge is seen* and what is considered important knowledge matters for what students are expected to learn. … How learning is *seen* influences how education is organized and for the pedagogical activities and tools that teachers use to support students learning. However, these *perceptions* also influence each other. How one *looks at knowledge* will have implications for how one learns … Therefore it is important to discuss *different ways of seeing knowledge and learning* and how they are related to each other.

(Elmgren & Henriksson, 2006, p. 17, translated from Swedish. Italics are ours)

Seeing as a phenomenon is closely interlaced to language use and imagination. In accordance with Professor Maxine Greene, imagination is a vital "means through which we can assemble a coherent world" since of all "our cognitive capacities, imagination is the one that permits us to give credence to alternative realities" (Greene, 1995, p. 3).

The meaning of language is created by people in social interactions where the use of language becomes a habit that comes naturally and involves a sense of certainty. Indeed, people often understand each other perfectly well seeing that they tend to organize language in familiar ways. If we say 'table' or 'democracy' certain images come into mind. At the same time there is a danger that we think we see the exact same thing while we don't, which often leads to confusion, misunderstandings and at times conflicts (see for instance Wittgenstein, 1953/2001 and Table 4.4). Table 4.4 visualizes two different ways of seeing a series of violent cases at a Swedish boarding school in 2011. One perspective comes from people at the boarding school and the other from the Swedish school Inspectorate:

The illusion of the duck and rabbit (see Figure 4.1) is a well-used image that can be interpreted differently depending where the eye rests. The original version was presented

Table 4.4 In order to grasp the consequences of various seeing, the following example can be used. In reation to violent cases at an elite boarding school in Sweden school staff and some pupils argued in relation to the left column while the Swedish School Inspectorate argued in relation to the right column (see Francia and Edling, 2016)

Elite Boarding School	Swedish School Inspectorate
All teachers and students need to do is to follow principles and rules	Rules are not enough. It is also important to pay regard to how values, cultures and norms come into expresssion in everyday life as well as their consequences for people
It is only a few who are guilty. Why do you punish the innocent majority?	It is not about punishing innocent people, but to stress that schools are environments constituted out of various dimensions that intersect and influence people's lives and learning
The boys just wanted to joke. They didn't have any intentions to harm others	Consequences of actions matter, not just good intentions
We are a good school that takes knowledge and discipline seriously	A good school needs to work with both knowledge and values
The pupils are like siblings and siblings tend to fight. Allow them and us to sort this out without any interference from the state	Since relations in private have consequences for questions the state has responsibility for, the state needs to interfere

Teacher professionalism and democracy 91

Figure 4.1 An illusion of Wittgenstein's Duck and Rabbit. It reveals two images depending on where the subjects chooses to focus (see).

in a German comic journal in October 1892 titled *Fliegende Blätter* but was later used for research of which Ludwig Wittgenstein is one of the most famous (McManus et al., 2010). The purpose of presenting it here is just to show how one and the same object can be interpreted differently depending on where the focus of our seeing is. Often we think we talk about the same things while in realty we don't and it is first when we start to communicate with each other that an alternative picture might appear.

The rabbit and duck image also reminds us of how quickly we reach certainty without pausing for a while and pondering about whether things can be viewed differently. There is a tendency amongst people in general to find quick answers to complicated questions. Kahneman (2013) makes a distinction between **fast** and **slow thinking** where the fast thinking is about providing quick answers and reactions based on an experience bank. Fast thinking is seductive because it does not demand a lot of energy, while slow thinking does. Fast thinking is also a necessary part of living well in life, it takes deep thinking and expenditure of energy out of many of the mundane tasks we need to do in everyday life that are repetitive, such as deciding how to dress ourselves from a wardrobe of options. Slow thinking is about slowing down and focus, like for example finding the answer to a mathematical problem, creating an educational seminar where various purposes are in balance, and finding out different ways about how democracy is described in a course book with a multitude of other information as well. Both of these ways of thinking are part of what it means to be human and are neither good nor bad in themselves. It is, however, a problem if we allow ourselves to be governed by fast thinking all the time often based on prejudice and simplified perceptions – at least if we think that the latter is un-welcome (ibid. in Edling 2012/2018, see also Chapter 6).

An inside-out-professionalism needs teachers who are willing to think slowly and not just merely act mechanically on impulse all the time like 'of course it is important to be kind', 'I'm kind', 'I actually think much in education is common sense', and 'of course I follow the democratic value foundation', but also try to understand the meaning of their profession more in depth and what it means to systematically and scientifically interpret the practice they are involved in as well as engage with the wider world of meaning-making and critically reading the world (see Chapters 3, 5 and 7).

There are various ways of approaching educational practice conceptually. Often people tend to approach the world through feelings implying that they react to their surroundings in terms of how they experience it: 'I'm so angry at that group', 'I'm happy I made some difference in Hannah's life today', 'I strongly dislike the immigrant children in class'. When the person is asked if s/he could elaborate s/he might describe the surroundings contrary to just expressing sentiments, for example: 'I began the class by talking to the students about democracy. Several of the children posed questions. Ann scribbled in her note book while Suzan and Carl seemed to look out the window and think about something else'.

Teaching involves the heart-work of teaching and learning and this requires recognized feminine qualities of empathy and care and capability to react emotionally to and with young people and with other actors. Teachers in this way build the affective structures of schools that are so important in community building as places of high trust and relational confidence (Lynch et al., 2012). However, the demands on intellectual teachers focusing an inside-out-professionalism is to also interpret what takes place around them with the help of counter-intuitive knowledge and theoretical frameworks and concepts (e.g. Arevik & Hartzell, 2013). For example:

- How does the teacher handle power and culture in the classroom (what kind of ways to grasp power and culture are there in research and what kind of conditions do they entail)?
- How is democracy approached by the students and teachers (what kind of ways to grasp democracy are there in research and what kind of conditions do they entail)?
- What kind of professionalism does the teacher express through his/her speech and practice (what kind of ways to grasp professionalism are there in research and what kind of conditions do they entail)?

Thinking through feelings, observations and science can be compared to having an **everyday language, academic language** and a **professional language**. Everyday language is the language we use in our everyday interactions that are not structured and are fuelled with feelings and observations. Contrary to this, academic language demands a systematized relationship to our surroundings and to knowledge stressing an awareness of analysis, transparency, well-grounded/scientifically grounded argumentation, and alignment between parts. Professional language is about being able to orient in a practice in constant movement with the help of academic language (e.g. Arneback, Englund & Solbrekke, 2017, in Edling 2012/2018). However, the inherent colonization and symbolic violence in this way of reasoning is that school life for teachers and young people is now elevated to a dominant syntax which rationalizes the affective and seeks to move teachers from former understandings of soul work, the moral goods of teaching and any notion of teaching as an itty witty feminized practice of care and personal development to a new inquiry-oriented stance as detached and disinterested teacher-researchers and an accompanying terror of performativity (Ball, 2003; Santoro, 2017).

Conclusion

In various places in the world democracy is regarded as an important dimension to include in teacher education programmes but there is a great variety in how this is to be understood and approached. Our focus for this chapter has been to elaborate on differences between broad and narrow approaches to democracy and their consequences for teacher professionalism. If the ethical dimension of democracy paying regard to plurality is to be taken into account, then narrow approaches to democracy are not sufficient. The broad approach to democracy on the other hand places a huge burden on teacher education, since student teachers need to learn more than merely knowledge and values about democracy. Regarding democracy from a broad stance, as a form of living, pleads for deep and slow learning as well as a deep and critical awareness that knowledge, values, socialization and equity/emancipation/subjectivity are interconnected.

Accordingly, the meaning of teacher professionalism is not given but depends on what kind of society is (politically) desired and thus what kind of skills, values, taste and knowledge citizens are to have. The very question of teacher professionalism is caught in the midst of various, contradictory values that cause dilemmas for teacher educators and student teachers in relation to theory/practice, values/neutrality, freedom/constraint, majority/minority, and order/disorder. This brings us to a discussion about democracy and knowledge which we will take up in Chapter 5.

Questions

1. What kind of spontaneous idea(s) did this chapter evoke in you? Can you put words on it/these using literature and concepts from the chapter as a point of departure?
2. Drawing on narrow and broad ways of grasping democracy can you locate colleagues' understanding, your family's understanding, and your teachers' understanding, based on what you have seen in their practice as well as their descriptions? What is your own understanding – try using the language from the chapter to describe this?
3. As concerns what you have read about teacher professionalism, what kind of professionalism is expected from you, drawing from policy, and how does it correspond with your perceptions? With your experiences in your practices? and with other teachers at the school setting?
4. Ponder about how you would handle the dilemmas mentioned in the chapter. Motivate your arguments based on what you have come to know and your own experiences. How does your argument hold when you consider research and readings in relation to the dilemma(s)?
5. How do you approach theory and meta studies and in what ways do you link it to practice? Give examples. Do you discuss issues like this with trusted critical friend(s)?
6. What kinds of change, if any, have you noticed in relation to how teacher professionalism is viewed at your higher education setting or at your school setting?
7. What kind of dilemmas in relation to the topic discussed would you like to add, and why?

Supplementary readings

1. Professor Maxine Greene speaking to new teachers about her broad democratic view of education and capacity to imagine and change
   Maxine Greene in 1988: Imagination, 03/04/2015

www.youtube.com/watch?v=b_raVMnP57w
2 ASTI Convention Wexford 2019 – Guest speaker Professor Kathleen Lynch Challenging Neoliberalism in Education: Care, Class and Equality of Condition, 01/05/2019
www.youtube.com/watch?v=D9FNyj4YDXo
3 The Late Bell When Teachers Can't Do the Work – Episode 2 featuring a conversation with Bowdoin Professor Doris A. Santoro
Demoralized: When Teachers Can't Do the Work with Doris Santoro, 12/08/2019
www.youtube.com/watch?v=hge42mWDQ8I
4 Dr. Geraldine Mooney Simmie, Senior Lecturer, School of Education, University of Limerick addresses the Association of Secondary Teachers of Ireland (ASTI) Convention in the INEC Centre, Killarney, Co. Kerry.
ASTI Convention 2017 – Dr. Geraldine Mooney Simmie, 28/04/2017
www.youtube.com/watch?v=q2-MvmUvevg

Notes

1 Parts of this chapter are freely translated from Swedish to English based on Edling (2016). *Demokratidilemman i läraruppdraget. Att arbeta för lika villkor [Democracy dilemmas in the teacher mission. To strive for equity]*. Stockholm.
2 The article can be found at: www.dn.se/nyheter/sverige/larare-forsvarade-fakta-kring-forintelsen-kritiseras/ [19.08.05]

References

Abbarno, G. John M. (2015). *Inherent and instrumental values. Excursion in value inquiry*. Lanham, MD & London: University Press of America.
Allodi, Mara (2010). The meaning of social climate of learning environments: Some reasons why we do not care enough about it. *Learning Environments Research*, 13(2), 89–104.
Arneback, Emma, Englund, Tomas & Solbrekke, Tone Dyrdal (2017). Att skriva sig till professionell identitet. Tre förskollärarstudenter. In P.-O. Erixon & O. Josephson (eds.), *Kampen om texten*. Lund, Sweden: Studentlitteratur.
Arevik, Sten & Hartzell, Ove (2013). *Att göra tänkandet synligt. En bok om begreppsbaserad undervisning*. Stockholm: Liber.
Armando, Luís Grandin & Apple, Michael (2002). Thin versus thick democracy in education: Porto Alegre and the creation of alternatives to neo-liberalism. *International Studies in Sociology of Education*, 12(2), 99–114.
Bagley, Carl & Beach, Dennis (2015). The marginalisation of social justice as a form of knowledge in teacher education in England. *Policy Futures in Education 2015*, 13(4), 424–438.
Ball, A. F. (2000). Preparing teachers for diversity: Lessons learned from the US and South Africa. *Teaching and Teacher Education*, 16(4), 491–509.
Ball, D. L. & Cohen, D. K. (1999). Developing practice, developing practitioners: Toward a practice-based theory of professional education. In G. Sykes & L. Darling-Hammond (eds.), *Teaching as the learning profession: Handbook of policy and practice*. San Francisco, CA: Jossey-Bass.
Ball, S. J. (1995). Intellectuals or technicians? The urgent role of theory in educational studies. *The British Journal of Educational Studies*, 43(3), 255–271.
Ball, S. J. (2003). The teacher's soul and the terrors of performativity. *Journal of Education Policy*, 18(2), 215–228.
Barber, B. (1997). Foreword. In G. Reher & J. Cammarano (eds.), *Education for citizenship. ideas and innovations in political learning*. Maryland: Rowman & Littlefield, pp. 4–9.

Barber, B. (2003). *Strong democracy. Participatory politics for a new age*. Berkeley, CA & London: University of California Press.

Biesta, Gert (2006). *Beyond learning: Democratic education for a human future*. Boulder, CO: Paradigm.

Biesta, Gert (2010). *What is education for? Good education in an age of measurement: Ethics, politics, democracy*. Boulder, CO: Paradigm.

Biesta, Gert, De Bie, Maria & Wildemeersch, Danny (2014). *Civic learning, democratic citizenship, and the public sphere*. Dortdrecht, The Netherlands; Heidelberg, Germany; London and New York: Springer.

Bingham, Charles W. & Sidorkin, Alexander M. (2004). *No education without relation*. New York: Peter Lang.

Borman, Kathryn, Danzig, Arnold & Gracia, David (2012). Introduction: Education, democracy, and the public good. *Education, democracy, and the public good. Review of research in education. American Educational Research Association*, 36, vii–xx.

Carr, Paul R. (2008). Educators and education for democracy: Moving beyond 'thin' democracy. *Inter-American Journal of Education for Democracy*, 1(2), 146–165.

Carr, Paul R., Thomas, P. L., Portfilio, B. & Gorlewski, J. (2016). *Democracy and decency: What does education have to do with it?*Charlotte, NC: Information Age.

Cherryholmes, Cleo H. (1988). *Power and criticism: Poststructural investigations in education*. New York: Teachers College Press.

Clark, C. M. & Peterson, P. L. (1986). Teachers' thought processes. In M. C. Wittrock (ed.), *Handbook of research on teaching* (3rd edn.). New York: Macmillan, pp. 255–296.

Cochran-Smith, M. (2011). Teaching in new times: What do teachers really need to know? *Kappa Delta Pi Record*, 47(1), 11–12.

Cochran-Smith, M. (2004). The problem of teacher education. *Journal of Teacher Education*, 55(4), 295–299.

Colnerud, Gunnel (2004). Värdegrund som pedagogisk praktik och forskningsdiskurs. *Pedagogisk forskning i Sverige*, 9(2), 81–98.

Colnerud, Gunnel & Granström, Kjell (2002). *Respekt för läraryrket. Om lärares yrkesspråk och yrkesetik* [Respect for the teaching profession. On teachers' professional language and ethics] (Updated edn.). Stockholm: HLS förl.

Colwell, Tom (1985). The ecological perspective in John Dewey's philosophy. *Educational Theory*, 35(30), 255–266.

Dahl, Robert (2002). *Demokratin och dess antagonister*. Stockholm, Sweden: Ordfront i samarbete med Demokratiakademin.

Dahlstedt, Magnus & Olson, Maria (2013). *Utbildning, demokrati, medborgarskap* [Education, democracy, and citizenship] (1st edn.). Malmö, Sweden: Gleerups.

Dewey, J. (1916). Democracy and education [Elektronisk resurs]. Retrieved from https://en.wikisource.org/wiki/Democracy_and_Education

Dewey, J. (2004 [1938]). *Experience and education*. Stockholm: Natur och Kultur.

Dewey, John & Bentley, Arthur F. (1949). *Knowing and the known*. Boston, MA: Beacon Press.

Doll, William, Jr. (2012). *Pragmatism, post-modernism, and complexity theory. The 'Fascinating Imaginative Realm' of William E. Doll, Jr*. New York & London: Routledge.

Edling, Silvia (2014). Between stereotypes and task complexity. Exploring stereotypes of teachers and education in media as a question of structural violence. *Journal of Curriculum Studies*, 47(3), 399–415.

Edling, Silvia (2016). *Demokratidileman i läraruppdrag. Att arbeta för lika villkor*. [Democracy dilemmas in the teacher mission. To strive for equity]. Stockholm, Sweden: Liber.

Edling, Silvia (2009). *Ruptured narratives: An analysis of the contradictions within young people's responses to issues of personal responsibility and social violence within an educational context*. Dissertation. Uppsala, Sweden: Acta Universitatis Upsaliensis (AUU).

Edling, Silvia (2012/2018). *Vilja andra väl är inte alltid smärtfritt. Att motverka kränkning och diskriminring i förskola och skola* [Wanting others' wellbeing is not always painless. To oppose violence and discrimination in preschool and school]. Lund, Sweden: Studentlitteratur AB.

Edling, S. & Liljestrand, J. (2018). Student teachers' task perceptions of democracy in their future profession – a critical discourse analysis of students' course texts. *Australian Journal of Teacher Education*, 43(7), 82–97.

Edling, S. & Mooney Simmie, G. (2017). Democracy and emancipation in teacher education: A summative content analysis of teacher educators' democratic assignment expressed in policies for Teacher Education in Sweden and Ireland between 2000–2010. *Citizenship, Social, Economics Education*, 17(1),1–15.

Elbaz, F. (1991). Research on teachers' knowledge: The evolution of a discourse. *Journal of Curriculum Studies*, 23(1), 1–19.

Elbaz, F. (1983). *Teacher thinking: A study of practical knowledge*. London: Croom Helm.

Elmgren, Maja & Henriksson, Ann-Sofie (2016). *Universitetspedagogik*. [University pedagogy]. Lund, Sweden: Studentlitteratur.

Endres, Benjamin (2007). The conflict between interpersonal relations and abstract systems in education. *Educational Theory*, 57(2), 171–186.

Englund, Tomas & Quennerstedt, Ann (2008). Linking curriculum theory and linguistics: The performative use of 'equivalence' as an educational policy concept. *Journal of Curriculum Studies*, 40(6), 713–724.

Francia, G. & Edling, S. (2017). Children's rights and violence : A case analysis at a Swedish boarding school. *Childhood*, 24(1), 51–67.

Fransson, Göran & Grannäs, Jan (2013). Dilemmatic spaces in educational contexts – towards a conceptual framework for dilemmas in teachers work. *Teachers and Teaching: Theory and Practice*, 19(1), 4–17.

Frelin, Anneli (2013). *Exploring relational professionalism in schools*. Rotterdam, The Netherlands; Boston, MA &Taipei, Taiwan: Sense.

Frelin, Anneli (2010). *Teachers' relational practices and professionality*. Uppsala, Sweden: Institutionen för didaktik, Uppsala universitet.

Frith, Chris & Frith, Uta (2010). Learning from others: Introduction to the Special Review Series on Social Neuroscience. *Neuron*, 65(6), 739–743.

Furman, Gail & Shields, Carolyn (2005). How can educational leaders promote and support social justice and democratic community in schools? In W. Firestone & C. Riehl (eds.), *New agendas for research in educational leadership*. New York & London: Teachers College Press.

Giroux, Henry A. & Penna, Anthony (1983). *Social education in the classroom: The dynamics of the hidden curriculum*. Berkeley, CA: McCutchan.

Gordon, J. A. (2006). From liberation to human rights: Challenges for teachers of the Burakumin in Japan. *Race Ethnicity and Education*, 9(2), 183–202.

Grannäs, Jan & Frelin, Anneli (2010). Present presence or absent presence? Counted and uncounted events in the managerial order of education. Paper presented at the AAACS Annual Meeting, 27–30 April, Denver, CO.

Green, Judith M. (1999). *Deep democracy: Community, diversity, and transformation*. Lanham, MD: Rowman & Littlefield.

Greene, Maxine (1995). *Releasing the imagination. Essays on education, the arts, and social change*. San Francisco, CA: Jossey-Bass.

Hadenius, Axel (2001). *Demokrati: en jämförande analys*. Stockholm, Sweden: Liber.

Håkansson, Jan & Sundberg, Daniel (2012). *Utmärkt undervisning. Framgångsfaktorer i svensk och internationell belysning* [Excellent education. Success factors from a Swedish and International perspective]. Stockholm, Sweden: Natur och Kultur.

Harber, C. & Serf, J. (2006). Teacher education for a democratic society in England and South Africa. *Teaching and Teacher Education*, 22(8), 9686–9997.

Hattie, J. (2012). *Visible learning for teachers: Maximizing impact on learning*. London & New York: Routledge.

Held, David (1987). *Models of democracy*. Cambridge, UK: Polity Press.

Honig, Bonnie (2007). Between decision and deliberation: Political paradox in democratic theory. *The American Political Science Review*, 101(1), 1–17.

Honig, Bonnie (1993). *Political theory and the displacement of politics*. Ithaca, NY: Cornell University Press.
Jackson, Philip Wesley (1990). *Life in classrooms*. New York: Teachers College Press.
Jönsson, Annelis & Rubenstein, Reich (2009). *Redo för läraryrket* [Ready for teacher education]. Lund, Sweden: Studentlitteratur.
Kahneman, Daniel (2013). *Thinking, fast and slow* (1st pbk. edn.). New York: Farrar, Straus and Giroux.
Letiche, H., Lightfoot, G. & Moriceau, J.-L. (eds.) (2016). *Demo(s): Philosophy – pedagogy – politics*. Rotterdam, The Netherlands: Sense.
Liljestrand, Johan (2011). *Demokratiskt deltagande: diskussionen som undervisning och demokrati*. Stockholm, Sweden: Liber.
Lonergan, J. (2016). Teacher professional learning: Contextual understandings and perspectives of secondary teachers in Ireland. PhD thesis. Limerick, Republic of Ireland: University of Limerick.
Lynch, Kathleen, Grummell, Bernie & Devine, Dympna (2012). *New managerialism in education commercialization, carelessness and gender*. New York: Palgrave Macmillan.
McManus, I. C., Freegard, Matthew, Moore, James & Rawles, Richard (2010). 'Science in the making: Right hand, left hand. II: The duck–rabbit figure' (PDF). *Laterality*, 15(1–2), 166–185.
Majhanovich, Suzanne & Malet, Régis (2015). *Building education through democracy and diversity*. Rotterdam, The Netherlands; Boston, MA & Taipei, Taiwan: Sense.
Mooney Simmie, G. (2020). The power, politics, and future of mentoring. In Beverly J. Irby, Linda Searby, Jennifer N. Boswell, Fran Kochan & Rubén Garza (eds.), *The wiley international handbook of mentoring: Paradigms, practices, programs, and possibilities* (1st edn.). Hokoben, NY: John Wiley & Sons, pp. 453–469.
Mooney Simmie, G. & Edling, S. (2016). Ideological governing forms in education and teacher education: A comparative study between highly secular Sweden and highly non-secular Republic of Ireland. *Nordic Journal of Studies in Educational Policy*, 2, 1–12.
Mooney Simmie, G. & Edling, S. (2018). Teachers' democratic assignment: A critical discourse analysis of teacher education policies in Ireland and Sweden. *Discourse Studies in the Cultural Politics of Education*. 40(6), 832–846.
Mooney Simmie, G. & Lang, M. (2020). *School-based deliberative partnership as a platform for teacher professionalization and curriculum innovation*. Routledge research teacher education series. London & New York: Routledge.
Mooney Simmie, G., Moles, J. & O'Grady, E. (2019). Good teaching as a messy narrative of change within a policy ensemble of networks, superstructures and flows. *Critical Studies in Education*, 60(1), 55–72.
Mouffe, Chantal (2000). *The democratic paradox*. London: Verso.
Oonk, W. (2001). Putting theory into practice: Growth of appreciating theory by student teachers. In M. van den Heuvel-Panhuizen (ed.), *Proceedings of the 25th Conference of the International Group for the Psychology of Mathematics Education* (Vol. 4). Utrecht, The Netherlands: Freudenthal Institute, pp. 17–24.
Östman, Leif (1995). *Socialisation och mening: No-utbildning som politiskt och miljömoraliskt problem* [Socialization and meaning: science education as a political and environmental-ethical problem]. Dissertation. Uppsala, Sweden: Uppsala University.
Östman, Leif & Almqvist, Jonas (2011). *What do values and norms have to do with scientific literacy?* New York: Routledge.
Pinar, William (2012). *What is curriculum theory*. London & New York: Routledge.
Ramsden, P. (2003). *Learning to teach in higher education*. London: Routledge Falmer.
Rancière, J. (1995). *On the shores of politics*. London & New York: Verso.
Säfström, Carl Anders & Månsson, Niclas (2004). The limits of socialisation [Symposium on curriculum theory and ethical questions]. *Interchange*, 35(3), 353–364.
Santoro, D. A. (2017). Cassandra in the classroom: Teaching and moral madness. *Studies in Philosophy of Education*, 36, 49–60.

Schön, Donald A. (1986). *The reflective practitioner: How professionals think in action*. New York: Basic Books.

Schulz, W., Ainley, J., Fraillon, J., Kerr, D. & Losito, B. (2010). *Initial findings from the IEA international civic and citizenship study*. Amsterdam: International Association for the Evaluation of Educational Achievement (IEA). Retrieved from: http://iccs.acer.edu.au/uploads/File/Reports/ICCS_10_Initial_Findings.pdf

Stanley, Edward & Stronach, Ian (2013). Raising and doubling 'standards' in professional discourse: A critical bid. *Journal of Educational Policy*, 28(3), 291–305.

Strike, K. A. (1999). Can schools be communities? The tension between shared values and inclusion. *Quarterly*, 35, 46–70.

Syal, Supriya & Andersson, Adam K. (2013). It takes two to talk: A second-person neuroscience approach to language learning. *The Behavioral and Brain Sciences*, 36(4), 439–440.

Thiessen, Dennis (2000). Developing knowledge for preparing teachers: Redefining the role of schools of education. *Education Policy*, 14(1), 129–144.

Thornberg, Robert (2013). *Det sociala livet i skolan : socialpsykologi för lärare* [The social life in school: social psychology for teachers. Stockholm, Sweden: Liber.

Torney-Purta, J. (2002). Patterns in the civic knowledge, engagement, and attitudes of European adolescents: The IEA civic education study. *European Journal of Education*, 37(2), 129–141. Retrieved from: http://onlinelibrary.wiley.com/doi/10.1111/1467-3435.00098/epdf

Wittgenstein, Ludwig (1953/2001). *Philosophical investigations*. Oxford: Blackwell.

Zeichner, Ken (2016). Advancing social justice and democracy in teacher education: Teacher preparation 1.0, 2.0, and 3.0. *Kappa Delta Pi Record*, 52(4), 150–155.

Zyngier, David, Delia, Maria & Murriello, Adriana (2015). 'Democracy will not fall from the sky'. A comparative study of teacher education students' perceptions of democracy in two neo-liberal societies. *Research in Comparative & International Education*, 10(2), 275–299.

5 Knowledge and democracy

Introduction

Education is a cross-disciplinary field rather than a well-defined 'learning' system, and in this way teaching is viewed at the crossroad between knowledge acquisition, socialization and **emancipation**. Our understanding of **emancipation** is the space for teachers and young people to be unique persons and to experience a sense of themselves that places being and becoming in the heart-work of education (e.g. Säfström, 2011) and educational praxis. We understand **praxis** as uneasy clashes and tensions in teaching between practice, experience, policy, theory and research that defy easy and simplistic explanations (Freire, 1971, see Supplementary reading). Tensions, contradictions and dilemmas require the intellectual and moral goods of teaching to be taken into account, such as rigorous critical thinking to interrupt and question routinized practices (Duarte, 2016; Nussbaum, 2010). Teachers interrogate themselves and their practices and need to mediate findings with wider social, moral and political issues of the day in order to secure a decent and vibrant democracy.

The current business-like Global Education Reform Movement's (GERM) pedagogy of 'visibility' (re)positions teachers to think of identity and the teaching assignment as different from an intellectually challenging assignment (Biesta, 2012; Giroux, 1988; Skerritt, 2018). Teachers are frequently described as not 'the sage on the stage' but rather the 'guide on the side'. An anti-intellectual stance has opened up and spawned a therapeutic emphasis on teachers as facilitators and social engineers as if schools were solely concerned with passing on technical skills and predetermined attitudes and no longer places with responsibility for the transmission and/or interrogation of a canon of existing powerful knowledge, culture and heritage, to the next generation. Former understandings of inextricable linkages between knowledge, values, knower's and ways of knowing have been broken as a new market-led discourse of education – from human capital theory (see Chapter 3) – has started to dominate the politics of knowledge and schooling (Bernstein, 2000).

We will structure the chapter as follows. First, we briefly examine the tensions and possibilities in relation to knowledge and democracy in teacher's assignments and show how various schools of thought reveal the deeply contested nature of the politics of knowledge and democracy in teacher education. Second, we show how GERM repositions teachers' assignment using new modes of knowledge, such as teachers' professional knowledge base, i.e. knowledge defined by a political-economic impetus as teacher identity, self-efficacy, communication and developmental psychology predominate with a live interest in the science of behaviour and achieving excellence in instruction. This is accompanied by downplaying other forms of knowledge such as foundational knowledge (history of education, sociology of education, philosophy of education), disciplinary

Table 5.1 An overview of dilemmas discussed in Chapter 5

Dilemmas
theory versus practice
objectivity versus subjectivity
self-confidence versus knowledge
politics of knowledge versus whose interest are served?
knowledge for democracy versus disciplinary regimen
knowledge-knowers inextricably linked versus separate
powerful knowledge/theory to interrupt versus routinized practices/atheoretical what works

knowledge, theoretical knowledge, and the arts and aesthetics (Biesta & Miedema, 2002; Nussbaum, 2010). In this chapter, we argue that mediation with other ways of knowing and with the wider world is currently erased from global reform policies and from the reform ensemble in Ireland and Sweden as it seeks to regulate teachers and young people in the direction of disciplinary order rather than stimulation of a democratic practice (Säfström, 2011). Connectivity to the wider world and multiple ways of knowing is what secures education's social responsibility for public interest values and a decent, just and vibrant democracy (Edling & Mooney Simmie, 2017; Mooney Simmie & Edling, 2016). Dilemmas in the chapter are concerned with this politics of knowledge, whose interests are served by current global and local reforms in education and democracy, how and in what ways the current framing of new entrepreneurial atheoretical knowledge forms in teacher education is contributing to securing a disciplinary regimen rather than emancipation and a vibrant democracy (see Table 5.1).

Teacher education, democracy and the demands for more complex knowledge

Teacher education as well as teachers have in many parts of the world been subjected to more or less fierce public critiques (Edling, 2014; Labaree, 2004; Paraskeva, 2011). The debate tends to circle around two major ideologies that at times overlap but often are treated in a dualistic fashion, namely: (a) the strife to stimulate a teacher education that creates a professional and democratic foundation for future teachers based on the ideas created in relation to K-12 curriculum standards and (b) those arguing that teacher education as a public institution should not have a monopoly on preparing future teachers, since there are other, conservative and private institutions, who could do it better. Whereas the term ideology is used as a bat to attack opponents

> both agendas are themselves ideological in the sense that they are driven by ideas, ideals, values, and assumptions about the purposes of schooling, the social and economic future of the nation, and the role of public education in a democratic society.
> (Cochran-Smith & Fries, 2001, p. 3, see Chapter 4)

These tensions are also related to whether teacher education should promote deep learning and capability to critique or narrow (shallow) learning and teaching. The former stresses the need to understand and actively take part in the formation of education/society based on well-grounded judgements whereas the latter approach is to solely be about mechanical transfer of knowledge fragments and inculcation of obedience (Britzman 2003; Säfström, 2011). This reasoning is also intimately connected to broad conceptions of democracy and teacher professionalism. Indeed, is **democracy** to merely **be taught about** or is **knowledge in** and **for democracy** equally important to pay regard to in education (see Chapter 4)?

What appears to have happened in Ireland and Sweden in relation to teachers' assignment is a reductionist approach to all forms of knowledge requirement, with the exception of professional (political) knowledge and its emphasis on teachers' capabilities to communicate and to rework teacher identity for a new actuarial and entrepreneurial self (Ball, 2003). We have shown in Chapter 4 how this reform policy ensemble has resulted in downplaying knowledge, such as disciplinary and theoretical knowledge and has instead fore-grounded situated/experiential knowledge for a practice turn, a new wave of policy compliance and adherence to regulations for generating a disciplinary order rather than stimulating emancipation and democracy (Edling & Mooney Simmie, 2017; Mooney Simmie 2012, 2014; Mooney Simmie & Edling, 2016, 2018; Säfström, 2011).

Higher education as a site for developing democratic societies is far from new. Besides, John Dewey Wilhelm von Humboldt argued that a central objective of higher education is to create spaces for **Bildung**, e.g. stimulating a harmony and a more mature relationship between mind and heart and hence between selfhood, identity, culture, and society at large. In this sense, knowledge and democracy played crucial roles in their potential for enlightenment and stimulating engaged, informed and critical citizens. Ideas of democracy within higher education are **normative** in the way that certain predefined steps are believed to lead to a desired outcome. However, a normative platform is problematic if it excludes difference, that is to say new ideas and ways of being to break into and redefine the normative order. This reasoning highlights tensions between higher education as an elite education and democracy based on an idea of folk rule that includes everyone (e.g. Biesta, 2013).

Public and policy demands on teachers' knowledge, skills, attitudes, capabilities and competences vary, depending on whether the compass needle points to broad or narrow ways of approaching education. In former times the expectations on teachers and subsequently teacher education were drastically lower than today. During the beginning of the 20th century the most important demands on an elementary teacher found in a teacher contract from the US, were to be unmarried and promise to avoid men altogether in their profession (Apple, 1987), which reflects a specific gender perspective. Currently, the demands on teacher and teacher educators have increased dramatically:

> In today's world, policy makers, politicians, educational leaders, the general public, and parents expect a great deal from teachers. Unlike our grandmothers' generation, we want teachers who know subject matter and know how to teach it to all students to world-class standards. We want teachers to be responsible for students' improvement on high-stakes tests, which in many states determines whether students will graduate and may determine teachers' salaries and future job status. We want teachers to be adept at all sorts of technology, to differentiate curriculum and instruction for students with special needs and disabilities, and to be thoroughly knowledgeable about multiple cultures. We expect teachers to teach students who do not speak English as a first language—without sacrificing attention to content and, in many cases, without long-term special programs. And the expectations for today's teachers don't stop there. In many instances, we expect teachers to work long hours at school and at home, doing lesson preparation and grading over the weekends, completing additional

coursework during the summers, and spending their own money for classroom resources. We expect teachers to participate in ongoing professional development and training for the implementation of new classroom strategies, curriculum materials, testing programs, assessments, and other new mandates from district, state, and federal regulatory agencies. We also expect teachers to communicate and collaborate with students, parents, guardians, caregivers, social workers, psychologists, specialist teachers, medical personnel, speech therapists, parole officers, supervisors, administrators, mentors, and community groups. We expect teachers to be effective members of the school's professional staff—working to prevent bullying, drug and alcohol use, pregnancy, and suicide. In addition to all these expectations, we want teachers who like children and can relate to today's youth.

(Cochran-Smith, 2011, p. 12)

The demands on teachers today, based on idealism, tend to brand teachers as constant failures, since no one is capable of attaining the high aims (Biesta & Säfström, 2011). Teachers are as such constantly caught in the struggle and/or embrace with imperfectness (Todd, 2009) while being asked to be perfect. At the same time it forces us to ponder about what kind of knowledge is required to meet the needs linked to a broad approach to democracy – at least if we argue that education matters?

Knowledge and theory

Teachers tend to say at times that teacher education has become too abstract, general, and distant from everyday education. Also when student teachers are asked about their relationship to theory they tend to value **practical knowledge** higher than **theoretical knowledge** (Allen, 2009; Zeichner, 2010).

The dualistic discourse existing within universities can also be described in terms of **everyday knowledge** and academic knowledge. Everyday knowledge is based on orally transmitted ideas that are elusive to their nature in that they do not build on a documented body of knowledge and it is a common sense practice in relation to practical goals. Contrary to this, **academic knowledge** is theoretical, specialized and developed in academic disciplines such as special education, sociology, mathematics and so forth. It is characterized by scientific structures and scientific language that appear abstract but have the potential to provide more systematic knowledge and concepts that help gain a sharper focus in the task to grapple with reality (Bernstein, 2000, p. 170–171). Other models to illuminate the dichotomy as regards knowledge are **vertical** and **horizontal discourse** (Player-Koro, 2012). While vertical discourse has been emphasized as important in the knowledge base for professional teachers in Sweden (Beach, 2011) this appears to have changed towards a horizontal understanding through a horizontal understanding, , hence marginalizing specialized (and theoretical) knowledge drawing on philosophy, economy, sociology, politics etc. (Beach & Bagley, 2012).

As such, many student teachers express insecurity in why theory is used and how they are going to apply this knowledge in their day-to-day education (Sjølie, 2014). This gives the impression that the abstract and general does not have a place in education but it also sheds light on challenges that appear when another regards something deemed as important by one part meaningless. Lately, the strong focus on evidence-based research in terms of large-scale empirical research has tended to push the use of theories to the margin in political and academic discussions that concern education. Theory widens perception and enables analysis of a complex practice and is important for critical thinking. In this regard the tendency to push it aside is highly problematic (Allan, 2014).

In an article in *Pedagogical Magasin* (*Pedagogiska Magasinet*) two previous student teachers asked why they had to read a range of different sociocultural theories during their education course, since these theories according to them lacked credibility. They argued that these theories are relative, and hence untrue and irrelevant to practice, while the mission in education is to teach truth and facts. Real knowledge, according to them is knowledge based on the evidence of large empirical research, and theories from this stance become nothing more than meaningless, imprecise and difficult to use as starting-points for education (André & Salmijärvi, 2015, in Edling, 2015).

This points toward the discrepancy between **practical and/or personal knowledge** and **theoretical and/or propositional knowledge**, i.e. knowledge that helps to focus and structure reality is important to be aware of when understanding knowledge (Higgs et al. 2001). In relation to this it is possible to distinguish between: knowledge-for-practice, knowledge-in-practice, and knowledge-of-practice (Cochran-Smith & Lytle, 1999). **Knowledge-for-practice** is the knowledge and theory generated through research that is provided by a canon of expert knowledge made elsewhere (e.g. the academy of teacher education and research) for teachers to improve their practice. Whilst knowledge-for-practice highlights knowledge as a commodity handed to teachers by experts, **knowledge-in-practice** is knowledge expressed in everyday practice and arising from reflections in, on and for practice, see Chapter 7 (Schön, 1983). There are those arguing that teachers learn from wiser colleagues when they follow their work in real-life classroom interactions (e.g. apprenticeships of observation). The third form of teacher learning is **knowledge-of-practice** that is to say neither just universal nor a question of reflection in and through practice. On the contrary, it interconnects the two forms of knowledge in the way that knowledge from research becomes a springboard for interpretation of practice while at the same time practice becomes a site for systematic investigation that exceeds previous research but communicates to a broader social and cultural body of knowledge and politics. In this latter view of knowledge-of-practice teachers become knowledge makers themselves, sense makers, culture makers and public intellectuals.

Cochran-Smith & Lytle's (1999) model of teachers' knowledge base can be compared to different ways of perceiving and using theory, which are important to be aware of when navigating the dilemmatic space of teacher education and the field of knowledge.

1 **Theory as a universal and generalizable model of real world**: What is emphasized here is the way theory is abstract and hence used to generalize, and simplify the complexity of practice in order to make it manageable and understandable. No theory can capture everything but is based on some kind of inclusion/exclusion. Theory is from this perspective a model or map based on some carefully selected parameters (Kvernbekk, 2005).

2 **Tested theory contrary to un-tested theory:** This way of approaching theory is based on a dualistic foundation where tested theory is a theoretical hypothesis that has been verified by empirical research and hence proved to be efficient. Theory from this stance becomes a description of a method that works. Contrary to this view are some theories from for instance the field of education that are deemed as to be quasi since they are not tested (Edling, 2015).

3 **Theory as a tool to navigate in relation to various purposes**: Whereas tested theory comes from natural science, there are those arguing that human and social

sciences where human practice is dynamic and complex need a different way of grasping theory than the dualistic one (Kvernbekk, 2005). From this stance practice and theory are interdependent in that there is no practice that lacks a way of thinking. In the latter approach, it is there accentuated that no theory has ever been constructed without a purpose and that this purpose needs to be taken account. Indeed, is the purpose of theory to problematize, critique, explain, describe, analyse, interrupt, disrupt routinized practices, justify etcetera? From this way of reasoning theories are in the service of humans rather than vice versa. Theories and theoretical maps can subsequently **be for practice**, that is to say be about providing a springboard for thought to interpret and interrupt and hence modify practice, but they can also be about providing **knowledge about practice** that makes student teachers more aware of how their practice is linked to society at large and its past (Kvernbekk, 2005; Sjølie, 2014).

Critique amongst teachers, student teachers and teacher educators as regards the role and place of theory and knowledge required are vital to pay regard to since, if people do not have a why, a rationale and cannot see their function, it renders the task of teaching meaningless and independent of good arguments. At the same time it is important to keep in mind that neither teacher educators nor students are simply passive victims to policy reforms. Individuals in teacher education and education writ large are also partaking in active reform work in various ways that contribute to producing dilemmas through productive use of discursive spaces for agency and activism (see Chapter 3).

Teacher educators as active reformers

Today, a range of reforms in relation to education tend to picture teachers and teacher educators as victims, but teaches and teacher educators are themselves carriers of values and ideologies that influence their practice. From this sense it is possible to argue that they too are active in reforming education on different levels. Indeed, teachers and teacher educators are involved in competing discourses for reform between **entrepreneurial reform, managerial reform**, and **democratic reform**. Whereas, the entrepreneurial reform is involved in finding new ways and places to perform teacher education there are educators actively working to create standards that are deemed universally accountable. Besides entrepreneurship and management, there are those teacher educators who are engaged in reforming (teacher) education to pay regard to broad democracy and equity (Cochran-Smith, et al., 2018a, 2018b). These different forms of reform work are in themselves complex and capable of generating dilemmas. For instance, there are those arguing that although democracy and equity are in themselves desirable they hamper teacher effectiveness (Crowe 2010).

At several teacher meetings at two teacher education institutions in Sweden a technical view on teacher education is constantly brought forward as a major problem for teaching amongst one group while others argue for the opposite. On one occasion teacher educators argued that the problem with education is that it is focused on constructive alignment and the machinery of achieving and measuring aims without being aware of the fact that some aspects in education cannot be measured and hence squeezed into the logic of new public management. During this meeting one teacher educator had chosen to have a test that required the students to learn a specific content by heart, which resulted in a major quarrel where the majority of the teachers saw the teacher as a bad teacher who had sold his soul to the devil. According to one teacher the most important work of teaching is to strengthen students' self-confidence rather than pump them up with fragmented knowledge.

Depending on purposes, a technical or mechanical approach to knowledge can be highly important and necessary. For instance, it is quite difficult to learn to play viola, learn a language or math without some kind of mechanical practice where words, phrases and movements are trained repeatedly in various ways until they are perfected. Also, depending on purpose knowledge learned by heart can also be vital in order to achieve a good education. The tendency to polarize education is problematic in that it overlooks nuances. In Swedish media, the debate about teacher education tends to mainly focus on why teacher education only presents abstract and obsolete theories rather than useful practical knowledge. Teacher education is pictured as non-scientific, abstract, and itty-witty due to the strong focus on theory rather than practical knowledge, and tried and tested effective methods coming from, for instance, brain-research and developmental psychology (Edling & Liljestrand, 2019). Student teachers have expressed the problem as that 'today's teacher education focuses far too much on abstract pedagogical theories and far too little on cognitive science and methodology'.[1] 'Woolly theories will not help new teachers or their pupils. A teacher education that actually teaches what it means to be a teacher is needed ... The pedagogical education is an orgy in woolliness. What is often taught are theories that are almost a hundred years old and are social constructivist in nature'[2]. Student teachers often struggle because the

> academisation of teacher education has gone too far in the sense that it is only devoted to theoretical pedagogy and very little to that which is practical. This means that when teachers enter the profession after five years of training they still don't know for certain how to teach in the classroom. It's absurd.[3]

They understand the problem is that

> today's teacher education focuses far too much on abstract pedagogical theories and far too little on cognitive science and methodology. The recent study 'The approach to knowledge and leading pedagogical theories in Swedish teacher education', in which the course literature used in numerous teacher education courses has been analysed, shows that research on how learning takes place based on knowledge from modern brain research and the psychology of learning is practically non-existent.[4]

Whereas the examples above highlight tensions created between various perspectives as regards the notion of knowledge and theory at teacher education there is also a point in shedding light on conditions for promoting knowledge and broad democracy

Conditions for promoting knowledge and broad democracy

The changing pace of teacher's relationship with knowledge and democracy and new understandings of teachers as extended professions engaged in partnership activities has started to emerge as tensions and dilemmas in practice settings (Ball, 2015). **Epistemology** describes everything to do with knowledge and understandings of the subjective or objective or in-between subjective–objective positioning in the nature of knowledge. The issue of **epistemic justice** is concerned with justice between persons in relation to knowledge (Fricker, 2007). It became a live issue in a doctoral study by Galvin (2016) when he examined the perspectives of community workers and residents whose disadvantaged area with a high crime rate was brought into the 'invited space' of an *Urban Regeneration Partnership* in Limerick City – with an aim of urban renewal along the lines of market forces rather than an emancipatory lens (Galvin & Mooney Simmie, 2017).

Groupings at the negotiating table were: residents and community workers from the community (popular everyday language), officials from the city council (professional language) and some academics/researchers from the university (academic language). Clashes with what Freire (1971) called the **dominant syntax** – in this case the specialist languages of professionals/academics – meant that residents felt unable to compete on an equal basis at the negotiating table and ended up feeling robbed of many community resources (e.g. houses were knocked down and families split up and moved to other parts of the city) – and residents were left with a felt sense of ethical suppression – their voices did not matter. A local resident, let's call her Madeline, expressed this as follows:

> I mean you're reared as the little people, you're trod on, on all your life … you bring that in, and you cower at a table and you go … I'm afraid to speak in case I say the wrong thing … that's the way you feel.
>
> (Galvin, 2016)

Education has a pedagogical and political imperative (Giroux, 2004) to critically engage with communities to offer alternative forms of social organization to the prevailing orthodoxy of market-forces. Findings from the study show contradictions between partnership presented in policy terms as 'transformative' and lived reality experienced by the residents. Galvin (2016) cautions against supposedly democratic partnerships that colonize using forms of logical rationalism that fail to acknowledge or agonize about dilemmatic issues of contradiction, such as, differential power relations, multiple ways of knowing, different cultural and value systems, and different knowledge forms (Cornwall & Coelho, 2006). Useful analogies can be drawn between this study and epistemic injustices in framing teachers as clinical practitioners using a dominant syntax of 'science' and at the same time keeping teachers in their place using a restricted practice turn (Chapter 4 and Chapter 6).

Another way teachers and school leaders can get a felt sense of being kept in their place, and removed from emancipatory spaces to interrupt dominant discourses, is in relation to the new wave of juridification with new laws and legislation replacing former educative spaces for contestation of issues and critical questioning of authorities (see Chapter 4). Keane's (2019) master's study in Ireland reveals the oppressive force of juridification when she examines the perspectives of school leaders undergoing a national system of training by the Centre for School Leadership – a partnership between the Department of Education and Skills and two professional bodies of school principals/deputy principals, National Association for Principals and Deputy Principals (NAPD) and Irish Primary Principals' Network (IPPN) – to act as mentors for newly appointed school principals/administrators in line with a new public (political) focus of school leadership. While the majority of respondents in her study (n=20) expressed satisfaction with the training programme the study revealed, the emphasis was decidedly on mentoring as a vehicle of reproduction – with a fixation on strong managerial, instrumental and scientific emphases on best practices and productivity rather than productive spaces for critical co-inquiry and emancipation (Gunter, 2001; Mooney Simmie & Moles, 2019). A discourse of professional (political) knowledge that needed to be primarily complied with rather than critically questioned is captured by a master's in education student in the following comment:

Competition is the order of the day and success in the system is seen as that which can be measured. Documentation from the inspectorate centres around schools evaluating themselves using LAOS 2016 by gathering evidence to inform school improvement plans. In this culture the education system now places the blame for failure with the individual, be it student, teacher or school principal, thus abdicating the State of any blame. [Policy] compliance is the new 'modus operandi' for school leadership thus eroding the space for critical reflection and critical co-inquiry that is vital to ensuring that the emancipatory purpose of education is not ignored.

(Keane, 2019, p. 25)

So far we can see that the field of education and teacher education is far from a crystal clear field of thought, theory and instruction and is imbued with diverse battles for the soul of the curriculum coming from policy actors, various schools of thought and ideological governing forms and resistances. Good intentions while important are clearly not enough in a field vulnerable to all types of real and symbolic violence and when a wholesome balance point between competing paradoxes becomes distorted and dysfunctional. It is to these various schools of thought that we now turn.

Schools of thought

The **politics of knowledge** is intimately connected with knowledge, ways of knowing and knower values, taste and questions of attitudes and dispositions. This makes knowledge invariably connected with differential power relations and with assumed and dominant ways of knowing, a dominant syntax and language. Whose knowledge matters and whose ways of knowing are marginalized? For example, this can be seen in the way popular and everyday knowledge holds a separate value and currency to expert knowledge and professional ways of knowing. Teachers' knowledge base draws from multiple fields, such as disciplinary and theoretical knowledge bases, from professional knowledge bases (see Chapter 4) and from situated experiential knowledge bases in the field of practice. So the question pertinent to this chapter, and to the book, is what knowledge bases, spaces and ways of knowing are needed so that teachers can enact a democratic assignment as discursive spaces to educate for a democratic and vibrant polity (see Chapter 3) rather than regulate for a disciplinary regime.

Knowledge is therefore a deeply contested and burning issue connected to the purposes of education. The current politics of knowledge and democracy reveals a new emphasis on the entrepreneurial self and a new market-led discourse that has results in what Bernstein (2000) called the commodification of knowledge. In order to make knowledge a commodity it needed to be separated and divorced from the knower and from knower values and taste. In this section we explore a number of schools of thought and show how they understand the deeply contested nature of the positioning and politics of knowledge and democracy in teacher education. Below, some examples of perspectives on knowledge are presented in a very simplified manner with the purpose to provide an overview of similarities and differences in relation to aspects such as purpose, teacher responsibilities and student learning.

Pragmatists

The pragmatists, moral philosophers are concerned with practical wisdom and with the overarching moral goods of education understood as a predominantly regulatory humanistic discourse. In this way the philosophical purposes of pedagogy involve a relational dynamic for holistic development where instruction is included rather than the overarching and dominant purpose: "The pedagogical task, understood as a concern for the whole person of the student, is the central and proper task of all educative processes, instruction included" (Biesta & Miedema, 2002, p. 181). A humanistic discourse in teacher education espoused by moral philosophers and pragmatics (e.g. practical philosophers) advances the role of inquiry and is inclusive of multiple teacher identities, such as found in becoming a moral and caring person, an instructional manager, a generous expert and a civic being (Conway et al., 2009). However, this inter-subjective positioning of knowledge, skills, norms and values does not consider education, teacher education and schooling as immersed in the political and within a rather messy narrative of change that needs to take into account complexity, layers of contexts, inter-sectionality between social class, race, gender etc.

A pragmatic understanding of the human encounter between teacher and student for 'good teaching' is fully described by rationalistic thinking and taking into account the moral goods of teaching. However, this mode of philosophical reasoning for the moral development of the individual fails to fully describe teaching and works in subtle ways to erase consideration of differential power relations and the many ways that teachers' moral agency and teachers' voices may be undermined in a hierarchical (paternalistic) system of education, where policy actors higher up the chain – e.g. politicians, policymakers, media experts, academic researchers etc. – can readily and easily dismiss teachers' concerns, claims and rebuttals as self-interest, laziness, unwillingness to embrace change or simply outdated thinking (Mooney Simmie, Moles & O'Grady, 2019; Santoro, 2017; Zipin & Brennan, 2003). For pragmatists the moral goods of teaching as a human encounter for individual holistic development are the sine qua non for teachers' assignment, and the messiness of knowledge-power-privilege contradictions, contexts, particularities, contestations and tensions are avoided and/or brushed aside.

Sociologists of education

Some sociologists and historians of education show that the tyranny of a market-led discourse of education is currently leading to a slow suffocation of democracy (Browning, 2018) in the real-world practice of higher education institutions and schools. This is done using deliberative plans to mandate reforms using the law and multiple forms of juridification for policy compliance with listings of predetermined measurable outcomes and to starve funds for non-desired activities.

The sociologist of education Basil Bernstein (2000) asserted there is a serious fault line that has been generated, since the turn of the century, by the new principle of the (neoliberal) market and its managers. It results in the divorce of knowledge from the knower, facilitating for the first time in education a schism that allows for the commodification of knowledge from the knower (the person), resulting in the ready replacement of one knower with another (p. 86). Bernstein was concerned that depriving teachers and students of intellectual goods, such as access to theoretical knowledge (theory) sealed students' fate toward a (post-modern) slave culture. When teachers fail to engage theory they no longer have a why (a rationale) for practice and instead are driven by a 'what works' mantra.

Bernstein (2000) provided a rich array of concepts and ideas which reveal inextricable links between curriculum, pedagogy and assessment, how power relays operate in the education system and how the gatekeepers of education ensure that access to knowledge forms is distributed and often denied. In his concept of the 'pedagogic device' he depicts an internal message relay between the official field of the policymakers and the pedagogical field where policy actors, such as teachers and teacher educators, operate to recontexualize knowledge, skills, norms, taste, capabilities and values.

Bernstein understood that a healthy and vibrant education system needed the presence of discursive gaps between the official recontextualizing field (ORF) of the state, state agencies and policymakers and the pedagogical recontextualizing field (PRF) of teacher educators and teachers and those primarily charged with the responsibility for policy enactment (Ball, Maguire & Braun, 2012, see Chapter 3). He understand that when the PRF is able to exert change independent of the ORF then the education system is an open-ended and productive system with authentic teacher autonomy and space for emancipation and democracy as a living entity. These discursive gaps contain the necessary spaces for assuring the beautiful risk of education (Biesta, 2013) and exist within a paradoxical understanding that while the official field of policy production works to control the unthinkable, at the same time, these discursive spaces allow the unthinkable to burst through from time to time. However, when the state, state agencies and supranational agencies move to exert epistemic dominance (over knowledge) and ontological dominance (over ways of knowing and values and taste) then the concepts of education and democracy are under threat and yield to a neoconservative system of pre-described outcomes and discipline.

Bernstein (2000) was concerned that education policy at the turn of the century was operating within "a new principle guiding the latest transition of capitalism" (p. 86), the principles of the market and its managers. He observed that this fixation with the economic principle resulted in a "fundamental break in the relation between the knower and the known" (p. 86). Whereas in the past knowledge was viewed as an "outer expression of an inner relationship …. a guarantee of the legitimacy, integrity, worthwhileness and value of the knowledge and the special status of the knower" (p. 86). Bernstein asserted that using the principles of the market knowledge was dehumanized: "once knowledge is separated from inwardness, from commitments, from personal dedication, from the deep structure of the self, then people may be moved about, substituted for each other and excluded from the market" (p. 86). Bernstein understood this divorce of knowledge from the knower facilitated movement from the moral good of education toward a commodification of education, and in turn, generated a new crisis where what is "at stake is the very concept of education itself" (p. 86).

He was particularly concerned with the loss of theoretical knowledge from the field, within an understanding that concepts, ideas and theories are useful to gain deeper perspectives on everyday practice and help educators and teachers articulate a sound educational rationale for the selection and justification of their practices. He argued that without theoretical understandings people are left not knowing why they are acting in one way rather than another – left without a why they are (postmodern) slaves to a 'what works' culture and with no modus operandi for challenging the status quo and the dominant syntax (see Freire in Supplementary readings). Theory as an important part of teachers' intellectual assignment, and its traditional role in supporting rigorous critical thinking and in interrupting practices and routines, is an important and recognized aspect of teachers' knowledge assignment for assuring emancipation and a vibrant democracy (Duarte, 2016; Nussbaum, 2010).

Critical pedagogy

Theorists and educationalists in the educational field of Critical Theory are concerned to ask whose knowledge matters? And whose interests are served? In this way researchers from the field of critical pedagogy, raise important political questions about differential power relations and the nature and purpose of hierarchical systems as well as knowledge systems embedded in curricular reforms and schooling systems. Using rigorous critical thinking these studies aim to critique and reveal how global and national reform policy efforts in schooling have in-built mechanisms to continue the hegemony of the dominant and to assure the continued advantage of those who are already advantaged (Allais, 2012; Apple, 2012; Freire, 1971; Giroux, 1988; Kincheloe, 2004; Lynch et al., 2012; McLaren, 2015). Education is positioned as a meritocratic system, where everyone's needs are thought to be served and where everyone is supposedly given an equal chance (by quality teachers).

Critical theorists reveal deep flaws in this meritocratic way of thinking and show that the playing field of education is far from being a level playing field of context and culture and inter-sectionality (e.g. social class, gender, race, ethnicity etc.). Instead schools, without equality of condition, are strongly tilted in favour of those who are more advantaged, those who already have better access to the social and cultural capital needed to succeed in what is described as a knowledge economy (Apple, 2012). This neoliberal and neoconservative policy imaginary repositions teachers and students as 'actuarial' 'self-disciplined' selves constantly seeking to improve themselves within the cruel optimism of a professional (political) system designed to keep this destination as a persistent, unobtainable and unachievable elusive goal. Rather than leading out the potential of all young people, this system of schooling works in the direction of reproduction, as it seeks to first identify and stratify 'learners', 'students', 'teachers' and 'schools' who are falling behind in order to mark, penalize, label, punish, reject and redirect. Critical pedagogy stresses the importance of asking who benefits in education systems, whose interests are being served? (Figure 5.1).

Figure 5.1 Critical understandings of the necessity of a Public Forum in education to question authority.

Feminists

Feminists, from the first wave, second wave, third wave etc. of the feminist movement, assert the predominance of gender in education and teacher education. They make the case for putting gender at the top of inter-sectionality issues in order to examine how education systems and teachers' practices are governed along gendered lines and in this chapter, the gendered nature and appearance of teachers' assignment for education and democracy (Nussbaum, 2010; Santoro, 2017; Santoro & Rocha, 2015). Within feminist theory, (social) solidarity matters as does equity, care and context, particularity and pluralism. For feminists the political-economic context matters and teaching is viewed as a "practice-based political and moral orientation for individuals engaged and committed to a collective, but non-identical, practice" (Santoro & Rocha, 2015, p. 417).

Earlier, we explored how pragmatic philosophers, educational psychologists and other theorists and educationalists suggest that the moral goods of teaching are of vital importance in teacher education – for the development of the moral and caring teacher bound by ethical codes of professional conduct for the welfare of students. However, in the same education systems there is often widespread ethical suppression of teachers' moral agency reported by the media and by policy actors with higher power in this hierarchical system of schooling, such as, from policy makers, politicians, positivistic researchers, administrators and media commentators (Zipin & Brennan, 2003). O'Neill & Bourke (2010) speak to the inherent danger in pre-scripted codes of conduct and ethics that are used by external agents to discipline teachers and, in some instances, in relation to the legal mandates of fitness to practice to dismiss teachers as found in an intention in the revised Codes of Professional Conduct in Ireland (Teaching Council, 2016). Santoro (2017) and Santoro and Rocha's (2015) critical feminist writings assert this ethical suppression of teachers' moral agency acts as a new form of moral madness in a feminized career where globally there are approximately 80% of female teachers working in hierarchical paternalistic schooling systems.

Teachers who dare to transgress and who dare to speak out, who foresee the dangers inherent in the loss of the public sphere, the loss of education's social responsibility for public-interest values and social justice, and a vibrant and decent democracy in the current concept of education as it is being evaporated by the new principle of the market and new debased modes of self-evaluation, become like Cassandra in the Greek Tragedy of Troy, who can foresee the dangers but when they speak out no one is prepared to listen as they are caught in a system where people with more power – school administrators, inspectors, educational researchers, the media etc. – dismiss this speaking out as unreflective protestations, fear of change, laziness and/or even self-interest (e.g. Santoro, 2017).

In this regard, feminist writers in education make the case that teachers' assignment in education and democracy is highly infused with and complicated by gender relations, especially when the education system is historically understood as conservative/paternalistic and hides behind the myths of pedagogy as an objective science of how young people learn and the moral (apolitical) goods of quality teaching.

Realists and critical realists

While educationalists and theorists mentioned so far have an issue one way or the other with recognition of knowledge as mere knowledge separated from power and values, social class privilege, gender privilege and/or an inter-subjective knower-knowledge balance point – social realists and critical realists take a different perspective on knowledge. Instead, they speak of the existence of a reliable canon of knowledge that is passed down through centuries as a bank of knowledge that is objective, neutral and independent of everyday life and contemporary social and political practices.

In this regard realists eschew the pedagogical notion of constructivism and the suggestion that all that is required of teachers is to set the scene for students to make actual 'discoveries' in the classroom. Guile, Lambert & Reiss (2018) writing about the work of Michael Young, and his book *Bringing Knowledge Back-In* (Young, 2007) argue that school knowledge needs to provide access for the vast majority of students to powerful knowledge, which though understood as reliable knowledge is also viewed as contested and part of a system of thought which can itself change. In this way social realists argue students need full access to disciplinary and theoretical knowledge forms and thus teachers' assignment is different from the (mundane) popular knowledge used in everyday life (Deng, 2018). Realists argue that this is the *raison d'être* of schools and imbues them with a distinctive knowledge assignment that is different from the popular/social knowledge forms shared in the family and everyday life. This knowledge assignment of schools and teachers can thus be framed as the transmission of disciplinary knowledge and the abstractions associated with theoretical knowledge.

This view of knowledge makes sense, especially in the part of the curriculum concerned with Science Technology Engineering and Mathematics (STEM) subjects as these disciplines traditionally work as a hierarchy of knowledge rather than a hierarchy of knowers. This knowledge base is always understood as partial and evolving and only when new knowledge is found is old knowledge discarded and superseded. By contrast, knowledge in education as a field of social study has traditionally been understood as a hierarchy of knowers, with names such as the French intellectuals Bourdieu and Foucault and prominent others playing a leading role in analysis and interpretation.

We assert that whichever positioning you take in relation to knowledge and democracy and teachers' assignment, it becomes hard to deny that there is in existence a canon of knowledge available to us through the centuries. We view this knowledge, not as a rigid static body of facts and values, but rather as reliable powerful knowledge that is being continually shaped, reshaped, adapted, changed and (re)imagined while, at the same time, understanding that powerful knowledge is somehow, if not always directly, connected to complex pathways of power, culture, intersectionality and contexts. Freire (see Supplementary readings) refers to this as the dominant syntax and argues the need for all learners to become familiar with this dominant syntax in order to resist oppression in all its forms.

Thus far we have been considering teachers' assignment as a contested construct in the politics of knowledge and knower dispositions, values and taste; we will now examine the way teachers' assignment is increasingly understood within a new global policy impetus for homogeneity and how this Global-local (**G-local**) landscape is influencing change in Ireland and Sweden (see Chapter 3).

Global Education Reform Movement (GERM)

Within GERM, education and teaching are changed to the new concept of 'learning' and the schooling system is reframed as nested 'learning systems' – redesigned as a system that values social harmony and cooperation between teachers and other policy actors – for an extended view of teacher professionalism see Chapter 4. However, this communal-orientation is understood to be for instrumental purposes of measurable outcomes. GERM presents good teaching as a 'perfect technology' that is ordered, predicable, categorized and controlled using well-defined codes, components, dispositions for knowledge application using diagnostics for risk-managed processes.

Educational psychologists and positivistic studies have become hailed in GERM for school improvement and teacher effectiveness and considered as the science of how young people learn – with no questioning of what is learning? why learning? why now? who is learning? for what purpose? and from whom? (Biesta, 2012, p. 36). The findings from these positivistic studies about quality instruction have become expediently and quickly used by policymakers, governments and politicians as the new way in human capital terms to 'squeeze' the asset, i.e. to extract from teachers' labour the desirable measurable products needed for the school as a high-performance learning system and for what is perceived as the requirements for national economic competitiveness.

World renowned educational research schools, such as Black and Wiliam's research school on classroom-based Assessment-for-Learning (AfL) in King's College London, appropriately called *Inside the Black Box*, assert that good teaching can be reduced to meeting students' needs and planning personalized courses of study that are individualized (Black & Wiliam, 1998). In their research work on formative assessment, Wiliam presents teachers' practices (Wiliam, 2014) as analogous to a modern-day pilot successfully landing an airline with great precision and with accuracy in a definite runway at a specified location in a busy international airport (Wiliam, see Supplementary readings).

In GERM, knowledge that has been divorced from the knower and teachers' autonomous localized judgement in the classroom setting is elided in favour of a fixation on data and hard evidence and outside experts. Moreover, there is a commodification of knowledge using the principle of the market. This supports skills-based knowledge and modes of social engineering of attitudes and dispositions understood as those required by employers in the workforce. GERM, as a linear rational system leads to the domestication of teachers' assignment as a disciplinary order, rather than to allow spaces for emancipation and democracy (Säfström, 2011).

Whatever GERM has included in the policy field, in its fixation on quality instruction, quality teaching and predetermined outcomes and metrics (Marcel, 2013; Muller, 2018), it is what GERM has excluded that is of particular significance when it comes to teachers' assignment in relation to education and democracy. Teachers need not only to interrogate their selves and their practice but to connect their practices with the wider world, to use affordances for discursive spaces for contestation of issues, for the PRF to make changes independent of the ORF, and for the beautiful risk of new possibilities breaking through and securing education's social responsibility for public-interest values, the notion of the public sphere and the public good of society.

In the next section, we interrogate how teachers' assignment has come under the influence of GERM in the dilemmas/tensions encountered by teachers and school leaders in Ireland and Sweden between the rhetoric of a diminished national policy landscape and the lived reality of G-local practices.

Critique of narrow approaches to democracy and higher education

In teacher education programmes, teachers are at times trained to think of themselves as involved in processes of knowledge application, taking knowledge made elsewhere and using diagnostic tools to arrive at well-defined pathways and solutions – researchers-in-practice (Cochran-Smith & Lytle, 1999). These processes confine teachers to interrogating themselves and their practices and offer no affordances for critically reading the world, questioning authority and working as public intellectuals within a dynamic polity moving in the direction of renewal, interruption and change (Giroux, 1988). GERM policy imperatives are delineated as places with no requirement for teachers to mediate practices with the wider world, moral, social and political issues of the day (Sexton, 2007).

Santoro and Rocha (2015) speak to the moral goods of education as they argue that schooling is organized using hierarchical chains of command: a paternalistic system where 'father' knows best and where teachers are increasingly denied moral agency in a system seeking to develop a moral (apolitical) individual rather than "trying to find a way to bridge moral, but apolitical, individualism with a practice-based political and moral orientation for individuals engaged and committed to a collective, but non-identical, practice" (p. 417).

Biesta and Miedema (2002) question the nature and purpose of pedagogy and what it means at a time of increasing interest in 'learning' and learning outcomes. They distinguish between broad understandings of education and pedagogy for holistic development of the young person as a primarily relational encounter and a reductionist view of schooling, training and instruction for predetermined products and outcomes. They show how a reductionist view (see Chapter 2), found in essentialist understandings of knowledge, results in the atomization of knowledge, skills, norms and values resulting in a false distinction between pedagogy and instruction. They argue that this split arises from a (Cartesian) dualistic schism between knowledge and skills, situated in the objective domain (with understandings of knowledge and skills as neutral and objective) from norms and values situated in the social domain. Biesta and Miedema (2002) advance a transformative conception of education which does not separate pedagogy from instruction using this dualistic way of thinking. In this way they argue for the inter-subjective nature of knowledge, skills, norms, taste and values.

Moreover, in Ireland there was a historically strong discourse of teachers as purveyors of knowledge, successfully helping students through state examinations and entry to college. Statistics showed a high percentage of students achieve places in higher education. The system showed itself to be traditional, conservative and authoritarian and unable to break the cycle of disadvantage (Lynch et al., 2012). The narrative of success is not repeated for every sector of society and those who are culturally, economically and socially disadvantaged get left behind. At the start of the century some schools were designated 'disadvantaged' and singled out for additional resources. However, the marking and labelling of these schools was to reframe poverty as a problem of the individual school/student rather than a shared societal and public values issue to be (politically) solved.

Quality teachers were becoming defined and regarded as learners committed to an 'actuarial' neoliberal self. This new soft skill of self-evaluation introduced by the OECD uses a performative discourse as it obliges teachers to showcase themselves as neoliberal subjects engaged in continuing cycles of learning and up-skilling based on competitive comparison (Brady, 2016, 2019). The quality teacher and autonomous school are becoming understood as the new third way of securing equity. There is no longer any moral obligation on the state, state agencies or civil society for further input of resources and/or for affordances for the necessary discursive spaces in schools for a dialectical development of a democratic and pluralistic society. In this regard, democracy is perceived as part of the existing police order, a duty of care and obligations for a compliant 'civic being' upholding a neoconservative politics of inevitability (Snyder, 2018).

Educationalists such as Michael Young plead for bringing knowledge back into the curriculum as they argue against the dubbing-down of disciplinary and theoretical knowledge in favour of competences and a new techné of skills (Young, 2007, see Supplementary readings). Freire (1971) posits that people need knowledge and fluency in the dominant syntax in order to argue for freedom from all forms of oppression. Apple (2012) and Gunter (2001) question the direction of current international policy reforms, the uneven playing field of schooling and the (re)distribution of knowledge-power in the direction of the advantaged (see Supplementary readings).

Concluding comments

The influence of GERM in the policy reform landscape of teachers' assignment reduced, if not completely eliminated, for example, any need for complex interplays with theoretical knowledge rigorous critical thinking, interrupting unreflective practices and for mediation with the wider world. This indicates a strong principle of the economy in operation and an equally strong (paternalistic) principle of communal-orientation among teachers in schools. This teacher communal-orientation is not primarily dedicated to holistic education and the development of a decent and vibrant democratic society but instead is expressed for instrumental purposes for predetermined learning outcomes and for a disciplinary regimen. Fielding (2007) argues that when schools adopt the typology of high-performance learning organizations there is an incalculable human cost and intellectual poverty.

Notwithstanding who is right or who is wrong in this debate in relation to teachers' assignment for education and democracy, we can conclude that teachers have a knowledge assignment that is distinctive from everyday (popular) knowledge, is somehow connected to forms of powerful knowledge (e.g. theoretical and disciplinary knowledge) and is inextricably linked with knower dispositions, values and taste assumed in the dominant syntax.

When teachers' assignment is bent toward the direction of securing a vibrant democratic society it requires access to multiple intellectual resources (e.g. theoretical knowledge) and capabilities for contestation and experiencing dilemmas for a felt sense of localized autonomous agency, for rigorous critical thinking, for drawing on theory to interrupt routinized practices and to mediate findings in classrooms and schools with wider social, moral and political issues of the day.

When this critical reading of the wider world is not proactively included, or deliberatively absented from policy documents and practices, then the seeds of authoritarianism and ecofascism are sown as teachers' moral agency and political activism for a democratic assignment is suppressed and democracy is slowly suffocated in schools and by implication in society.

Questions

1. What kind of spontaneous idea(s) did this chapter evoke in you? Can you put it into words using literature and concepts from this chapter as a point of departure?
2. Why might we need to turn to tensions between knowledge and knower dispositions and values to better grasp dilemmas in the present and to open new spaces for the future?
3. What do you think about GERM as a live reduction mechanism of complexity and plurality in relation to (teacher) education and democracy?
4. Can you see patterns of oppression for people who are partaking in systems that focus more on everyday (situated) knowledge and communication than on powerful knowledge?

5   What kind of philosophical struggles or ideas can you see in current practices and contexts you have taken part in that inspire you to critically question education and democracy?
6   In relation to what you have read in this chapter regarding the dangers of divorcing knowledge from knower dispositions and values how would you handle it as a teacher?
7   What kind of dilemmas in relation to the topic discussed would you like to add, and why?

Supplementary readings

1   Professor Michael W. Apple Dean's Lecture at the Melbourne Graduate School of Education, 12/10/2012
    Michael Apple: Why we should be worried about current educational reforms, 30/01/2013
    www.youtube.com/watch?v=dLcwXDT2Vew
2   Paulo Freire's last public lecture
    Paulo Freire – An Incredible Conversation, 30/12/2009
    www.youtube.com/watch?v=aFWjnkFypFA
3   Professor Michael Young's Lecture on Bringing Knowledge Back In, 15/05/2013, Institute of Education, London
    Powerful Knowledge (Michael Young), 20/11/2013
    www.youtube.com/watch?v=r_S5Denaj-k
4   Professor Helen Gunter's Lecture at BELMAS conference 21 November 2012 Leadership and Policy in Education 'Looking back to look forward'
    Helen Gunter, 18/01/2013
    www.youtube.com/watch?v=_GufhDEeN_w

Notes

1 "Pedagogerna bör stängas ute från lärarutbildningen." *Svenska Dagbladet* 26 September 2017. Author: secondary school teacher Isak Skogstad (in Edling and Liljestrand, 2019).
2 "Usel utbildning ger usla lärare". *Expressen*, 24 July, 2017. Author: freelance reporter Naomi Abramowicz, (in Edling and Liljestrand, 2019).
3 "Björklunds betyg på 'sin' lärarutbildning: Undermålig". *Svenska Dagbladet* 25 September, 2017. Author: reporter Karin Thurfjell, (in Edling and Liljestrand, 2019).
4 "Pedagogerna bör stängas ute från lärarutbildningen." *Svenska Dagbladet* 26 September 2017. Author: secondary school teacher Isak Skogstad, (in Edling and Liljestrand, 2019).

References

Allais, S. (2012). 'Economics imperialism', education policy and educational theory. *Journal of Education Policy*, 27(2), 253–274.
Allan, Julie (2014). Making a difference in theory in Sweden and the UK. *Education Inquiry*, 5(3), 319–335.
Allen, J. M. (2009). Valuing practice over theory: How beginning teachers re-orient their practice in the transition from the university to the workplace. *Teaching and Teacher Education*, 25(5), 647–654.
André, Joel & Salmijärvi, Susanna, (2015). Lärandeteorier som akademisk fernissa. *Pedagogiska Magasinet*. Retrieved from https://pedagogiskamagasinet.se/tag/larandeteori/
Apple, M. W. (2012). *Education and power*. New York: Routledge.

Apple, M. W. (1987). The de-skilling of teachers. In F. Bolin & J. M. Falk (eds.), *Teacher renewal: Professional issues, personal choices.* New York: Teachers College Press, pp. 59–75.

Ball, S. J. (2015). Education, governance and the tyranny of numbers. *Journal of Education Policy,* 30(3), 299–301.

Ball, S. J. (2003). The teacher's soul and the terrors of performativity. *Journal of Education Policy,* 18(2), 215–228.

Ball, S. J., Maguire, M. & Braun, A. (2012). *How schools do policy: Policy enactments in secondary schools.* London: Routledge.

Beach, Dennis (2011). Education science in Sweden: Promoting research for teacher education or weakening its scientific foundations? *Education Inquiry,* 2(2), 207–220.

Beach, Dennis & Bagley, Carl (2012). The weakening role of education studies and the re-traditionalisation of Swedish teacher education. *Oxford Educational Review,* 38(3), 287–303.

Bernstein, B. (2000). *Pedagogy, symbolic control and identity: Theory, research, critique.* Oxford: Rowman & Littlefield.

Biesta, G. J. J. (2012). Giving teaching back to education: Responding to the disappearance of the teacher. *Phenomenology & Practice,* 6(2), 35–49.

Biesta, G. J. J. (2013). *The beautiful risk of education.* London: Routledge.

Biesta, G. J. J. & Miedema, S. (2002). Instruction or pedagogy? The need for a transformative conception of education. *Teaching and Teacher Education,* 18, 173–181.

Biesta, Gert & Säfström, Carl-Anders (2011). A manifesto for education. *Policy Futures in Education,* 9(5), 540–547.

Black, P. & Wiliam, D. (1998). Assessment and classroom learning. *Assessment in Education: Principles, Policy & Practice,* 5(1), 7–74.

Brady, A. M. (2019). Anxiety of performativity and anxiety of performance: Self-evaluation as bad faith. *Oxford Review of Education* (Online). doi:10.1080/03054985.2018.1556626

Brady, A. M. (2016). The regime of self-evaluation: Self-conception for teachers and schools. *British Journal of Educational Studies,* 64(4), 523–541.

Britzman, Deborah P. (2003). *Practice makes practice: A critical study of learning to teach.* Albany, NY: State University of New York Press.

Browning, C. R. (2018). The suffocation of democracy. *New York Review of Books,* 25 October issue, 65(16), 14–17.

Cochran-Smith, Marilyn (2011). Teaching in new times: What do teachers really need to know? *Kappa Delta Pi Record,* 47(1), 11–12.

Cochran-Smith, Marilyn, Cummings Carney, M., Stringer Keefe, E., Burton, S., Chang, W. C., Fernandez, M. B., Miller, A. F., Sanchez, J. G. & Baker, M. (2018b). *Reclaiming accountability in teacher education.* New York: Teachers College Press.

Cochran-Smith, Marilyn & Fries, Mary Kim (2001). Sticks, stones, and ideology: The discourse of reform in teacher education. *Educational Researcher,* 30(8), 3–15.

Cochran-Smith, Marilyn & Lytle, S. L. (1999). Relationships of knowledge and practice: Teacher learning communities. *Review of Research in Education,* 24, 249–305.

Cochran-Smith, Marilyn, Stringer Keefe, Elizabeth & Cummings Carney, Molly (2018a). Teacher educators as reformers. Competing agendas. *European Journal of Teacher Education,* 41(5), 572–590.

Conway, P. F., Murphy, R., Rath, A. & Hall, K. (2009). *Learning to teach and its implications for the continuum of the teacher education: A nine-country cross-national study.* Report commissioned by teaching council. Maynooth, Republic of Ireland: The Teaching Council, Ireland, University College Cork.

Cornwall, A. & Coelho, V. S. P. (2006). Spaces for change: The politics of citizen participation in new democratic arenas. In A. Cornwall & V. S. P. Coelho (eds.), *Spaces for change: The politics of citizen participation in new democratic arenas.* London: Zed, pp. 1–33.

Crowe, E. (2010). *Measuring what matters: A stronger accountability model for teacher education.* Washington, DC: Center for American Progress.

Deng, Z. (2018). Bringing knowledge back in: Perspectives from liberal education. *Cambridge Journal of Education,* 48(3), 335–351.

Duarte, M. (2016). Educating citizens for humanism: Nussbaum and the education crisis. *Studies in Philosophy of Education*, 35, 463–476.

Edling, Silvia (2014). Between stereotypes and task complexity. Exploring stereotypes of teachers and education in media as a question of structural violence. *Journal of Curriculum Studies*, 47(3), 399–415.

Edling, Silvia (2015). Två förhållningssätt till teorier på (lärar)utbildningar i relation till lärares förutsättningar att motverka våld [Two strategies to theories at (teacher) education in relation to teachers' assignment to oppose violence]. In C. Ljunggren, I. Unemar & T. Englund (eds.), *Kontroversiella frågor i samhällsundervisningen*. Malmö, Sweden: Glerups.

Edling, S. & Liljestrand, J. (2019). Let's talk about teacher education! Analysing the media debates in 2016–2017 on teacher education using Sweden as a case. *Asia-Pacific Journal of Teacher Education* (Online). Retrieved from www.tandfonline.com/doi/full/10.1080/1359866X.2019.1631255. doi:10.1080/1359866X.2019.1631255

Edling, S. & Mooney Simmie, G. (2017). Democracy and emancipation in teacher education: A summative content analysis of teacher educators' democratic assignment expressed in policies for Teacher Education in Sweden and Ireland between 2000–2010. *Citizenship Social & Economics Education*, 17(1), 1–15.

Fielding, M. (2007). The human cost and intellectual poverty of high performance schooling: Radical philosophy, John Macmurray and the remaking of person-centred education. *Journal of Education Policy*, 22(4), 383–409.

Freire, P. (1971). *Pedagogy of the oppressed*. London: Penguin Books.

Fricker, M. (2007). *Epistemic injustice: Power and the ethics of knowing*. Oxford: Oxford University Press.

Galvin, M. (2016). Whose knowledge matters: An exploration of citizen participation, meaning construction and expansive learning in an urban regeneration process. PhD dissertation. Limerick, Republic of Ireland: University of Limerick.

Galvin, M. & Mooney Simmie, G. (2017). Theorising participation in urban regeneration partnerships: An adult education perspective. *Journal of Education Policy*, 32(6), 809–831.

Giroux, H. A. (2004). Cultural studies and the politics of public pedagogy: Making the political more pedagogical. *Parallax*, 10, 73–89.

Giroux, H. A. (1988). *Teachers as intellectuals: Toward a critical pedagogy of learning*. Westport, CT: Bergin & Garvey.

Guile, D., Lambert, D. & Reiss, M. J. (2018). *Sociology, curriculum studies and professional knowledge new perspectives on the work of Michael Young*. Abingdon, UK: Routledge.

Gunter, H. (2001). Critical approaches to leadership in education. *Journal of Educational Enquiry*, 2(2), 94–108.

Higgs, J., Titchen, A. & Neville, V. (2001) Professional practice and knowledge. In J. Higgs & A. Titchen (eds.), *Practice knowledge and expertise in the health professions*. Oxford: Butterworth-Heinemann, pp. 3–9.

Keane, M. G. (2019). Exploring the contextual understandings of post-primary school principals in a formal mentoring programme of new appointed school principals. M.Ed. dissertation. Limerick, Republic of Ireland: University of Limerick.

Kincheloe, J. (2004). The knowledges of teacher education developing a critical complex epistemology. *Teacher Education Quarterly*, Winter, 49–66.

Kvernbekk, T. (2005) *Pedagogisk teoridannelse: insidere, teoriformer og praksis*. [Construction of pedagogical theories: Insiders, theory forms and practice]. Bergen, Norway: Fagbokforlaget.

Labaree, David (2004). *The trouble with ed schools*. New Haven, CT: Yale University Press.

Lynch, K., Grummell, B. & Devine, D. (2012). *New managerialism in education commercialization, carelessness and gender*. New York: Palgrave MacMillan.

McLaren, P. (2015). *Pedagogy of insurrection from resurrection to revolution*. New York: Peter Lang.

Marcel, J.-F. (2013). Critical approach to the contribution made by education research to the social construction of the value of teaching work. *Policy Futures in Education*, 1(3), 225–240.

Mooney Simmie, G. (2014). The neo-liberal turn in understanding teachers' and school leaders' work practices in curriculum innovation and change: A critical discourse analysis of a newly proposed reform policy in lower secondary education in the Republic of Ireland. *Citizenship Social & Economics Education*, 13(3), 185–198.

Mooney Simmie, G. (2012). The pied piper of neo liberalism calls the tune in the republic of Ireland: An analysis of education policy text from 2000–2012. *The Journal for Critical Education Policy Studies*, 10(2), 485–514.

Mooney Simmie, G. & Edling, S. (2016). Ideological governing forms in education and teacher education: A comparative study between highly secular Sweden and highly non-secular Republic of Ireland. *Nordic Journal of Studies in Educational Policy*, 2016(1), 1–12.

Mooney Simmie, G. & Edling, S. (2018). Teachers' democratic assignment: A critical discourse analysis of teacher education policies in Ireland and Sweden. *Discourse Studies in the Cultural Politics of Education*, 40(6), 832–846.

Mooney Simmie, G. & Moles, J. (2019). Teachers' changing subjectivities: Putting the soul to work for the principle of the market or for facilitating risk? *Studies in Philosophy and Education* (Online), 1–16. doi:10.1007/s11217-019-09686-9

Mooney Simmie, G., Moles, J. & O'Grady, E. (2019). Good teaching as a messy narrative of change within a policy ensemble of networks, superstructures and flows. *Critical Studies in Education*, 60(1), 55–72.

Muller, J. K. (2018). *The tyranny of metrics*. Princeton, NJ: Princeton University Press.

Nussbaum, M. C. (2010). *Not for profit: Why democracy needs the humanities*. Princeton, NJ: Princeton University Press.

O'Neill, J. & Bourke, R. (2010). Educating teachers about a code of ethical conduct. *Ethics and Education*, 5(2), 159–172.

Paraskeva, João M. (2011). *Conflicts in curriculum theory: Challenging hegemonic epistemologies*. New York: Palgrave Macmillan.

Player-Koro, Catarina (2012). Reproducing traditional discourses of teaching and learning mathematics: Studies of mathematics and ICT in teaching and teacher education. PhD dissertation. Gothenburg, Sweden: Department of Applied Information Technology.

Säfström, C. A. (2011). Rethinking emancipation, rethinking education. *Studies in Philosophy and Education*, 30, 199–209.

Santoro, D. A. (2017). Cassandra in the classroom: Teaching and moral madness. *Studies in Philosophy of Education*, 36, 49–60.

Santoro, D. A. & Rocha, S. D. (2015). Review of Gert J. J. Biesta, The Beautiful Risk of Education. *Studies in Philosophy of Education*, 34, 413–418.

Schön, D. (1983). *The reflective practitioner: How professionals think in action*. New York: Basic Books.

Sexton, M. (2007). Evaluating teaching as a profession – implications of a research study for the work of the teaching council. *Irish Educational Studies*, 26(1), 79–105.

Sjølie, Elsa (2014). The role of theory in teacher education: reconsidered from a student teacher perspective. *Journal of Curriculum Studies*, 46(6), 729–750.

Skerritt, C. (2018). Discourse and teacher-identity in business-like education. *Policy Futures in Education*, 17(2), 1–19.

Snyder, T. (2018). *The road to unfreedom*. London: Penguin Random House.

The Teaching Council (2016). *Code of professional conduct for teachers* (Updated 2nd edn.). Maynooth, Republic of Ireland: The Teaching Council.

Todd, Sharon (2009). *Toward an imperfect education: Facing humanity, rethinking cosmopolitanism*. Boulder, CO: Paradigm.

Wiliam, D. (2014). Dylan Williams: Formative assessment. YouTube video clip. Retrieved from www.youtube.com/watch?v=sYdVe5O7KBE

Young, M. (2007). *Bringing knowledge back in: From social constructivism to social realism in the sociology of education*. Abingdon, UK: Routledge.

Zeichner, K. (2010) Rethinking the connections between campus courses and field experiences in college- and university-based teacher education. *Journal of Teacher Education*, 61(1–2), 89–99.

Zipin, L. & Brennan, M. (2003). The suppression of ethical dispositions through managerial governmentality: A habitus crisis in Australian higher education. *International Journal of Leadership in Education*, 6(4), 351–370.

6 Darwinian strength[1]

Introduction

Fundamental in understandings of modern democracy is its ethical core stressing the need to protect everyone's equal and intrinsic value and shield the existence of plurality (see Chapters 2, 3 and 4). Besides seeing everyone's equal value as intrinsic it is also approached in an instrumental fashion where research shows that safe environments, environments where individuals are not afraid of being hurt, strengthens possibilities for learning (e.g. Nakou, 2000; Ungdomsstyrelsen/Swedish Agency for Youth and Society, 2013, p. 2; Kochenderfer & Ladd, 1996; Slee, 1994; Frelin, 2015).

There is however less research highlighting how difficult it can be to encounter people who (temporarily) radiate weakness, in the sense that they feel subordinated, sad, exposed and/or vulnerable. Indeed, it is easy to forget that the right not to be exposed to discrimination and violation endorsed by the United Nations, the European Union and translated into Educational Acts in many European countries risks evoking anger and at times disgust (Edling, 2009, 2012/2018). There are unavoidable gaps between espoused policies and the lived reality of practice and it is in these gaps and discursive spaces that actual relationships between people take place (Bernstein, 2000).

Accordingly, parallel to the increase of acts promoting democracy and contesting various forms of bullying and violence there are also reactions against these acts, vented in the media and in people's everyday discussions. It can be in the form of comments like "It always has to be someone who is violated", "Do I dare to say this or do you think someone is going to be offended?", "All this political correctness, I am so tired of it, people can no longer speak their mind", and "Do we have to care about violated people, I mean really get a grip man". What seems to be forgotten is that work against, for instance, oppression, bullying and inequality involves dealing with people who can be perceived as weak and also those who are provoked by being forced to restrain themselves for the sake of others (see Edling, 2016).

Education and teacher education are not liberated from these tensions, seeing that they are a part of society, and these tensions generate dilemmas that are important to highlight (see Table 6.1).

This chapter is divided into three parts. To begin with the first part revisits arguments from Chapter 2 highlighting the ways a strict focus on narrow perceptions involving either/or thinking risks enhancing violence. In this case a dualistic and essentialist notion of weakness and strength are in focus along with their consequences for action. In the second part, ways in which weakness and strength are linked to femininity and masculinity are brought to attention and problematized. Contrary to simplified either/or images,

Table 6.1 An overview of dilemmas that will be discussed in Chapter 6

Dilemmas
Strength versus Weakness
Femininity versus Masculinity
Body versus Mind
Conscious versus Unconscious
Intimacy versus Distance
Purity versus Complexity
Conserve versus Change
Monism versus Pluralism

the third part aims to provide alternative routes to approach weakness and strength by turning to philosophy, psychoanalysis, cognitive (psychology) research, intersections and history research.

Weakness and strength in dualistic terms: central in societies supporting violence

Weakness within philosophy and empirical research has generally been described either as *mental incapability* when it comes to taming strong emotions and as such act in a socially desired way (Evans, 1975; Hoffman, 2008; Levy, 2011; Mele, 2012) or like *physical weakness* it is thought to occur due to a lack of training or some form of illness (Sanderson, 2012). **Mental weakness** is often described as a weakness of will and is also frequently associated with relational aspects, such as being dependent upon others and experiencing feelings and desires such as longing, powerlessness, empathy and soft sentiments like love and care (Freire, 1971). Contrary to this, strength is pictured as something desirable and linked to traits like reason, power, autonomy, control, impartiality and dominance (e.g. Stenqvist, 2005; Young, 1990a).

This way of separating human traits and the world into two parts, when one grouping is dominant and the other grouping is subservient, originates from a **dualistic world-view** and is one of the main reasons why bullying, violence and suppression come into expression. Accordingly, one of the main reasons for why the World Wars and post-wars could happen was not primarily due to efficient weapons but because of people's **perceptions** guiding the weapons, that is to say ways of seeing the world which influence how we act and reason (e.g. the United Nations Educational, Scientific and Cultural Organization, UNESCO).

An example of dualism can be found in the Austrian-German politician and leader of *Nationalsozialistische Deutsche Arbeiterpartei* (NSDAP): Adolf Hitler's autobiographical manifesto *Mein Kampf* (first published in 1925 and 1926). Over the years, several researchers have analysed its content and one early analysis is made by Norwegian moral philosopher Harald Ofstad in 1969 (see Ofstad, 2012), published in his book *Our Contempt for Weakness: Nazi Norms and Values – and Our Own*. Central in his reasoning is that Nazism as an ideology is created by people's values, norms, and hence perceptions of the world. This implies that in order to prevent the ill deeds from the past from happening again in the present it's important to become aware of values, norms and ways of seeing the world that support the ethical dimension of democracy, which implies opposing suppression and violence towards those who are deemed in any way different, and the implication that they are hence of lesser worth (weak).

In his analysis, Ofstad found that Hitler mainly argued in a black and white manner that lacked nuances and complexities in ways that made it possible to turn people against each other without bad conscience. Hitler is far from unique. This rhetoric is quite common in war tactics and is a means for taking control and is thus actively applied by current authoritarian leaders (see Rydgren, 2018, p. 2). On one side, he positioned democrats, communists and pacifists, which he described as evil devils, while on the other side the German people as a race were portrayed as practically divine and representatives of goodness. Hitler was possessed with the concept of 'racial purity'. Since devils *per se* are evil and dangerous they need to be made extinct, which implies that any kind of violence against those who represent these malicious traits are something necessary and good (the opposite of evil). He even maintained that the German people, who are good and great, have a divine duty to make these groups of people extinct to save the world from evil.

Following Ofstad, dualistic reasoning was also used by Hitler to project German peoples' shadow side and violence onto those who were perceived as the enemies. His thinking suggested that if the German people hurt others, they did it out of goodness while Democrats and other enemy groups did it due to their inherent violent and bullying nature. However, in the shadow of this radiant self-image constructed out of certain norms and values, several million people were killed and tortured, which indicates that people's seeing is interwoven with their acting and that this interconnection needs to be acknowledged if everyone's equal value is to be acknowledged and suppression and violence is to be opposed (Ofstad, 2012, p. 96).

Central in Hitler's writing were also questions about **biological determinism**, i.e. those who are strong should dominate and conquer those who are weak and in contrary terms those who are weak should be dominated and in the long run be rendered extinct: "[t]he entire nature is a powerful struggle between strength and weakness – the strong for ever conquering the weak" (Bullock, p. 347, cited in Ofstad, 2012, p. 50, translation from Swedish). This chain of logic bears resemblance to Darwin's famous expression 'natural selection' and which Spencer interpreted as 'the survival of the fittest' (e.g. Offer, 2014).

A tendency to provide people with a fixed essence is part of the dualist logic of **essentialism**. From this way of reasoning some people are by their nature weak while other people are strong, some are devils while others are angels, some should be despised and hated while others should be loved and so forth. Everything in the Nazi ideology was constructed in a black and white logic that provided a sense of safety and protection against various forms of dilemmas. Those propagating Nazism were strongly against the *idée* that the world is full of shades and nuances, that multi-layered interpretations are possible, that various values exist and might collide, and that different rationalities and ways of thinking take form due to the fact that people are different from each other: "[a]ll these signs of decadence are finally just due to a lack of one firm and generally accepted world-view" (*Mein Kampf*, 1932/2006, p. 292, cited in Ofstad, 2012, p. 142, translation from Swedish). This idea can be found in current radical right movements too, which are defined as political extremists because they are anti-pluralists and prefer **monism**: the belief in singular explanation models or that everything can be defined through one lens/principle. "Despite the radical right's acceptance of procedural democracy, its ideal society is ethnocracy, which in many ways runs counter to the pluralistic values of liberal democracy" (Rydgren, 2018, p. 2).

Why should educators care about Hitler and Nazism?

At this stage you might wonder aloud as to why we are writing about Nazism and Hitler – why do we think this discussion is necessary for all educators and teachers and what has it to do with education as a social responsibility when democracy is discussed? We are not claiming that all teachers who struggle with a contempt for weakness are to be denigrated – however we are arguing for capability for a reflexive consciousness and 'wide-awakeness' in all teachers and teacher educators so that we understand that education is imbued with potential for symbolic violence and as such good intentions however worthy are never enough (Freire, 1971; Greene, 2008; Pillow, 2003; see also Chapter 7).

In this regard we are required as educators to come face to face with our own '**unfinishedness**', the fact that each and every individual is far from perfect and as such has the possibility to take responsibility for her or his shortcomings (Freire, 1971; Todd, 2009). This implies a possibility to seriously engage in the tough personal journey of excavation in order to reveal to ourselves our own reflexive blind spots. An ongoing reflexive process allows us to remain engaged with the 'uncomfortable' reflective process of owning our own shadow side (Pillow, 2003). This process is a very different process from the current policy requirements of remaking an 'actuarial' self for self-evaluation and reporting successful outcomes to policymakers and a sceptical public. Brady (2016) called this latter reflective work a debased form of self-interrogation as the criteria are set by others from the outside.

What is at stake here is to become conscious that well-used slogans like 'respect everyone's equal value' and 'oppose discrimination' are directly linked to people who can be regarded as (temporarily) weak and that it is imperative to think about what this implies. Research shows that violence tends to increase and become more accepted when strength is regarded as desirable and weakness is seen as disgusting and in need of being crushed or made extinct (Ofstad, 2012). For example, the number of incidents of hate crimes due to race and diversity in the UK has grown exponentially since the UK voted for BREXIT based on a nationalistic desire to better police and control borders and to keep out illegal immigrants and others considered unworthy of entry to the nation state (Burnett, 2017).

What we are saying is that the content for weakness can come into expression in all of us and serve as a reminder that the ethical dimension of democracy is very fragile – linked to people's perceptions, day-to-day struggles and, at times, shortcomings. One such reoccurring perception is that men are the strong sex and that women are the weak sex.

Weakness and strength in relation to masculinity and femininity

The **dualistic** and **dichotomist** discussion between weakness and strength also has a **gender dimension**, that is to say influenced by culturally created perceptions of how women and men are and ought to be. The purpose here is not to pin down the nature of men and women, but to remind us of the cultural-historical heritage that is ours. This dualistic perception tends to nestle into the choices of daily action in often subtle ways that impact on people's life conditions.

For example, both from a Swedish context and internationally, boys in various ages tend to be bullied (violated) and bully (violate) others more often than girls (e.g. Cook et al. 2010; Mitsopoulou & Giovazolias 2015; Thornberg & Wänström, 2018). This trend is also supported by a meta-study where five large cross-national data bases where compared and analysed (Smith & Brain, 2000; Smith et. al., 2004). Now and then firm ideas about masculinity and femininity colour the discussions at teacher education institutions, for example:

> A couple of years ago, during a seminar about democratic values and sustainability in Sweden, a heated discussion with pre-school student teachers erupted. One of the men, whom we can refer to as Johan, highlighted that it is both interesting and strange that he was one out of only six men in the entire cohort of pre-school teachers that semester. One woman (Anna) responded that it could be due to the fact that women are better equipped when it comes to caring for small children because of their feminine nature and that many men feel this and avoid applying. Johan became irritated along with some other women, arguing that it is a very narrow way of reasoning that overlooks ways in which both women and men can be caring as well as hurt others.

This gendered view of care is often found within teaching as a feminized profession and within the assumed (unrecognized) responsibility teachers carry for generating harmonious affective structures in schools. It is particularly observable in *Early Childhood Care and Education* (ECCE). A doctoral study by Murphy (2018) in Ireland reveals the dilemmas and contradictions found in relation to the rhetoric of ECCE official policy calling for an ideal professional practitioner (which the state seeks to hold publicly accountable using an extensive rubric of standards) and the lived reality of early childhood education and care (ECEC) workers (a vulnerable precariat workforce on low wages and poor working conditions in what are publicly-supported private centres).

At policy level, the ideal early childhood practitioner is envisioned as an accomplished technician (Moss, 2006, p. 35) implementing an early year's curriculum, working to prescribed, performative standards, meticulously accountable and ever ready for inspection. Simultaneously, the public perception of early childhood practitioners is typically one of a 'substitute mother' (Moss, 2006, p. 34) within which traditional and stereotypical conceptualizations of working in ECCE are understood as feminine, intuitive and vocational (Chang-Kredl, 2018, p. 266). This study shows the lived reality of early childhood practitioners to be oppressive, precarious, undervalued and conflicted with regulatory demands for performative, educative outcomes requiring prioritisation over meeting children's care needs (see Murphy, 2018).

Indeed, culturally and historically strength has been interconnected to masculinity and weakness interconnected to femininity. Masculinity and femininity should not be seen as men and women but as values grouped in two gendered boxes (James, 1997):

> Johannes: There is no place for weak people, and especially weak men. Men become aggressive of [weak people], they get reminded about aspects in themselves they worked all their lives to oppose …
> (*Dagens Nyheter*, pp. 7–8, cited in Edling, 2016, translated from Swedish)

From a biological perspective this might not be surprising seeing that men's bodies generally have more muscles than women's, but the labelling has gone far beyond biology. This dualistic and dichotomist division has contributed in structuring social life in many countries along the lines of gender in various ways, not the least in difficulties showing soft emotions like love, care or sadness. Similar to the quotations above, a male professor of education, at a university in Sweden, once described to me an event that arose in a course he was giving about 'the pedagogy of violence' where he felt and expressed strong emotions that left him feeling ashamed in front of the students:

> The course was held during the evenings and, being the year 1998, the professor decided to use some examples from the turbulence in Northern Ireland during 1998. The Good Friday Peace Agreement was being negotiated. All the while, one of the main movers of the process, President Bill Clinton, was embroiled in the Monika Lewinsky affair. The specific evening in question, he was trying to describe for the students how fragile a peace process can be, how one of the fundamentals of democracy can easily crumble and disappear. The specific situation, the juxtaposing of the two events (a real hope of peace and a sordid sexual affair) triggered something in him and he began to cry in front of the students, sniffling at first and then uncontrollably. The students surrounded the professor and tried to comfort him. He could hear comments like 'we should stop for today' and 'who'll take care of him?'. After a while he was able to pull himself together. He described how he felt afterwards – really stupid and almost ashamed.
>
> (Translated email from a Swedish professor)

The categorization of male strength and female weakness can be found in the Bible where Eve did not have the strong will to resist the snake's persuasions to bite the apple. Her bodily desires and feelings took control over her capability for reasoning and made her fall for temptation (Avsenik-Nabergoj, 2009). The idea that women are mentally weaker than men, along with their comparative physical weakness, has been a recurring topic, well emphasized in popular culture (Jönsson, 2009).

Hand in hand with these categorizations, weakness has come to be despised and strength cherished, which has entailed that female values automatically have come to be depreciated and male values described as something to be aspired to. This gendered pattern created in a distant past and polished over the centuries has come to influence not only how women should act but also what counts as masculinity. Historically men have been **socialized** to not show any signs of either mental and/or physical weakness.

To ask for help, to express a sense of being violated, or to show any signs of bodily weakness are, from this way of perceiving weakness, utterly unthinkable and has at times led to situations where men see themselves or want the world to see them as invincible. Violent sports like rally driving, boxing, karate and ice hockey as well as an idealization of violence linked to bar fights and being gang members has cost a lot of men their lives (Buchholz & Boyce, 2009; van den Hoopaard, 2009).

Another example is from a section from a Swedish newspaper describing the outrage of British people in August 2019 for having a prince attending to his toenails and talking about feelings:

> Harry used to be a real guy – he dressed sloppy, loved drinking and didn't care a shit about how he looked ... Now ... Harry tries to save the world barefooted instead of in Apache helicopters. What is more, he talks about feelings with disturbing comfort.[2]

This perception of manliness as strong **hegemonic masculinity** can often be found in elite boarding schools (Poynting & Donaldsson, 2005) and military schools (Larsson, 2005) and is a cornerstone for the establishment of violent and oppressive cultures. According to Brandt and Henry (2012), an increase of authoritarian ideas also increases gender inequality. Contrary to this, countries with low authoritarian views appeared to be more gender equal (ibid.). A dominant competitive culture of meritocratic individualism with cooperation, solidarity and equity become 'unthinkable' and 'unsayable' (Bernstein, 2000).

Soldiers in the Second World War

Studies of Schutzstaffel (SS) soldiers' behaviour and world-view during the Second World War indicate that they were based on a **hyper masculinity** where men came to see themselves as absolute opposites of women and people who were similar to the ideals of femininity and stood for peace and democracy. A soldier's manly toughness was placed in direct contrasting relation to female weakness and Christian tolerance. Strength was not merely about external aggression but was also described as an inner toughness, a capability to control one's will, follow principles and to actively work to supress soft values like feelings of love, tolerance, sadness, care and so forth since they were regarded as utterly disgusting (see Figure 6.1).

Figure 6.1 The image symbolizes a 'manly' arm hitting a Jew, with the text 'Der Schlag muss sitzen' (approximately translated as: 'the blow must be perfect').

Table 6.2 Examples of how values are split into a dualistic model, where some values are connected to women/femininity and other to men/masculinity

Women/femininity	Men/masculinity
Weak (in will)	Strong (in will)
Emotional, sentimental, unreasonable	Unsensitive, unsentimental, reasonable
Stupid	Smart
Obedient	Authoritative
Passive	Active
Peaceful	Violent
Dependent on men	Independent of others

The guidelines governing the concentration camp in Dachau came to play a significant role within the ideologies of Nazism since the camp functioned as a training school for SS soldiers where they were taught to be violent. The SS guards were given certain written directives, which they had to obey, which amongst others included sentences like '[t]olerance means weakness' (Dillon, 2013, p. 375). A common conviction was that tolerance makes people weak/soft and since weak/soft people are incapable of killing other human beings in cold blood they are reprehensible and not sufficiently manly.

The school socialized the soldiers to cherish violence, which can be contrasted with many post-war countries where youth and children are fostered to be tolerant and empathic. Several empirical studies show that when this type of hyper masculinity or hegemonic masculinity comes into expression in the actions of men and women it stimulates violence and racial hatred because it rewards aggression (Poynting & Donaldsson, 2005; Francia & Edling, 2016) (see also Figure 6.1).

Consequently, hyper masculinity is not just something men can express, it is also something that women can display. For example, in a major Swedish newspaper, Anna Hagwall, a member of parliament maintained that women who are physically bullied and beaten by their men should not complain but instead take their responsibility and leave the offending man. In this way, the focus of the aggression becomes the person being hit rather than the offender, the one that hits. This means that it is not the violence that is problematized but rather the weak one who is being hit and responds by whining. Whining is pictured as a sign of weakness and those who actively do something are regarded as strong.

> In the interview with P4 [radio] she makes clear that it is very much up to the 'women themselves'. Both to be more active in their work life – as leaving the men that beat them. 'There's no one forcing a women to stay in such a relationship, it is up to her. I think you shouldn't whine so much, rather we should really think that "what's my role in this, what is my responsibility in this, that I'm oppressed?"' she says in the radio interview.
> (*Svenska Dagbladet*, 15 July 2014, translated from Swedish by the author)

This black and white reasoning can seem appealing in its simplicity: instead of being weak, passive and whiny there is a point in being strong, active and taking full personal responsibility for succeeding in the world. When this argument is placed in a broader context and compared to the vast range of research that exists on the matter, this reasoning collapses. Both men and women can in certain situations be caught in a sense of learned helplessness where the step to ask for help requires an immense strength (e.g. Buchholz & Boyce, 2009; Lombard & McMillan, 2013; Messerschmidt, 2004).

There has been quite a lot written to date about this dualism and by some it might be regarded as suffocating and/or out of date. However, since this world-view not merely still exists, but is enhanced due to conservative and nationalistic forces growing stronger, it is important to be aware of it as it risks hurting both men and women. The division between female and male traits in a dualistic fashion has nothing to do with how women and men actually are.

Attempts to fixate different groups of people to these abstract and in many ways banal characteristics functions in a dominating and conservative manner. Accordingly, one group is allowed to suppress another and any kind of change in these structures and symbolic ways is not regarded as desirable or even possible. **Soft values** like empathy, care, tolerance, feelings of love and desire for peace is from this chain of logic weak and feminine and can in some cases be ridiculed for being airy-fairy, childish and associated with hippy women with long skirts and tambourines singing 'we shall overcome'.

At the same time, there is an extensive body of evidence, for example, from peace research, history, minority research and research about various forms of violence that feelings for others are necessary for people to live side by side without hurting each other. In the aftermath of the Second World War there was a general understanding and idea that those who committed the brutalities in the concentration camps were not normal people but psychopaths and evil people who enjoyed hurting others.

Contrary to this idea, several research projects have shown otherwise. In the book *Eichmann in Jerusalem: A Report on the Banality of Evil* (Arendt, 2006 [1963]), the political theorist Professor Hannah Arendt analysed the trial of Adolf Eichmann in order to gain a deeper understanding of why a human being is capable of committing brutalities against other human beings. Adolf Otto Eichmann was a Nazi SS officer in Germany and described as one of the major organizers of the mass murder of dissidents, mainly Jews, during the Second World War. What characterized his trial was that he felt no remorse for what he had done because he considered himself as being moral and, as such, doing his duty and what he understood as doing good. He expressed a lot of love for his family. Eichmann's thinking displayed parts of Kant's imperative, namely the idea that goodness has to do with obeying general laws, which he later interpreted as following Hitler's demands. Arendt noticed that Eichmann was reluctant to think for himself, loved the sense of belonging to something larger than himself, and seemed to feel that his contribution in logically organizing the Holocaust complemented his lack of knowledge in education (ibid.). He felt weak but compensated it by becoming strong in a brutal sense.

A central conclusion in Arendt's analysis of the trial was that evil is not something residing in certain people, rather it is expressed in a lack of responsibility for others' life situations, canonized in the belief that the moral is about duty and rules and following orders. If a person blames all his or her actions on majority rule and/or a totalitarian power, even the most ordinary of men and women can become evil. Similarly, the historian Christopher Browning (1998) found in his study of the Reserve Police Battalion

101 in Poland that middle-aged men committing brutal acts, against mainly Jews, were ordinary men stemming from working-class backgrounds. They were not hurting other people because they enjoyed blood, fuelled a hatred against Jews, and loved torturing others, but because they found it important to obey authority and to follow norms existing in their peer group in order to 'fit in' and experience a sense of belonging and fraternity.

Based on the chain of logic of these and other similar studies, the philosopher Emmanuel Levinas (1981) came to the conclusion that theories about ethics risk being brutal if they are grounded in ideas of universal truth and social convention rather than a sense of responsibility for the Other. In his ethics of alterity, oppressed feminine values like uniqueness, sensing, love, feelings for others and so forth were revived in order to handle the fact that violence tends to increase when we distance ourselves from the alterity and intensive presence of the Other.

More complex images of weakness and strength

Within the black-and-white (dualistic) way of perceiving strength and weakness and subsequently weak people versus strong people, there is a belief that some people are close to perfect while others are imperfect and due to their imperfections become disturbing and in need of being cleansed. This thinking feeds into the neoliberal policy imaginary we discussed earlier in Chapter 3 where the policy influence today is on education for the development of meritocratic individualism, expressed as a new human ideal – a highly functioning entrepreneurial 'actuarial' self who takes responsibility for their own lifelong learning and is not dependent on anyone and/or most of all any notion of a dependent society and/or social welfare. It encapsulates the concept of education as a private good for the development of a person with a career aim of a trajectory of flexibility, adapting endlessly to the vagaries of unfettered markets and with no misconceptions or entanglements about the nation state as a decent caring place.

As a (future) teacher you are expected to deal with children or students' who can be perceived as weak and full of flaws as well as keeping questions of democracy alive in the classroom or kindergarten. Compare, for instance, this experience from a student teacher, who we will refer to as Patricia:

> She described that during her VFU (Verksamhetsförlagd utbildning/vocational training) at a primary school in Sweden she had a teacher who believed that it is healthy to let children fight and sort out their differences, since they have to learn how to become tougher. According to him, a lot of parents and teachers spoil children and thus make them more whining and sensitive for violation. 'You can't even make jokes, because then parents are filing complaints that I've violated their children'.
>
> (Observation from a real life situation)

Hence, in order to move beyond a dominating dualistic image, there is a rationale for turning to research that demonstrates how human perfection is impossible to attain – which is not the same as anything goes. Understanding our human 'unfinishedness' instead calls us as educators to dedicate time and energy over a lifetime to the often 'uncomfortable' work of reflexivity, which we discuss in Chapter 7 (Pillow, 2003). Freire (1998) argues for the political nature of education and its connection to what he calls the 'radical unfinishedness' of the human condition:

the real roots of the political nature of education are to be found in the educability of the human person. This educability, in turn, is grounded in the radical unfinishedness of the human condition and in our consciousness of this unfinished state.

(p. 100)

The idea is not to give a full-fledged overview of existing research, but rather to provide examples, which can be used as starting points for further discussion.

Beyond abstract forms of humanism

The categorization between those deemed as humans and those deemed as non-humans can be said to be one important motivator for accepting and carrying out torture and mass murder. During the Second World War, some groups of people, such as Jews, Roma people, Jehovah's witnesses, homosexuals and disabled people were described as different and with certain unwelcome characteristics in need of extinction. Often images of rats and vermin where used as projections of these groups of people in ways that reduced their human value and stimulated ideas of radical extermination to prohibit damage to what was perceived as the normal population (see Figure 6.2). The process of dehumanization is one of the strongest reasons for motivating violence against others (Haslam, 2006; Bar-Tal, 1989; Goof et al., 2008), although other factors intersect. For example:

'Perhaps when we were raping her, we looked at her as a woman … but when we killed her, we just thought of her as something like a pig.'

(Chang, 1998, pp. 49–50)

Repeatedly the rhetoric during the Second World War pictured those who were characterized as defective people as weak while strength became associated with those regarded as normal. Strength was also linked to masculine traits like force, violence, superiority, striking back and hence not allowing oneself to be emotional, sensitive, subordinate and so forth. Accordingly, the vision of strength versus weakness was based on a dualistic logic that supported the right of the German people to cleanse the world of the unwelcomed. The German people were depicted by Hitler as divine through God's will and since God is good and almighty those who were against God's will could only be seen as the enemy – and as devils (see Hitler's *Mein Kampf* in Ofstad, 2012).

Violence from the Second World War is often used as an example in research and education, but it is important to remember the multitude of genocides taking place in history:

the genocide of the Armenians at the hand of the Turks, the race wars such as in those Homewood, Florida, and Tulsa, Oklahoma (as just two events that marked the extensive murder and subjugation of African-Americans throughout the United States during the twentieth century), the Nazi genocide of European Jewry, the Nazi genocide of the Roma, the widespread murder and oppression of Poles and Slavs also by Nazi regime, the rape and murder of Chinese people by Japanese troops in Nanking, the Cambodian genocide initiated by the Pol Pot regime, the massacre of Timorese civilians by the Indonesian army and militias supported by that army, the 'ethic cleansing' attempted in Bosnia and Kosovo, the slaughter in

Figure 6.2 An example of a propaganda used in the Third Reich picturing violence as something desirable [*Der Schlag muss sitzen*/The hit must be perfect].

Rwanda of Tutsis by Hutus, the murderous violence of the apartheid regime in South Africa, the extensive slaughter of indigenous people in Guatemala – and this list is by no means exhaustive!

(Simon, 2012, pp. 185–186)

Overall patterns of how violence occurs are very similar worldwide, and dehumanization is one central aspect in enabling the process to accentuate and take form in everyday life. In accordance to the American psychologist and professor from Harvard University, Gordon Allport (1954), people tend to divide the world into inside-groups (majorities) and outside-groups (minorities). Inside-groups have an inclination to express prejudices (stereotyped perceptions) of people seen as out-groups, which risk hurting these groups of people physically and/or psychologically. Based on his empirical observations he highlights five steps of prejudices in a hierarchical fashion:

1. **Antilocution**: has to do with a majority group who jokes about minorities using negative stereotypes. Often the majority tend to see this as not harmful, while studies show that it is a starting point for more serious expressions of prejudices against minorities.
2. **Distancing**: which is about a majority group who avoids people stemming from a minority group. Even though the intention is not always conscious but unconscious it can provide harm in that people from the minority group are isolated.
3. **Discrimination**: is about stereotypes which are turned into given truths about minority groups, which entails that individuals from these groups tend to be treated differently than individuals from the majority group in a similar situation. The result of such action is that people from minority groups risk facing harsher conditions than those in the majority group.
4. **Physical attack**: has to do with the majority groups harming minority groups and their property through different kind of violence, such as kicking, setting things on fire, bombs and graffiti.
5. **Extinction**: is when the majority group strives to get rid of minority groups through extinction or/and deportation (Allport, 1954).

The possibilities to oppose negative stereotypes require awareness of these patterns in everyday life in order to create situations where people from the outside and inside are working together towards similar aims (Allport, 1954). As a teacher educator and teacher student, what do you see in the social contexts around you when it comes to the use of prejudices?

The process to dehumanize some people was made in the name of humanism and came through the system of dualism to represent the Good. When trying to scientifically grasp the horrors of the Second World War, the dangers of Humanism defining who is human and not human was regarded as one important reason why this brutality was accepted and was able to accelerate (e.g. Aitken & Valentine, 2006; Arendt, 2004; Bauman, 2000). Emanuel Levinas' (1981) notion of an *Ethics of Alterity* can be grasped as a direct response to the cruelty created due to an overreliance and unquestioning acceptance of the power of human categorization (p. 203).

In several of his books, Lévinas systematically explores the narrow image of ethics as character building where different ethical theories subsume that individuals automatically become better when they come to act in ways that do no harm to others simply through knowledge about how humans and societies are. Without claiming that character building is unimportant, he underscores that violence is difficult to counteract without being aware that it is always created towards a face – a radically unique subject. One of his main contributions to the field of ethics is the way he highlights the unavoidable presence of alterity and intimacy in the midst of ethical relations (e.g. Lévinas, 1987, 1998).

Drawing on Lévinas, Bauman (1993) argues that mental and physical distance assists people distance themselves from people's life conditions and sufferings (pp. 168–179). He uses the term cloakroom communities, which is about ways in which a society applies **adiaphorization**. Adiaphorization means processes in a society to create feelings of belonging by reducing plurality and increasing a sense of similarity and an engagement to preserve this similarity. The active distancing from Others' differences risks enhancing violence towards those that do not fit into the idea of sameness (Bauman, 2000, pp. 192–201). Increasing a strong loyalty and feeling for one's own community automatically creates a distance to other communities (Bauman, 1995, pp. 149–155).

Consequently, if there is an authentic desire to avoid violence, Bauman argues there is a point in approaching communities and hence morality differently than simply starting from socialization and the commons. In interconnection with socialization (distance) is the capability of sensing the Other as a face (intimacy) and it is in this relational encounter that a unique human being's fate is decided (Bauman, 1993, pp. 69–78 and 85–92).

Thus, central in an ethics of alterity is to take into account the responsibility that awakens when we encounter the face of the Other, which opens up ethics to existential questions of how we react and act when we, for instance, see and sense the sufferings of others like refugees. During 2015, one image of Alan Kurdi was published in newspapers all over the world to give face to the brutalities that accompanies people who flee from war and poverty. The image and reactions amongst some right-wing people were discussed at a seminar in teacher education problematizing the notion of *intimacy* and *distance* as well as journalists' ways of writing.

The teacher students were asked to read an article where radical right-wing youth were interviewed:

> 'We cannot just let our societies perish'.
> When we meet, the body of Alan Kurdi has washed up on the beach of Bodrum. The picture of the Kurdish boy has hit a whole world.
> – Sob stories [*snyfthistorier*]!
> X sounds angry. The veins on the forehead are tense (*spänner*).
> – It's not relevant! It's not relevant with a single boy who has drowned!
> – That media doesn't report a shit about the fact that [a] million people have been killed in [the] Congo in the last years, it's too complicated with all the tribes who [beat] each other to death here and there.
> – But to take a photo of a little boy who's drowned – that's very simpl[e] for media to take advantage of for their higher purposes. That is to say, to make Europe more multicultural. There is no rationality. I'm a rational human being. And it is quite easy to look through arguments based on feelings.
> (*Dagens Nyheter*, 19 December 2015, interview with a member of Sverige Demokraternas Ungdomsförbund (SDU), translated from Swedish)

While people within a rational discourse of humanism are pictured as perfect and/or possible to mould to perfection, research about various forms of mental and physical violence show the importance of keeping the imperfections of people and ideas alive along with consequences of action. For instance, when evidence-based (empirical) studies found, for example, in the new construction of teaching as a clinical (medicalized) practice, are presented as absolute reflections of realities there is a real risk of actual and symbolic violence and people getting hurt in multiple ways. While striving to prevent girls' physical health declining, all girls in a study were treated as being at risk of bad health, which actually made some girls become ill due to the negative stereotyped categorizations (Wickström, 2013). Accordingly, the tendency to regard a vision of what it means to be 'a perfect human' as a solution for human suffering, risks causing violence since it overlooks the fact that humans are imperfect. Consequently,

> it is often taken for granted that humanity is itself the remedy for violence, as if violence could be divorced from the actual human subjects who commit it. Indeed, humanity has been conflated with human life and goodness in such a commonplace way, that imperfection has been expunged from its meaning.
>
> (Todd, 2009, p. 2)

Indeed, to gain knowledge is important but it is not the same thing as absolutely knowing how individuals concretely experience the world, how they think and feel. Consequently, the inclination within ideas of humanism to subsume that all people share a common identity and that being human can be reached through behaving in a certain manner can in itself be counter-productive and generate situations where people are being hurt or prohibit the possibilities for equal conditions.

In order to handle and grasp the various ways in which human relations come into existence there is a point in acknowledging peoples' differences and keeping peoples' imperfections alive in education.

The unavoidable presence of the body

Seeing that violence comes into expression in various ways, one theoretical model of explanation is never enough. One dimension to understand the complexity of violence is to turn to research about embodiment (Grosz, 1995; Grosz & Probyn, 1995; Mohanty, 1989; Nussbaum, 1997; Young, 1990b). While research generally tends to emphasize cognitive or emotional aspects of being human, research about embodiment stresses that people are never just walking heads but always walking bodies where thoughts, emotions, desires, dreams and expectations are conjoined and influence each other. Since we cannot escape our bodies and since this affects our actions and ways of being towards others it is worth recognising its presence (e.g. Aldama, 2003; Arturo & Arteaga, 2003).

In order to explain why people do not always act in the manner of rational choice, Julia Kristeva (Kristeva, 1984, 1991, 2000, 2010) turns to psychoanalysis and comes to the conclusion that irrationality is due to our conscious and subconscious parts – interconnected like waves crashing on the shore. With the help of language, the conscious part tries to understand the world while the subconscious uninvitedly breaks into our meaning-making and disturbs it from within. Kristeva calls the gap between the conscious and subconscious the metaphor, where bodily reactions built up from past experiences break into how we reason and act in the present, often without our awareness.

It is often only when we gaze back and reflect on what we have said and done that the subconscious can be rendered visible and become accounted for. In this sense we can never know how other people and we ourselves react, i.e. we are always in some terms surrounded by strangers and are also *Strangers to ourselves* (Kristeva, 1991). This can be seen as a weakness, which we are forced to live with one way or another. For example, during a talk with a colleague a teacher could feel that she became irritated by one of the male teachers. When she was asked why she was irritated she responded by saying that he reminded her of a nasty relative. Similarly, teachers and students can react instinctively towards others' presence, generating spontaneous feelings of love/hate and without being aware of and problematizing these reactions they can cause a lot of damage (e.g. Britzman, 1998).

When asking young people about how they respond to others' life situations, practically all of the young people stressed that they wanted to promote others' well-being while at the same time, in their narratives, described situations where they for instance found silent people irritating, enjoyed bullying others, hated those contradicting them and so forth (Edling, 2009). Subsequently, research about embodiment can help teachers and students to slow down, turn the gaze back to what they might themselves have said and done, and thus become aware of the processes in which we project our own perceptions and feelings onto others without being aware of it. Rather than merely giving in to hatred, irritation, annoyance etc., there is a point in asking why these feelings occur in our bodies.

Contemporary research indicates that expressions of hatred towards dissidents like journalists and minorities in societies are increasing today (eMORE, 2017; Clark & Grech, 2017; Foxman & Wolf, 2013; Waldron, 2014).[3] Hate speech is a strong emotion that erupts and silences those who think and act in ways that do not correspond with the perpetrators' own ways of thinking and feeling. Hate as an emotion is not *per se* rational, since rationalism as a philosophy stands for thinking and logic separate from feelings (e.g. Descartes). Yet hatred erupts in seemingly reasonable conversations in the public, media and institutions and disturbs in ways that threaten the very fibres of democracy, which is dependent upon freedom of speech and open dialogue (Waldron, 2014; Heinze, 2016).

Ponder about the following examples said in different contexts by both young people and adults:

1. I think it is important to help others – weak and whiny people irritate me.
2. I think it is important to be kind – I jump the queue in the cafeteria since no one dares to confront me.
3. I think it is important to be tolerant towards immigrants – it feels a bit threatening when immigrant boys stand in group in front of the store since Swedish people don't do that.
4. I understand that refugees have a tough life – those who come from Syria have the violence in themselves.
5. It is no question that we in Sweden should fight for the rights of homosexuals – I shudder with disgust when Gustav speaks in his feminine voice.

(Edling, 2016, p. 108, translated from Swedish)

A class of student teachers, during a seminar about the Swedish democratic value foundation, were asked to write about how they understood their future profession as teachers in relation to the task of upholding the given and politically defined values. One young woman raised her hand and said that she found the task problematic in that it forced her and others to reply according to the book: 'you need to be kind and good hearted and bla bla ... it's like we're forced to be politically correct while overlooking how we really feel. It feels fake. The suffocating goodness kills the spirit at times, I'm not sure if you understand what I mean but that is how I feel' [notes taken by the author after the seminar].

(Observations from everyday life)

Similarly a journalist in a Swedish newspaper recently wrote an article titled 'The return of the house woman – and the forbidden seduction of conservatism':

After the peak woke (which we in Sweden call the 'politically correctness' days of glory) – let us say that it was during 2014 that the trend was, perhaps if not the strongest [but strong] ... But which now and then appeared to be dreadfully wholesome in its urge to always do *so* right ... I understand them. It is easy to look through a house woman – in more or less transparent ways she gets advantages through sucking up to the power, be in collusion with the enemy and betray one's own. It is not a very sympathetic characteristic, but it is as if there is a seduction even in that. Do I have to be sympathetic then? Can't I be selfish! Can't I be … as conservatives always have been in public life?

(*Dagens Nyheter*, 181021, "Huskvinnans återkomst – och konservatismens förbjudna lockelse"/"The return of the house woman – and the forbidden seduction of conservatism", Greta Thurfjell, translated from Swedish by the author)

It can also be part of a chain of logic and empiricism that works to slowly 'suffocate democracy' in the classroom and in society (Browning, 2018; Mooney Simmie, 2020). If the focus in education policy and practice is constantly aimed at doing and being good it can be suffocating, since there are other feelings underneath that get suppressed and repressed. How can these mixed emotions be handled in education? What do you think?

Brain/cognitive research and human complexity

It is not just philosophers or those working with psychoanalysis that have come to the conclusion that people are unique and that conclusions about how people are in universalist terms is problematic as a starting point for action. Cognitive research and neuroscience have shown that every brain is unique – even identical twins – and that the brain we are born with constantly changes with an evolving plasticity throughout our lives through a variety of stimulus and learning (Goswami, 2006). In this sense cognitive research and neuroscience contributes to challenging the notion of fixed one-size-fits-all solutions, and instead rather encourages teachers and educators to slow down and think.

Similarly, research in psychoanalysis studies about the brain indicate that there is no clear-cut border between cognitive capacities, feelings, the subconscious and the conscious. How people feel impacts what they learn. This implies amongst other things that people's possibilities to learn will be impeded if they feel threatened, worried, or in fear of being hurt. Similarly, there is no distinct border between parts, unity, facts, experience, focus and periphery, they intersect and influence each other in a dialectical fashion, which encourages teachers and students to take this into consideration (e.g. Caine & Caine, 1991; Goswami, 2006; Caine, Caine, McLintic & Klimek, 2005; Gilkey, 2014) (see Table 6.3).

Professor Daniel Kahneman's (Kahneman, 1973; Kahneman, Slovic & Tversky, 1982; Kahneman & Tversky, 2000) cognitive studies based on statistical significance also point to a weakness/flaw built into the fabric of being human. One of the questions his research takes an interest in is how people make judgements, which clearly has great relevance for teachers' professional work. According to Kahneman, people's judgements can be controlled by a *fast thinking system*, which he calls System 1, and a *slow thinking system*, which he refers to as System 2. These two systems are not separated units but are symbiotically interconnected. System 1 is the judgement that happens on autopilot, it is constantly active and does not require much effort. The judgement in System 1 is about quickly locating stored information as well as making fast connections and associations between ideas. It can be about a) seeing how close or far away an object is from another, b) trying to distinguish the location of a sudden noise, c) wrinkling one's forehead when someone tells you something troubling, d) finding rhymes, e) noticing when someone sounds friendly or threatening, f) knowledge that works on autopilot, like 2×2, g)

Table 6.3 A selection of how the brain works and how it influences learning

Research about the brain	Suggestions in education
Every brain is unique and changeable. The structure of the brain changes through experience and learning.	Vary the pedagogical strategies to stimulate as many as possible and let the students use their hearing, vision, and their tactile and emotional preferences.
Learning engages the entire body. Physics, development, personal comfort, and one's emotional state affect the ability to learn.	Be aware of the fact that children and students develop individually at their own pace and that actual age does not mirror the child's/student's readiness to learn. Incorporate aspects stimulating health like physical training and stress management into education.
The search for meaning is something we are born with. The mind's natural curiosity can be moved by complex and meaningful challenges.	Stimulate seminars and activities that awaken the mind's search for meaning and problem solving.
The brain is created to perceive and create patterns.	Present information in a context in order to allow the student to identify patterns and get in touch with previous experiences.
Emotions and cognition cannot be separated. Emotions can be vital for storing knowledge and regaining information.	Enable a classroom environment that promotes positive attitudes amongst students and teachers and in relation to school work. Encourage students to be aware about their emotions and how the emotional climate in the classroom influences their learning.
Every brain can perceive parts and units in parallel (i.e. all at the same time).	Avoid isolating information from its context since this impedes learning. Create activities that demand full brain activity and communication.
Learning involves both focused and periphery attention.	Place materials (for instance posters, art, information) outside the students' immediate focus. Even though they are in the peripheral they influence learning. Be aware of the signals that you, as a teacher, radiate externally to what is said since it signals what is important to learn.
Learning always implies that conscious and subconscious processes transect.	Use hooks or other motivating techniques to stimulate personal connections. Reflection and metacognition can help students to become conscious about their learning.
We have at least two types of memory: spatial that registers daily experiences and rote learning that treats facts and acquisition in isolation.	Separating information and competences from previous experience forces the student to be dependent on rote memory. Avoid a strong focus on rote learning since it makes it difficult to stimulate understanding.
Learning is stimulated through challenges and is hampered through threats.	Try to create an atmosphere of relaxed awareness with low risk and high challenge.

Source: Adapted from Caine and Caine, 1991; compare also Goswami, 2006.

hearing the name Dewey and automatically citing 'learning by doing', h) driving a car without other cars nearby, and i) understanding simple sentences.

Contrary to System 1 that makes fast (reflexive) judgements possible and helps with all the mundane repetitive chores and choices of everyday life (e.g. What will I wear tomorrow?), System 2 thinking requires concentration and slow thinking. It is about being in the present, systematization, and logical puzzling but is constantly disturbed by the impulsive System 1. Judgements made with the help of System 2 can, for instance, be about a) just focusing on how democracy is described in a text, b) locating and listening for a specific person's voice in a crowded room, c) making connections between concepts and practice, d) comparing two or more ways of understanding democracy, e) seeing if a logical argument is valid, f) solving a mathematical problem, g) driving a car in a very crowded street, and h) deconstructing a text to understand the pieces. System 2 thinking requires effort and focus, and it often gets seduced by the impulsive auto pilot of System 1 thinking (Kahneman, 2013).

If you as reader of this book let your thoughts drift now and then rather than give your full concentration to the content it can be understood as an internal battle between System 1 and 2 thinking – where the impulsive System 1 thinking is attracted by easy and fast solutions. Perhaps it is time for a cookie now? Or just a tiny break with a cup of coffee?

However it would be wrong to think that System 1 thinking is just a lazy system that is spontaneous and needs to be banished. System 1 thinking, as an impulsive system worthy of listening to, has supported the survival of humankind in harsh competitive times, it has helped people in the past and in the present read and respond to a threatening stimulus and whenever there is a call for a 'fight or fight' response. It assists people to work on autopilot in their daily routines and frees up creative energies for higher-order pursuits. For example, Barack Obama as former President of the United States is reported to have used a capsule wardrobe to make it easier to devote his energies to all the important occasions and presentations he was expected to deliver during his presidency. This System 1 thinking system greatly helped his daily practices as president. Having to deal with substantive issues and also having to battle with your wardrobe of clothes on a daily basis is one practical example of System 1 thinking.

However, what research has shown is that people have a general tendency to rely too much on System 1 thinking, which sometimes leads to situations where other people are judged without connection to facts and without taking all the facts into consideration. System 1 thinking makes conclusions based on 'all I see is all that exists', without finding out if there are other knowledge forms, evidence, or other aspects that can be of relevance to understand the situation better.

If individuals do not activate their slow thinking System 2 more often there is a real risk that they themselves are readily manipulated and that they risk hurting others. Some of the risks are as follows:

- If we hear certain phrases or expressions many times System 1 has a tendency to take them for truth, for instance teacher education is bad, brain research is evil, Miranda is smart, Karl is stupid. If the brain has heard it many times it creates a sense of recognition and the information is incorporated to that which is seen as familiar and safe. This knowledge is often used by advertisement and political campaigns and dictatorships all over the world.
- System 1 easily seduces our minds because its easy black-and-white logic creates a feeling that the puzzle pieces fit nicely together. It creates a treacherous feeling of

140 *Darwinian strength*

self-confidence because the more knowledge we gain, the more it becomes difficult to simply state 'this is how it is': "[i]ndeed, you will often find that knowing little makes it easier to fit everything you know into a coherent pattern" (Kahneman, 2013, p. 87).

- System 1 is fast in registering norm deviation. If you are used to being surrounded by people who speak quietly, System 1 thinking might automatically react as if there is something wrong with a person speaking louder than that which you have implicitly registered as normal. System 1 signals that the person is rude or simply not normal. System 2 could help System 1 to understand that there might be several reasons for the other person to speak loudly. The other person might not be aware of it, have learnt to speak loudly in order to be heard at all, have a hearing problem, have lived near people with hearing problems, and so forth.
- In relation to the point above, System 1 thinking is easy in judging others beforehand (see stereotypes and prejudice) based on the device 'all I see is all that exists' and the easiness to judge without taking other options into consideration.
- If there is something in another person that is conceived as nice, positive and joyful, System 1 has a tendency to glorify the entire personality without paying regard to nuances and taking other opinions/options into consideration. This is called the Gloria Effect (Kahneman, 2013, in Edling, 2016, pp. 111–112) (see also Table 6.4).

In accordance to Kahneman the impact from System 1 thinking will never cease, which might be interpreted as a sign of human weakness. However, there is a huge difference between giving into the seductive and often pragmatic impulse of System 1 thinking and slowing down the impulsive urge to go on autopilot in order to wrestle with the surrounding world in a more thoughtful and measured way using System 2 thinking.

Table 6.4 An example of how a Gloria Effect is created. Put your hand above the right-side column and think for yourself what kind of thoughts and emotions the left column causes to arise. Take away your hand and add the new information to the previous one. What happens?

Hitler 1	*Hitler 2*
Likes children	He despises weakness
Likes dogs	He considers Nazis to be good since they stimulate the natural extinction of weak people
He is a passionate and skilled in rhetoric	He is responsible for 55 million people's deaths and suffering
He really take interest in the best of the nation	Considers people to be uneducated since they are easier to manipulate
Johanna 1	*Johanna 2*
Is skilled in maths	She has bullied Ted since preschool
Dresses very elegantly	She has difficulties with people who are silent
Talks calmly and argumentatively	She is happy when she exerts power over others
Is often volunteering as a class representative	Pokes her nose where no one sees

Source: The tables can be found, in Swedish, in Edling, 2016, pp. 112–113.

This section has highlighted how a narrow either/or world view, i.e. where people are seen as either weak or strong in an essentialist fashion is an illusion that ignores people's 'radical unfinishedness' (Freire, 1998, p. 100) and embodied imperfectness (see also Table 6.4). Since people cannot escape their imperfections, their shadow side – nor can they escape from the embeddedness of their own bodies, where the conscious and subconscious as well as Systems 1 and 2 are in constant symbiosis with each other – it becomes important to include all these multiple ways of knowing into the midst of education. In the section below the attention shifts from our bodies and brains to discursive intersections that might explain how images of people being strong and/or weak changes from context to context.

Caught in the web of intersections

Studies that direct attention to people's daily interactions show that individuals often are categorized differently from context to context. A person seen as weak in one context can just a couple of hours later be seen as strong depending on the people and situation s/he encounters. Categorizing and categorization can be seen as a natural part of meaning-making and a natural part of the way language is structured. By using the words weak and strong we signal that there are those who are strong and those who are weak (e.g. Bauman, 1999). Yet, just because categorizations are part of meaning-making there is a point in being careful with how categorizations are used to determine how people we encounter really 'are' (Pickering, 2001).

In daily interactions people tend to be given and give each other different identities, which automatically places individuals in different categories and boxes, such as woman/girl, coloured, intelligent, fat, teacher, weak or pupil. The intersectional perspective was born because coloured women in the US found that women often were treated as a homogenous group which overlooked the nuances in the group. Many women were not mistreated merely due to their female sex but also due to the fact that they were, for example, coloured or lesbians or from a poor background and therefore economically dependent. In order to describe this process, the term 'intersection' was used to signal a point where various lines (categories) meet (intersect).

Intersectionality as a research concept is intimately connected to a desire to change different forms of injustices, such as the production and reproduction of oppression. A central starting point is that people's identities, image(s) of who they are do not have to be singular or forever fixed. On the contrary, they can change depending on the people we encounter and situations we find ourselves in, that make the borders of who we are fuzzier and changeable. In some situations, class/gender/ethnicity influence my condition due to the way people treat me, in other contexts people treat me as a geek or fat (e.g. Arriaza, 2003; Crenshaw, 1998; Kumashiro, 2001; Shields, 2008).

There are differences in how intersectionality is understood and used by researchers (Hancock, 2007; McCall, 2001) and there are those who have criticized the difficulties for the intersectional perspective to handle people's differences outside the notion of identity and categorization in general (e.g. Lykke, 2004; McCall, 2005). Intersectionality can be linked to Michael Foucault's theories about discourses, which can generally be described as frames of understanding the world that is shared by others and which defines the borders of what should be seen as good or bad, right or wrong.

Discourses are not fixed but change over time and from place to place, which has made it possible to question aspects of the world with the help of knowledge that previously has been taken as true. Discourses come into expression through language (writing, speech, body language) through the way they define how things are and creates the frames for people's life conditions (de los Reyes & Martinsson, 2005). When student teachers speak about children they are going to teach, various discourses can be interpreted. The most common one is:

> I'm really happy to become a teacher and work with children since all children are so cute and cuddly. It feels as if they have nothing bad in their little bodies … they aren't as ruined as we adults are, but pure and unspoiled.
>
> (Inspired by Edling, 2016, p. 114)

This frame of understanding can be compared to descriptions like:

> Children are undeveloped creatures who really need the firm hand of an adult that guides their steps so they can develop properly. When I become a teacher the children will certainly know what's right and wrong, not like my teachers who just let them do anything they wanted.
>
> (Ibid.)

There are also student teachers who maintain that:

> I love being a teacher but it is a scary business since children, like adults, are unique personalities. They are full of thoughts and ideas from the start and I think my job as a teacher will be to gently guide them … but I guess sometimes they probably guide me as well.
>
> (Ibid.)

If one of these discourses is particularly strong in a group it can become very tense when someone ventilates a contradictory way of grasping children and teaching. Have you tried saying that children can be horrible in a group where the majority has just established how cute and adorable all children are? How do you think, and what kind of discourses do you detect in your surroundings? People in general all partake in upholding certain discourses that they are influenced by, but they can also resist them. In order to understand how people's preconditions change dependent upon how they discursively are categorized, the use of language patterns can be observed in your environment. Can you detect language patterns? What is included or excluded in the discourses? Can you see when a discourse changes from context to context? Can you see if and how discourses influence people's life condition? Can you detect any resistance? (e.g. de los Reyes & Martinsson, 2005).

Bernstein's (2000) pedagogic device used is a powerful explanatory framework to understand power relays when knowledge moves in circular ways from the field of official policy into the pedagogical field and back again through modes of assessment and evaluation and he spoke of defining in the pedagogic device what was the 'thinkable' and what was the 'unthinkable'. Critical theorists advance this argument through asking whose thinking is acceptable, whose voice matters, whose voices are silenced, who benefits (Apple, 2012; Giroux, 1988; Gunter, 2001; Kincheloe, 2004; McLaren 2015).

Compare the following examples of how a student teacher is categorized as weak in one context and strong in another:

> **Example 1**: Maja and Jens were at the same upper secondary high school during their VFU and shared the same supervisor, a middle-aged woman named Sandra who

was a math and history teacher. According to both Maja and Jens, Sandra tended to favour Jens. She often turned to him during conversations and highlighted his strengths and competences in front of the students. On one occasion the teacher wanted the pupils to watch a film about the French Revolution and turned to Jens for help: 'Jens, I would guess you're a master of these things being a guy and all, could you please start this while I write some questions on the white board for students to ponder?'

Example 2: The school had a room with colourful sofas and some armchairs, where the teachers could meet over a cup of tea or coffee during their breaks. Halfway through the practice-based education, Maja came to sit beside the school principal, Christine. They came by chance to talk about the importance of digitally enhanced schools due to current challenges and Maja told the principal she had taken several courses about programming and IT before she started her teacher education programme and that she'd even won a prize for the best IT innovation in 2015. The principal was really thrilled and asked if Maja wanted to present this innovative idea at the next teacher council the coming Monday. Late on Monday the principal introduced Maja as both a student teacher (novice) and as an expert in IT and whose competence could (be shared) at the school.

Research about intersectionality provides powerful examples of risks in approaching people as if they only belong to one category, without consideration to changeable intersections of social identities in daily relations that are forced upon us whether we desire it or not and which we at times impose on others. These categories are not harmless but set the frames for our life condition (Crenshaw, 1998).

The power of authority, belonging, and the desire to stop thinking

A critical question asked after the Second World War is how come ordinary men and women that appeared to have been given a normal upbringing, had well-paid jobs, were polite and perceived as nice people suddenly could accept and uphold concentration camps and genocide. The American social psychologist Stanley Milgram (1975) asked similar questions before he conducted his famous experiment regarding obedience. Milgram explained to people who wanted to participate in the study that it was about a desire to promote learning and that they wanted to examine which method worked best to pursue this aim. The research group arranged a false lottery procedure to choose a group that would represent teachers and a group that would represent learners. Those selected as pupils were actors already instructed to act as pupils beforehand thus rendering the role of teacher to be the only position available for the newcomers.

The group of teachers consisted of women and men from various professions: students, workers and businessmen. They were to read different words to the pupils whose sole mission was to repeat these and when the pupils managed to do a series of cards, they went on to the next series. During this process the teachers were instructed to punish the pupils if they did something wrong with the help of electric shocks. The shocks were not real, but the skilful members of the group acted as if they were hurt. The level of the electric shocks accelerated successively for every mistake that was made. The lowest was 15 volts and the highest was 450 volts, which was deadly and the subjects were informed about this at an early stage.

Despite this knowledge and despite the fact that the pupils stopped reacting after 300 volts, the teachers continued increasing the strength until it reached 450 volts because the researcher who asked them to conduct this study asked them to do this with a firm authoritative voice. The subjects in the study appeared to blindly follow authority. This study stirred many reactions and was copied in several other countries including Sweden – always with the same results. Not all subjects, but the majority, continued sending out volts even when they knew these voltages jeopardized the life of the student.[4]

This human tendency to blind obedience has been studied in other research fields as well. For example, the American historian Christopher Browning (1998) wrote a book called *Ordinary Men*, where he analysed the Reserve Police Battalion 101 in the Lublin district of Poland during the Second World War. The Reserve Police Battalion in Lublin consisted of older men who had volunteered to partake in the genocide and were responsible for the killing of 38,000 Jews and for sending 45,000 Jews to concentration camps. None of these men were trained soldiers or had an armed gun pointed to their heads, the phenomenon that took place could rather be explained as blind obedience through group pressure. They wanted to fit into governing norms but also to quickly advance on the social ladder without any thought about consequences. One of the conclusions Browning makes is how easy it is to simply follow the flow and accept a group's norms as good and as the truth (Browning, 1998). This tendency to be violent without thinking can be seen as a form of weakness since it takes much more strength to slow down, say no, and go against the flow (e.g. Wu, 2003).

The possible conclusions to draw from both Browning's and Milgram's research is that people generally have a tendency to go with the flow, to blindly obey a group/authority without much consideration of other people's well-being. How can this then be understood from an educational point of view? How can it be understood from the perspective of education's social responsibility for public interest values and for the development of a vibrant democracy? What of the extensive 'uncomfortable' work of reflexivity required of teacher educators/teachers so that educators do not become mere functionaries of a system blindly following orders, becoming punitive and careless rather than enacting emancipatory practices? It is to this dilemma that we turn in the next chapter.

Conclusion

The purpose of this chapter has been to revive shortcomings in dualism (dichotomy) and essentialism – this time in relation to the notions of weakness and strength. There is a tendency in various societies to cherish strength over weakness, which in accordance to research risks increasing interpersonal violence. At the same time the ethical dimension of democracy stresses the importance of acknowledging everyone's equal value, plurality, and hence implicitly people's weaknesses, which can create tensions and provocations, not least in (teacher) education. Weakness and strength are intimately interlinked with femininity and masculinity as well as a belief that they are fixed traits in women and men (essentialism) and thus important to keep separated (dichotomy). Without claiming that either strength or weakness are solutions to education, this chapter elaborates alternative ways of approaching weakness and strength by turning to philosophy, psychoanalysis, cognitive (psychology) research, intersections and history research.

Questions

1   What kind of spontaneous idea(s) did this chapter evoke in you? Can you put it into words using literature and concepts from this chapter as a point of departure?

2   If you turn your attention to your friends, family, course books, newspapers etc., what kind of images of weakness and strength, as well as femininity and masculinity, are expressed? Use concepts from this chapter to analyse these findings.
3   Reflecting on the notion of intimacy and distance, can you detect a movement between these in education and teaching? If so, please explain in what ways.
4   How do you handle your fast and slow thinking and how can they be related to education? Can you give examples?
5   It is possible to approach weakness and difference in various ways. Drawing on the concepts from this chapter, what can you see in your surroundings (see, for example, the notion of an ethics of alterity, consciousness/subconsciousness, intersections)?
6   Have you encountered any examples of Darwinian strength in the way your teaching practices are understood, either in policy, in higher education settings or in your school settings?
7   What kind of dilemmas in relation to the topic discussed would you like to add, and why?

Supplementary materials

1   Holocaust and Genocide Spring Lecture Series – Professor Christopher Browning, PhD "Ordinary Men as Perpetrators A Reappraisal After Twenty-Five Years", 5 June 2019
https://www.youtube.com/watch?v=aoqsRno-Xzg
2   "Professor Castleberry's Philosophical Lecture Shorts: Emmanuel Levinas and the Face of the Other", 15 November 2013
https://www.youtube.com/watch?v=S-YqKLZDf34
3   Facing Uncertainty in Education – one of the most pressing concerns identified in current European educational discourse
"ECER 2015 Keynote by Sharon Todd", 22 October 2015
Professor Sharon Todd, Head, School of Education, NUI Maynooth, Ireland
https://www.youtube.com/watch?v=Le0sw-PJBG0
4   "Daniel Kahneman: 'Thinking, Fast and Slow' | Talks at Google", 11 November 2011
https://www.youtube.com/watch?v=CjVQJdIrDJ0

Notes

1   Parts of this chapter are freely translated from Swedish to English based on Edling, Silvia. (2016). *Demokratidilemman i läraruppdraget. Att arbeta för lika villkor [Democracy dilemmas in the teacher mission. To strive for equity]*. Stockholm: Liber.
2   *Dagens Nyheter*, 190811, "Britterna har svårt att hantera en kunglighet som vill vara politisk" ["The British people have difficulties handling a royalty who wants to be political"], Katrine Marcal, p. 19, translated from Swedish.
3   See also https://www.vox.com/identities/2017/11/13/16643448/fbi-hate-crimes-2016 (22 October 22 2018); https://www.regeringen.se/regeringens-politik/samling-mot-hot-och-hat/ (22 October 2018).
4   A video of the experiment can be found at: https://www.youtube.com/watch?v=W147ybOdgpE.

References

Aitken, Stuart & Valentine, Gill (2006). *Approaches to human geography*. London, Los Angeles, CA, California & New Delhi: Sage.
Aldama, Arturo (2003). *Violence, bodies, and the color of fear*. Bloomington, IN: Indiana University Press.

Allport, G. W. (1954). *The nature of prejudice*. Reading, MA: Addison-Wesley.
Apple, Michael W. (2012). *Education and power*. New York: Routledge.
Arendt, Hannah (2006 [1963]). *Eichmann in Jerusalem: A report on the banality of evil*. New York: Penguin Books.
Arendt, Hannah. (2004). *The origins of totalitarianism* (1st edn.). New York: Schocken Books.
Arriaza, Gilberto (2003). Overview: The intersection of ideologies of violence. *Social Justice*, 30(3), 1–3.
Arturo, Aldama & Arteaga, Alfred (2003). *Violence and the body: Race, gender and the state*. Bloomington, IN: Indiana University Press.
Avsenik-Nabergoj, Irena (2009). *Longing, weakness, and temptation: From myth to artistic creation*. Newcastle: Cambridge Scholars Publishing.
Bar-Tal, D. (1989). Delegitimization: The extreme case of stereotyping and prejudice. In D. Bar-Tal, C. Graumann, A. Kruglanski & W. Stroebe (eds.), *Stereotyping and prejudice: Changing conceptions*. New York: Springer.
Bauman, Zygmunt (1999). *Culture as praxis* (New edn.). London: Sage.
Bauman, Zygmund (1995). *Life in fragments. Essays in postmodern morality*. Oxford: Basil Blackwell.
Bauman, Zygmunt (2000). *Modernity and the Holocaust*. Ithaca, NY: Cornell University Press.
Bauman, Zygmund (1993). *Postmodern ethics*. Oxford: Basil Blackwell.
Bernstein, B. (2000). *Pedagogy, symbolic control and identity: Theory, research, critique*. Oxford: Rowman & Littlefield.
Brady, A. M. (2016). The regime of self-evaluation: Self-conception for teachers and schools. *British Journal of Educational Studies*, 64(4), 523–541.
Brandt, Mark J. & Henry, P. J. (2012). Gender inequality and gender differences in authoritarianism. *Personality and Social Psychology Bulletin*, 38(10), 1301–1315.
Britzman, Deborah (1998). *Lost subjects, contested objects: Toward a psychoanalytic inquiry of learning*. Albany, NY: State University of New York Press.
Browning, Christopher (1998). *Helt vanliga män: Reservpolisbataljon 101 och den slutliga lösningen i Polen* [Ordinary men: Reserve Police Battalion 101 and the Final Solution in Poland]. Stockholm: Norstedt.
Browning, Christopher (2018). The suffocation of democracy. *New York Review of Books*, 25 October issue, 65(16), 14–17.
Buchholz, Zachary & Boyce, Samantha (2009). *Masculinity: Gender roles, characteristics, and coping*. New York: Nova Science.
Burnett, Jon (2017). Racial violence and the Brexit state. *Race and Class* [*Institute of Race Relations*], 58(4), 85–97.
Caine, Renate Nummela & Caine, Geoffrey (1991). *Making Connections: Teaching and the human brain*. Alexandria, VA: Association for Supervision and Curriculum Development.
Caine, Renate Nummela, Caine, Geoffrey, McLintic, Carol & Klimek, Karl (2005). *Brain/mind learning principles in action. The fieldbook for making connections, teaching and the human brain*. Thousand Oaks, CA: Corwin Press.
Chang, Iris (1998). *The rape of Nankin. The Forgotten Holocaust of World War Two*. London: Penguin.
Chang-Kredl, S. (2018). Challenging public perceptions of childcare teachers through Cixous' ecriture feminine. *Gender and Education*, 30(2), 259–272.
Clark, Marilyn & Grech, Anna (2017). *Journalists under pressure. Unwarranted interference, fear and self-censorship in Europe*. Brussels: Council of Europe.
Cook, C. R., Williams, K. R., Guerra, N. G., Kim, T. E. & Sadek, S. (2010). Predictors of bullying and victimization in childhood and adolescence: A meta-analytic investigation. *School Psychology Quarterly*, 25(2), 65–83.
Crenshaw, Kimberle (1998). Demarginalizing the intersection of race and sex: A black feminist critique of antidiscrimination doctrine, feminist theory, and antiracist politics. In A. Phillips (ed.), *Feminism and politics*. Oxford & New York: Oxford University Press.
Dillon, Christopher (2013). 'Tolerance means weakness': The Dachau concentration camp SS, militarism and masculinity. *Historical Research*, 86(232), 373–417.

Edling, Silvia (2016). *Demokratidilemman i läraruppdraget. Att arbeta för lika villkor* [Democracy dilemmas in the teacher mission. To strive for equity]. Stockholm: Liber.

Edling, Silvia (2009). Ruptured narratives: An analysis of the contradictions within young people's responses to issues of personal responsibility and social violence within an educational context. Dissertation. Uppsala, Sweden: Acta Universitatis Upsaliensis (AUU).

Edling, Silvia (2012/2018). *Vilja andra väl är inte alltid smärtfritt. Att motverka kränkning och diskriminring i förskola och skola.* [Wanting others' wellbeing is not always painless. To oppose violence and discrimination in preschool and school]. Lund, Sweden: Studentlitteratur.

eMORE (2017). An overview of hate crime and hate speech in 9 EU countries. Towards a common approach to prevent and tackle hatred. Project co-funded by the Rights, Equality and Citizenship Programme (2014–2020) of the European Union. Retrieved from www.emoreproject.eu/wp-content/uploads/2017/11/Emore_CountryReport_Nov17web.pdf

Evans, Donald (1975). Moral weakness. *Royal Institute of Philosophy*, 50(193), 295–310.

Foxman, Abraham H. & Wolf, Christopher (2013). *Viral hate. Containing its spread on the Internet.* New York: Palgrave Macmillan.

Francia, Guadalupe & Edling, Silvia (2016). Children's rights and violence: A case analysis at a Swedish boarding school. *Childhood*, 24(1), 1–17.

Freire, P. (1998). *Pedagogy of freedom.* Lanham, MD: Rowman and Littlefield.

Freire, P. (1971). *Pedagogy of the oppressed.* London: Penguin Books.

Frelin, Anneli (2015). Relational underpinnings and professionality – a case study of a teacher's practices involving students with experiences of school failure. *School Psychology International*, 36(6), 589–604.

Gilkey, Joseph William (2014). Brain and learning. *Journal of Arts and Humanities*, 3(1), 50–56.

Giroux, H. A. (1988). *Teachers as intellectuals: Toward a critical pedagogy of learning.* Westport, CT: Bergin & Garvey.

Goof, Phillip, Eberhardt, Jennifer, Williams, Melissa & Jackson, Matthew (2008). Not yet human: implicit knowledge, historical dehumanization, and contemporary consequences (PDF). *Journal of Personality and Social Psychology*, 94(2), 292–306.

Goswami, Usha (2006). *Cognitive development: The learning brain.* New York: Psychology Press.

Greene, Maxine (2008). *The dialectic of freedom. New introduction by Michelle Fine.* New York & London: Teachers College Press, Columbia University.

Grosz, Elizabeth (1995). *Space, time, and perversion: Essays on the politics of bodies.* New York: Routledge.

Grosz, Elizabeth & Probyn, Elspeth (1995). *Sexy bodies: The strange carnalities of feminism.* London: Routledge.

Gunter, H. (2001). Critical approaches to leadership in education. *Journal of Educational Enquiry*, 2(2), 94–108.

Hancock, A.-M. (2007). When multiplication doesn't equal quick addition. *Perspectives on Politics*, 5(1), 63–79.

Haslam, Nick (2006). Dehumanization: An integrative review. *Personality and Social Psychology Review*, 10(3), 252–264.

Heinze, Eric (2016). *Hate speech and democratic citizenship.* New York: Oxford University Press.

Hoffman, Tobias (2008). *Weakness of will, from Plato to the present* (Vol. 49). New York: The Catholic University Press.

van den Hoopaard, Deborah (2009). *'I was the man'. The challenges of masculinity for older men.* New York: Nova Science.

James, Christine A. (1997). Feminism and masculinity: Reconceptualising the dichotomy between reason and emotion. *International Journal of Sociology and Social Policy*, 17(1/2), 129–152.

Jönsson, Kutte (2009). Fysisk fostran och föraktet för svaghet. En kritisk analys av hälsodiskursens moraliska imperativ. *Educate*, 1(7), 7–20. Retrieved from http://dspace.mah.se/dspace/handle/2043/8421

Kahneman, Daniel (1973). *Attention and effort.* Englewood Cliffs, NJ: Prentice-Hall.

Kahneman, Daniel (2013). *Thinking, fast and slow* (1st pbk edn.). New York: Farrar, Straus and Giroux.
Kahneman, Daniel, Slovic, Paul & Tversky, Amos (1982). *Judgment under uncertainty: Heuristics and biases.* Cambridge & New York: Cambridge University Press.
Kahneman, Daniel & Tversky, Amos (2000). *Choices, values, and frames.* New York & Cambridge: Russell Sage Foundation, Cambridge University Press.
Kincheloe, J. L. (2004). The knowledges of teacher education: Developing a critical complex epistemology. *Teacher Education Quarterly*, Winter Edition, 49–66.
Kochenderfer, B. J. & Ladd, G. W. (1996). Peer victimization: Manifestations and relations to school adjustment in kindergarten. *Journal of School Psychology*, 34(3), 267–283.
Kristeva, Julia (2010). *Hatred and forgiveness.* New York: Columbia University Press.
Kristeva, Julia (1984). *Revolution in poetic language.* New York: Columbia University Press.
Kristeva, Julia (1991). *Strangers to ourselves.* New York: Columbia University Press.
Kristeva, Julia (2000). *The sense and non-sense of revolt.* New York: Columbia University Press.
Kumashiro, Kevin (2001). *Troubling intersections of race and sexuality: Queer students of color and anti-oppressive education.* Lanham, MD: Rowman & Littlefield.
Larsson, Esbjön (2005). *Från adlig uppfostran till borgerlig utbildning Kungl. Krigsakademien mellan åren 1792 och 1866* [From Nobel upbringing to bourgeois education]. Uppsala, Sweden: Acta Universitatis Upsaliensis (AUU).
Lévinas, Emmanuel (1987). *Collected philosophical papers.* Dordrecht, Netherlands: Kluwer Academic.
Lévinas, Emmanuel (1998). *Entre nous: On thinking-of-the-other.* New York: Columbia University Press.
Levinas, Emmanuel (1981). *Otherwise than being: Or, Beyond essence.* Dordrecht, Netherlands: Kluwer Academic.
Levy, Neil (2011). Resisting 'weakness of the will'. *Philosophy and Phenomenological Research*, 82(1), 134–155.
Lombard, Nancy & McMillan, Lesley (2013). *Violence against women, current theory and practice in domestic abuse, sexual violence and exploitation.* London: Jessica Kingsley Publishers.
Lykke, N. (2004). Between particularism, universalism and transversalism: Reflections on the politics of location of European feminist research and education. *NORA: Nordic Journal of Women's Studies*, 12(2), 72–82.
McCall, L. (2001). *Complex inequality.* New York: Routledge.
McCall, L. (2005). The complexity of intersectionality. *Signs*, 30(3), 1771–1800.
McLaren, P. (2015). *Pedagogy of insurrection from resurrection to revolution.* New York: Peter Lang.
Mele, Alfred (2012). *Backsliding: Understanding the weakness of will.* Oxford & New York: Oxford University Press.
Messerschmidt, James W. (2004). *Flesh and blood: Adolescent gender diversity and violence.* Lanham, MD: Rowman & Littlefield.
Milgram, Stanley (1975). *Lydnad och auktoritet: [experimentsituationer, resultat och utvärdering].* Stockholm: Wahlström & Widstrand.
Mitsopoulou, E. & Giovazolias, T. (2015). Personality traits, empathy and bullying behavior: A meta-analytic approach. *Aggression and Violent Behavior*, 21, 61–72.
Mohanty, Chandra Talpade (1989). On race and voice: Challenges for liberal education in the 1990s. *Cultural Critique*, 14, 179–208.
Mooney Simmie, G. (2020). The power, politics and future of mentoring. In Beverly J. Irby, Linda Searby, Jennifer N. Boswell, Fran Kochan & Rubén Garza (eds.), *The Wiley international handbook of mentoring, paradigms, practices, programs, and possibilities* (1st edn.). Hoboken, NY: John Wiley, pp. 453–469.
Moss, P. (2006). Structures, understandings and discourses: possibilities for re-envisioning the early childhood worker. *Contemporary Issues in Early Childhood*, 7(1), 30–41.
Murphy, D. (2018). Rhetoric-reality contradictions: Examining the discursive positioning of early child care and education practitioners in the Republic of Ireland. PhD thesis. Limerick, Republic of Ireland: University of Limerick.

Nakou, I. (2000). Elementary school teachers' representations regarding school problem behaviour: Problem children in talk. *Educational and Child Psychology*, 17, 91–106.
Nussbaum, Martha Craven (1997). *The feminist critique of liberalism*. Lawrence, KS: Department of Philosophy, University of Kansas.
Offer, John (2014). From 'natural selection' to 'survival of the fittest': On the significance of Spencer's refashioning of Darwin in the 1860s. *Journal of Classical Sociology*, 14(2), 156–177.
Ofstad, Harald (2012). *Vårt förakt för svaghet*. Stockholm, Sweden: Karneval förlag.
Pickering, Michael (2001). *Stereotyping: The politics of representation*. Basingstoke, UK: Palgrave.
Pillow, W. (2003). Confession, catharsis, or cure? Rethinking the uses of reflexivity as methodological power in qualitative research. *International Journal of Qualitative Studies in Education*, 16(2), 175–196.
Poynting, Scott & Donaldsson, Scott (2005). Snakes and leaders: Hegemonic masculinity in ruling-class boys' boarding schools. *Men and Masculinities*, 7(325), 325–346.
de los Reyes, Paulina & Martinsson, Lena (2005). *Olikhetens paradigm: Intersektionella perspektiv på o (jäm)likhetsskapande*. Lund, Sweden: Studentlitteratur.
Rydgren, Jens (2018). The radical right. An introduction. In Jens Rydgren (ed.), *The Oxford handbook of the radical right*. Oxford: Oxford University Press.
Sanderson, Kath (2012). Health education in schools: Strengths and weaknesses in relation to long-term behaviour development. *Perspectives in Public Health*, 132(1), 19–20.
Shields, Stephanie (2008). Gender: An intersectionality perspective. *Sex Roles*, 59, 301–311.
Simon, Roger (2012). The pedagogical insistence of public memory. In Peter C. Seixas (ed.), *Theorizing historical consciousness*. Toronto, Canada, Buffalo, New York & London: University of Toronto Press, pp. 183–201.
Slee, P. T. (1994). Situational and interpersonal correlates of anxiety associated with peer victimization. *Child Psychiatry and Human Development*, 25, 97–107.
Smith, J. D., Schneider, B., Smith, P. K. & Ananiadou, K. (2004). The effectiveness of whole-school anti-bullying programs: A synthesis of evaluation research. *School Psychology Review*, 33, 548–561.
Smith, P. K. & Brain, P. (2000). Bullying in schools: Lessons from two decades of research. *Aggressive Behavior*, 26(1), 1–9.
Stenqvist, Catharina (2005). *Simone Weil och det okränkbara. Krig, våld och föraktet för svaghet*. Lund, Sweden: Nordic Academic Press.
Thornberg, Robert & Wänström, Linda (2018). Bullying and its association with altruism toward victims, blaming the victims, and classroom prevalence of bystander behaviors: A multilevel analysis. *Social Psychology of Education*, 21(5), 1133–1151.
Todd, Sharon (2009). *Toward an imperfect education: Facing humanity, rethinking cosmopolitanism*. Boulder, CO: Paradigm.
Ungdomsstyrelsen/Swedish Agency for Youth and Society (2013). *Tio orsaker till avhopp*. Retrieved from www.mucf.se/sites/default/files/publikationer_uploads/tioorsaker.pdf
Waldron, Jeremy (2014). *The harm in hate speech*. Harvard, CA: Harvard University Press.
Wickström, Anette (2013). From individual to relational strategies: Transforming a manual-based psycho-educational course at school. *Childhood*, 21(2), 215–228.
Wu, Kuang-ming (2003). Violence as weakness: In China and beyond. *Dao: A Journal of Comparative Philosophy*, 3(1), 7–28.
Young, Iris Marion (1990a). *Justice and the politics of difference*. Princeton, NJ: Princeton University Press.
Young, Iris Marion (1990b). *Throwing like a girl and other essays in feminist philosophy and social theory*. Bloomington, IN: Indiana University Press.

7 Teacher reflexivity

Introduction

In former times, requirements for teachers to become reflective were connected to the moral goods of education and were concerned with developing ethical and caring teachers with capabilities to think and reflect on their practices (Santoro, 2017). According to Brookfield (1995), teachers do reflective work drawing from four lenses simultaneously: self-evaluation, evaluation with a peer/critical friend, evaluation from their students and, finally, connection to the literature. A number of educationalists, from their understanding of the politics of knowledge (see Chapter 5) suggest that teachers need to interrogate their positioning at a far deeper reflexive level, to do the hard and often uncomfortable work of inner development in order to reveal personal bias and prejudices and to enact pluralistic practices (Pillow, 2003). Schooling has changed dramatically from a former honour system encompassing the moral goods of teaching to a new value system of competitive individualism, the principle of the market and the primacy of the economic goods of teaching (Bernstein, 2000; Brady, 2016, 2019; Sidorkin, 2016; Tan, 2014). We show how this has reframed reflection and reflexivity as a debased mode of self-evaluation for a performativity turn (Ball, 2003; Brady, 2016, 2019).

Reflection, reflexivity and critical reflexivity, and the role of value systems and ethics in education, has its origins in the work of Dewey and experiential co-enquiry and has generally been considered an important feature of teacher education programmes in higher education (Dewey, 1933). However, the case for reflection and reflexivity has not always been grasped by every teacher educator and policymaker as the same thing and it has proved rather elusive. Functional notions of schooling differ from any understanding of education as an emancipatory and societal practice. Functional views are aligned with a fixation on metrics and with conservative ideologies and serving immediate needs, i.e. the political and economic requirements for a project that secures the status quo and does so, consciously or unconsciously, along the lines of reproduction and colonization (Fielding, 2007; Freire, 1971; McLaren, 2015; Muller, 2018).

Mordal-Moen & Green (2014) speak to a broad-based understanding of reflection and reflexivity along a spectrum of possibilities – from weak reflection connected with a concept of skills, to a mid-way concept of reflection as moving beyond skills to ways of better informing oneself about practice selections and justifications to modes of strong reflection as self-awareness, which are closer to the virtues and values of reflexivity. The notion of the teacher as a reflective and/or reflexive practitioner implies a teacher who is willing to use a double take on their practice experiences, working with themselves and with critical friends, to unlearn, relearn, improve and change. In this regard teachers are not merely partaking in an unthinking practice as clones and functionaries where there is the ever-increased possibility for real and symbolic violence, for unethical practices, for bullying and for reproduction of disadvantage and inequity.

We distinguish between teachers understood as self-evaluators and teacher-researchers for clinical practices (Brookfield, 1995; Macbeath et al., 2000), and teachers engaging with the often uncomfortable work of critical reflexivity, positioning themselves and their practices within a world-orientation and cultural milieu for teaching with heart and integrity, engaging in intellectual activity that requires a clash between theory, practice, research and experience and operating at the risk-laden interface between the personal and the public, with compassion and insight and what Greene (2017) called 'wide-awakeness' for those experiencing oppression (Ball, 2003; Nussbaum, 2010; O'Neill & Bourke, 2016; Palmer, 1997; Santoro & Rocha, 2015).

We have sub-divided the chapter into three sections. First, we interrogate the role of values in education and democracy and the case for reflexivity and show how the new teacher appraisal systems recommended in the *Global Education Reform Movement* (GERM) is influencing policies and practices in teacher education. Second, we examine four different yet inter-related teacher positionings in relation to reflection, reflexivity and critical reflexivity: teacher-as-scientist stance; teacher-as-coach; teacher-as-action researcher and a critically reflexive teacher positioned for an emancipatory and transformative practice. Third, we discuss dilemmas we have encountered as teacher educators with student teachers and experienced teachers in Ireland and Sweden, and our understanding of the inter-sectionality between teacher reflexive practices and the dynamic development of a vibrant, pluralist and decent democracy.

Contemporary notions of teacher appraisal

Different groupings of educationalists and theorists share an interest in teacher reflection – communitarians, positivists and critical scholars – and each school of thought has a different emphasis.

Communitarians take a humanistic and communal-orientation view of education and concentrate on the moral goods of teaching and teacher reflection. They understand reflection as work that takes place on a number of different levels (Korthagen & Vasalos, 2005) and using a wide number of different 'tools', such as written reflections, analysis of stories, reflective diaries, logs of critical incidents and conceptual mapping (Gray, 2007). They are interested in preserving the status quo and cultural heritage and have no aspiration for schooling to contribute to changing society or for allowing something new in the social order to break through (Apple, 2013). In fact communitarians for the most part dismiss outright any notion that schooling and teachers can influence, affect or even begin to change a democratic society in the direction of social justice and equity "possessing the ability and inclination to critically reflect on their roles as educationalists alongside the desire to effect change at the personal, professional and political levels – has been revealed as a vain hope" (Mordal-Moen & Green, 2014, pp. 415–416).

Positivistic scholars focus for the most part on the instrumental and the technical-rational (scientific). Teacher self-regulation is understood as drawing from empirical data to self-evaluate, both self and practices, and is inextricably connected to the policy reform direction desired, and possibly mandated by policymakers and supported by large scale developmental psychology studies. Empirical studies and the notion of the teacher as researcher-in-action aligns well with a neoliberal ideology of competitive individual

Table 7.1 An overview of dilemmas discussed in Chapter 7

Dilemmas
Interplay between reflection versus reflective practitioner
Reflexivity connected to the moral goods of education
versus
Critical Reflexivity connected to emancipatory practices
versus
Self-Evaluation underpinned by performativity

and new modes of teacher appraisal for public accountability that are based on teachers working continually on themselves in predetermined policy directions to show evidence (e.g. data) of continuing improvement and attainment of prescribed outcomes (Ball, 2003, see also Merzano in Supplementary materials). Within this positioning, reflective practice follows a mantra emanating from *Human Capital Theory* that fosters non-recognition of a wider society and/or the role of the school in the generation of a vibrant democracy (Apple, 2013; McLaren, 2015; Lynch, 2015; Tan 2014). Here every teacher is classified as a 'worker' and 'lifelong learner' dedicated to entrepreneurial self-improvement as an 'un-dependent' competitor rather than an inter-dependent individual with proactive membership of a vibrant democratic society. Within the dominant influence of GERM policies, teachers are required to engage in self-evaluation of themselves and their practices and with no explicit requirements for capabilities to critically read the world (Freire, 1971, see also Fielding in Supplementary materials).

By contrast, critical scholars drawing from a number of critical and feminist fields of study understand education as pedagogical and political. They argue that the current new politics of reflection needs to be replaced with a principled politics of resistance. This requires teachers to look at the same time both inward at a deep reflexive level and outward in a world-orientation in order to accurately interpret the world and to change it in the direction of equity and democracy (Freire, 1971; Bleakley, 1999; Lynch, Grummell & Devine, 2012; Mooney Simmie, 2020; Nussbaum, 2010; Santoro, 2017).

In Chapter 5, we showed how the current epistemic dominance of trans-national agencies, such as the World Bank, the Organisation for Economic Co-operation and Development (OECD) and European Commission (EC) are re-shaping schooling and teacher education in the direction of market-led values, competences and skill-sets. The widespread influence of these policy actors is brought about by a small number of pedagogic devices, in particular the method of constant comparison and an over-reliance and fixation on the value of scientific studies and metrics in positivistic research (Muller, 2018; Sellar & Lingard, 2013). These latter studies are purporting to be objective and value-neutral and offer straightforward, manageable and measurable solutions in classrooms and school settings to what are complex, cultural, political and sophisticated educational dilemmas and problems (see Table 7.1).

Method of constant comparison

While international comparison in education systems has been a widespread practice since the 1800s, it has only recently taken on the significance of an exact science and a system of 'datafication' that makes claims of reliability and validity between nation states (OECD, 2013). This can be seen in the high esteem of education systems in different countries – such as Finland, Korea and Singapore – and the international high stakes rivalry to imitate and surpass measurable outcomes and rankings.

This approach of global constant comparison uses new teacher appraisal systems that are soft sculpted by policymakers and the inspectorate and presented as increasing teacher freedom and autonomy (Brady, 2019). These soft sculpted modes require, and often mandate, teachers practices in communal orientation (e.g. structured observations, peer-feedback, peer-coaching) following tightly regulated and prescribed curricula and reporting outcomes of their self-evaluation in oral ways (e.g. public presentations, peer observation), in written ways (e.g. portfolio assessment) and generally in very public ways that support a constant comparison gaze by external policy actors (e.g. inspectors). In this neoliberal imaginary teachers act as self-regulating entrepreneurs (Ball, 2003) showcasing desired outcomes as carbon copies of what has already been established as 'best practices'.

This method of constant comparison has reframed former notions of teachers as reflective practitioners – more connected to practical philosophy than psychology of education – and replaced this with notions of teaching as an evidence-based clinical practice, as a new mode of teacher public accountability and set within an empirical field of laboratory experimentation and (action) research and repositioning the teacher-as-scientist, teacher-as-action-researcher and teacher-as-coach.

Over-reliance on scientific research

Nowadays, insistence by policymakers and positivistic researchers alike that teaching is fully described as an exact science set within a value-neutral field of data analysis is supported by replacement of the terminology of education with a new language of learning for a clinical practice (Biesta, 2012). Developmental psychology has grown in importance as the science capable of showing how all young people learn with definable characteristics of the quality teacher. In this way, the arts and humanities are downplayed, such as history of education (e.g. culture and heritage) and philosophy (asking why and reasoning about meaning-making), as teacher identity, self-efficacy and professionalism are foregrounded (Nussbaum, 2010).

Greenbank (2003, p. 791), using a model by Rokeach considers values as a multi-dimensional cluster of moral, competency, personal, social and political values. He makes a good argument for positivistic researchers to be required to share their reflexive positioning. These researchers claim value-free neutrality that does not require them to inform readers where they are positioned. Positivistic researchers claim to search for the objective 'truth' versus Foucault's notion of regimes of truth, and to do this from a value-free and disinterested positioning, claiming personal freedom from political, social and educational beliefs and expectations. These positivistic claims of value-free neutrality and objectivity are challenged as delusional and arise from a flawed positioning. While it is recognized that a positivistic approach often fails to "provide adequate insights into the social and contextual complexity of the educational process" (Greenbank, 2003, p. 793), it has worryingly, in the last decade, gained far higher status among governments and research funders than it had before. Positivists hold a dominant positioning and power of influence with policymakers and politicians as the global search is underway for measurable, market-oriented, reproducible and manageable solutions to complex dynamic real-world moral, social and political problems in education.

In this chapter, we are not arguing for conducting biased research that is susceptible to the selective use of information but instead we are making the case that all researchers are coming from somewhere and as such it is necessary for all educational researchers, including positivistic researchers, to publicly share their reflexive positioning. This ethics of research also applies to teachers, especially when we consider recent notions of the teacher-as-scientist, teacher-as-researcher and teacher-as-action-researcher undertaking a clinical practice (Simić, Jokić & Vukelić, 2019). Playing dual roles of teacher and researcher may have unintended consequences and may in some instances undermine the relationship of trust and asymmetrical power relations between teachers and students. Greenback asserts students may feel short-changed and/or deceived by teachers who take an interest in them not for altruistic reasons but for research purposes – for objectification as part of a data-mining operation.

Teacher positioning

In the next section, we examine four possible positions of teacher reflection and reflexivity depending on whether or not the approach taken is concerned within an understanding of good teaching as a moral (apolitical) individual endeavour for an evidence-based clinical practice (teacher-as-scientist stance; teacher-as-coach) or as a moral (apolitical) individual endeavour connected to a communitarian-orientation inclusive of the technical-rational (teacher-as-action-researcher) or for a notion of good teaching as a moral and political orientation for a collective (and non-identical) endeavour that includes deliberative spaces for the aesthetic and the ethical risk of education, spaces for challenging the status quo, for critical reflexivity and holistic reflection (Biesta, 2013; Giroux, 1988). Theses ontological and epistemological positions (i.e. vales and knowledge-based positions) have been similarly articulated by Bleakley (1999) as the technical-rational (which we understand as the teacher-as-scientist); the postmodern deconstructive (which we define as teacher-as-coach); humanistic emancipatory (which we have called teacher-as-action-researcher) and radical phenomenological (for critical reflexivity).

Teacher-as-scientist stance

The teacher-as-scientist stance has grown rapidly and exponentially in GERM policy literature in the last decade (OECD, 2013). This stance perceives good teaching as a clinical practice tied to empirical findings. The teachers' stance as a scientist is to effectively operate a technocratic practice of visible learning and to relay successful outcomes of best practices using data and hard evidence. In this regard, a teacher's reflective role is understood as a compact of technical competences for self-evaluation, based on an improvement model for the competitive individual (MacBeath et al., 2000; see also Merzano in Supplementary materials). Within this positioning the teachers' task is to engage in self-reflection using straightforward policy implementation of pre-specified policy imperatives and directives for well-rehearsed learner-centred pedagogies (see Chapter 3). These include structured observations and oral peer-feedback mechanisms, experimental (enquiry) activities using formats, such as portfolio development that showcases progress and has affordances for constant comparison with other teachers and schools to continually report successful outcomes in standardized formats to policy actors, such as school administrators, parents and inspectors.

Good teaching and reflection, using this positioning becomes a highly-skilled performative task of self-evaluation that has a practice turn and is grasped as situated learning and applying research that informs 'what works' as it seeks to arrive at a well-defined destination and known solutions that are already well charted (Black & Wiliam, 1998; Wiliam, 2014). The teacher is continually planning, diagnosing, measuring and regulating themselves and their practices against a 'charter' of definitive metrics, weights and measures that are already worked out in this model seeking to achieve excellence in instruction and training. Education and teaching are understood as learning systems – as the science of how young people learn and how quality teachers apply standardized knowledge – using results and data from psychology and behaviour studies for school effectiveness and improvement (Hattie, 2012).

A study by Simić et al. (2019), funded by the Ministry of Education to "prepare teachers to be agents of education reform and thus educate them for reflective practice" (p. 1) reported on an intervention in pre-service teacher education, where 36 student teachers undertook an 8-hour alternative programme based on developmental psychology. The aim of the intervention was to advance the teacher-as-scientist stance and to teach students the importance of cooperating with others "to continually question and improve themselves" (p. 14). The researchers claimed that once a teacher is well intentioned and uses 'good reflection' and has the know-how to be a 'good scientist' then that is all that is required to assure quality learning:

> both a good 'person-as-scientist' and a good 'reflective practitioner' are aware that there are no privileged positions, but that it is necessary to approach different viewpoints in a critical manner, in order to check them and revise one's own beliefs and acts, if necessary.
>
> (Simić et al., 2019, p. 2)

The intervention used skilled psychology interventions to develop trust and support students in opening up their personal backgrounds to group scrutiny so that a zone of collective meaning-making could be established: "what we identified as a potential zone for negotiation over meaning is the implicative dilemma we described with the superordinate construct *personal-professional*, with both poles of the construct implying both a *good* and a *bad* teacher" (p. 9). However, this process often appeared akin to psychotherapy and brought some students "to tears and caused strong emotions" and for others "this technique was too threatening and overwhelming" (p. 14).

Teacher-as-coach

In a similar view to the teacher as quasi-scientist, the teacher-as-coach continues a practice turn only this time the message of reflective practice relies on an apprenticeship of observation, structured observations and coach-led feedback loops. The novice teacher is learning how to conduct their self-evaluation from observing, copying and imitating a master teacher, presented as an expert teacher who is acting as coach. As there are no affordances or possibility within this stance for critically reading the world, the world of school and/or the wider world, this runs the risk of student teachers becoming clones of experienced teachers who can in many instances use differential power relations in oppressive ways and with serious employment consequences (Sundli, 2009).

Here the successful application of knowledge relies on modes of social constructivism and a communal orientation of reflection among teachers. Teachers are positioned as lifelong learners, continually re-working and self-regulating themselves and their practices and doing it along a continuum of teacher education for a well-defined life cycle with stages that start with *Initial Teacher Education* and move to *Induction Teacher Education* and then later to *In-Career Teacher Education*.

While research generally shows that experienced teachers are not that highly regarded, being seen for the most part as out-of-touch, out-of-date and even lazy to take on reform demands, they are nonetheless, within this understanding of teacher-as-coach, credited with having tacit knowledge (reflection-in-action) that needs to be relayed to novice teachers through modes of direct observation, structured observations and reflective coach-led practices and this it appears can be done unproblematically and uncritically. Fielding's (2007) typology of schooling for a *High-Performance Learning Organization* shows how this teacher-as-coach stance, embedded in an evidence-based practice for the (competitive) individual, is aligned with the exchange value of a market-led discourse of schooling, training and instruction rather than emancipation and community building (see Supplementary materials).

Teacher-as-action-researcher

The notion of the teacher-as-action-researcher takes a softer view of reflection than previously discussed stances of teacher-as-scientist and teacher-as-coach. Reflections gets positioned in the field of practical philosophy and a communitarianism that acknowledges the 'swampy lowlands' of practice (Schön, 1983) and the need to display artistry and style rather than skills (Brookfield, 1995). According to Bleakley (1999), the failure of Schön's model (see Meirdirk talking about Schön's writings in Supplementary materials) was not that it prized the indeterminate swampy zones of practice as an artistry involving 'uncertainty, uniqueness, and value conflict' (p. 315) but that it promoted a form of non-rigorous enquiry. Situated reflection that fails to connect with a theoretical knowledge base and fails to abstract for an advanced practice keeps practitioners stuck in cycles of practice-based mundane knowledge. According to Bernstein (2000), being left without theory and the capability for abstraction is to be left without an overview and a why, which can be taken as akin to a mode of postmodern slavery.

Within this humanistic (empowerment) movement practitioners interrogate the inherent contradictions of their living practices and do this using steps and stages that redirect the teacher-as-action-researcher toward an iterative cycle of *Planning, Action and Reflection* (PAR) (Whitehead, 1989). The teacher-as-action-researcher is required to subject themselves to a continuing interrogation of their self and their practices for personal empowerment and professional development (Edge, 2011). Bleakley (1999) problematises this notion of developmentalism as:

> progressivism, stages, steps, skills and knowledge hierarchies, spiral curricula, and overarching dogma that one must always proceed from the simple to the complex. Such developmentalism denies the value of suffering the complex right from the start, perhaps relishing open endedness, chaos, or unpredictability in learning, and valuing its ambiguities, paradoxes and twists.
>
> (p. 318)

Teacher-as-action-researcher fulfils neoconservative requirements of a conduct of conduct (Petersen & Millei, 2016) as it gestures in the direction of good teaching as an evidence-based communitarian practice. Reflective teachers within this positioning are expected to exercise a confined agency that is tightly regulated and prescribed by a hierarchy of

Figure 7.1 Reflection generally tells you what you look like?

knowledgeable others. A recent study in Australia, by Ryan et al. (2019) grasps good teaching as being about an application of knowledge using notions such as sometimes 'teachery' and at other times 'researchery'. While the study claims to take power relations into account, it fails to problematise differential power relations and the relative weightings given to knowledge forms by various actors. The study notices some epistemic pitfalls and calls for better brokerage of spaces between different institutions in education.

Studies of reflection within this teacher-as-action-researcher stance situate the teacher within a given context and understand reflective practice as a relational endeavour that requires a combination of artistry, communal orientation, situated learning, value interrogation and technical rationality (see Figure 7.1). However, this positionality while communitarian is concerned with teaching as a moral (apolitical) endeavour within a hierarchical system of knowers that fails to connect teachers' practices with a world-orientation (political) and thereby works to secure and to reproduce the status quo.

Teachers' critical reflexive positioning

The fourth positioning connects the teacher and their practices to a world-orientation – as critical reflexivity – where there is connectivity to intellectual, critical and caring approaches and an extensive toolkit needed for problem posing and radical interruption of practices and consideration of the wider moral, social and political issues of the day. The teacher understood within this critical reflexive positioning is involved in emancipatory and dynamic practices, where in addition to acting as cultural workers and public intellectuals – passing on cultural heritage and new forms of knowledge and value systems – they are using and making spaces that set the scene for a new social and political order to burst through. The educator therefore works within the paradox of a principled politics of resistance, looking back to the past while making space for the future in a holistic, ethical, aesthetic, political, moral, social and emancipatory view of reflection and education.

Reflexivity can be understood as teachers seeking to position themselves inside multi-dimensional value systems taking the cultural milieu into account and, at the same time, developing sufficient detachment from practices to achieve a trustworthy even if unfinished awareness of self, practice and world-orientation (Greenbank, 2003; Mordal-Moen & Green, 2014). Some educationalists believe that greater reflexivity in research is "at best self-indulgent, narcissistic and tiresome" (Pillow, 2003, p. 176) and others suggest that reflexivity is not a panacea for transcendence and its limits need to be acknowledged. Pillow presents this reflexive work of self-analysis and political awareness as a necessary and yet imperfect way to do reflexivity that takes dilemmas into account, where "messy texts are many sited, intertextual, always open ended, and resistant to theoretical holism, but always committed to cultural criticism" (pp. 187–188). Pillow problematises "reflexivities of discomfort" (p. 188) for a "positioning of reflexivity not as clarity, honesty, or humility, but as practices of confounding disruptions – at times even a failure of our language and practices" (p. 192). Pillow argues this is a better way of being accountable to peoples' struggles and our own self-representation:

> this is not easy or comfortable work and thus should not be situated as such. The qualitative research arena would benefit from more 'messy' examples, examples that may not always be successful, examples that do not seek a comfortable, transcendent end-point but leave us in the uncomfortable realities of doing engaged qualitative research.
>
> (Pillow, 2003, p. 193)

(See also Pillow and others in Supplementary materials.)

Critical reflection and critical reflexivity are not about securing the status quo, but about using theory and an extensive intellectual and caring toolkit to interrupt and to ensure that classrooms and schools do not become unwittingly, and often unconsciously, agents of reproduction of inequity, whereby reforms simply result in more advantage for the already advantaged and continue to disadvantage the disadvantaged. We are reminded by Apple (2013) that an age-old question of the purpose of education has always been about whether society changes schools – given that curriculum is defined as a selection from culture – or whether schools can have an impact and change society? This is concerned with education's social responsibility for public interest values (Lynch, 2015). This concern is particularly pertinent today when there is a slow suffocation of democracy in the public sphere globally (Browning, 2018) and where in public schooling, teachers' democratic assignment has been reduced to simply teaching for or about democracy and about becoming compliant civic beings where citizenship is viewed as participation and duty with no affordance for questioning authority or critically reading the world (Edling & Mooney Simmie, 2018; Mooney Simmie & Edling, 2016, 2019).

What is at stake is the hard and uncomfortable work of critical reflexivity (see Figure 7.2) for a holistic and emancipatory view of education and teaching (Biesta & Miedema, 2002). This involves being willing to do the hard work of reflexive positioning of self as well as the work of interpretation of the wider world. Bleakley (1999) grounds his construct of critical reflexivity for holistic reflexivity in radical phenomenology, in the aesthetic rather than the functional, as a "fourth-order, as a radical reflection, or holistic reflexivity, that, as Sontag

Figure 7.2 The psychiatrist's couch symbolizes the uncomfortable work of critical reflexivity.

observes, offers a state of grace, a gift of aesthetic sensitivity and elegance that also constitutes a monitoring as a reflexive awareness" (p. 326). In this way, he offers a definition of holistic reflexivity as "reflection-as-action + aesthetic co-intentionality + ethical reflexivity (or ecological co-intentionality), within a house of being that is language at its limits" (p. 328). Bleakley's construct of holistic reflexivity is an "inclusive ecological or caring act of reflection as well as an appreciative gesture, with an explicit concern for otherness and difference" (p. 328).

There are few examples of application of approaches of critical reflexivity in the research literature. One study by Thomas & Vavrus (2019) problematises this uncomfortable hard work of critical reflexivity by two international scholars involved in advocating for and promoting *Learner-Centred Pedagogy* (LCP), as a new reform in week-long workshops with Tanzanian teachers, between 2008 and 2015. During their critical reflexive study, the researchers started to question the prescribed nature of this universal pedagogy for its capacity to act as a Western colonization project, its uncritical stance in relation to allowing affordances for alternative pedagogies to be considered and its eschewing of traditional teacher-centred practices of Tanzanian teachers in their contexts, particularities and cultures.

Another critical reflexive study reveals disinclinations involved for skills-minded teacher educators to proactively engage with critical thinking, critical consciousness and a higher level of abstraction and theoretical knowledge for successful interruption of routinised practices. The study demonstrates Physical Education teacher educators' pragmatic skill-based mind-set and their reluctance to engage in depth with reflexivity in one teacher education institute in Norway (Mordal-Moen & Green, 2014).

Dilemmas in practice

Final year undergraduate students in Ireland grappling with understandings of teacher professionalism tended to opt for moral (apolitical) understandings of becoming a critically reflective teacher. This positioned undergraduate teachers as engaging in relational practices with a strong emphasis on being a moral and caring person but without grasping or problematising any wider democratic assignment. It appears from comments below that teachers' democratic assignment was not considered a live dynamic issue worth troubling, and where it was considered it was quickly reduced to social reproduction, maintaining an existing fixed and static (police) order rather than offering any 'agonistics', interruption or resistance in order to allow something new to burst through. One male student teacher suggested that he would like to develop the image of caring and moral person:

> I feel I could develop this aspect of my teaching by focusing on being fair and equal to all students. I would try to develop this image by building greater understanding and relationships with the students. When you are a new teacher to a school it can be hard to build relationships at the beginning until you get to know the students a bit better … I would look to become involved in any sports or other communities which would help build relationships with students outside the classroom.
> (Student teacher comment at a tutorial on becoming a teacher in Ireland)

Another male student teacher in Ireland felt comfortable with a view of himself as a caring and moral person:

> I feel that if in some way I show qualities and kindness it may develop them as a person. I would ensure I was one hundred percent fair and non-biased of how I treated students. I would conduct myself in such a way that my qualities would be projected onto the students as many see the educator as a role model. As a[n] NQT (Newly Qualified Teacher), you are new to the school you must develop the respect of the students. I would rely heavily on the opinion of experienced teachers in school already to seek guidance.
> (Student teacher comment at a tutorial on becoming a teacher in Ireland)

A female student felt that this was the most striking for her and that the notion of acting as a:

> civic and cultural being was the least striking for me. I think this is because I am not highly engaged with politics etc. However, I feel it is necessary to keep up [to] date on what will/is affecting us in society. I connected least with this one. Also my manner and attitude in lessons meant students enjoyed lessons and worked well because they felt comfortable. Students were not anxious expressing troubles or difficulties. I related back to my own educational experience where I learned and developed much more when the teacher/professional was genuinely interested in students' well-being and took the time to get to know their students.
> (Student teacher comment at a tutorial on becoming a teacher in Ireland)

Lonergan's (2016) doctoral study examined understandings and perspectives of secondary school teachers in Ireland in relation to a new construct of Teacher Professional

Learning. Lonergan described something of the struggle she underwent to reveal her critical reflexive positioning:

> I aimed to reflect critically on the influence of my own background, assumptions, positioning, feelings, behaviour while also attending to the impact of wider organisational, discursive, ideological and political contexts. … while I was teaching abroad in [country X] the curriculum of the school was highly structured and prescribed. … teachers taught one concept at a time using the schools' 'Points System'. A system of academic tracking, a computerised method of detecting 'gaps in knowledge', allowed the school administration to closely monitor the progress of each individual on a weekly basis. [This] was a stifling system of surveillance and monitoring because there was no room for creative and imaginative teaching outside a technocratic system of performativity. … I feel this is why the work of Michael Fielding (2007) connected with me.
>
> (Lonergan, 2016, p. 17)

The experienced teachers partaking in her study (n=162), located through the Teaching Council expressed concern about their practices undergoing rapid change – from primarily about the moral goods of education to becoming governed by the principle of a new market-led discourse. This is captured by a male business teacher of 17 years in the study:

> I spent months this year reading this book and that book and this paper and that paper, you can't tell that to the IMF (International Monetary Fund) so I understand why you know for economic reasons they have to bring in box ticking bureaucratic CPD (continuous professional development). I've got friends in the UK and they show me all this stuff about individual targets and graphing this and that, and it's just rubbish.
>
> (Lonergan, 2016, pp. 221–222)

Amy, an Art teacher for 20 years in a community college talked about the gaps between "in-service training and then coming back to the school and realising it's about results" (p. 222). However she was conscious that changes were not culturally confined "it's not just about individual schools, it's about every school in society". John felt that prescribing reflection missed the point and only served to reveal at any one time the political, philosophical and economic agenda underpinning education: "[the preferred notion of reflection at any one time] and this here is my cynical bit often seems to follow a very, very prescribed political and economic agenda [more or less stating] reflect the way you're expected to" (Lonergan, 2016, p. 222).

In this book we have shown how the preferred policy imperative for contemporary self-evaluation is interlaced with an expressed urgency for teachers to become neoliberal subjects (Ball, 2003; Brady 2016, 2019). While many experienced teachers in Lonergan's study claimed to draw from theory in their practices there was no teacher who explicitly understood their role as problem-posing and troubling wider moral, social and political (emancipatory and democratic) issues. However, experienced teachers were aware of differential power relations and shared how they understood what Santoro (2017) and others named the ethical suppression of teachers' agency and voices within a fixation on metrics and elevation of empirically based evidence in good teaching. Peter, a physical education and biology teacher with seven years of teaching experience captured this in his comment that:

> Research is usually funded by somebody who wants the results. ... the commissioner of the research might not necessarily listen to the experiences of the teacher, once the decision was made by those in power. There's not much we teachers can do because we don't have the power, we might have the power if we go through the (trade) unions. ... but you can see what's happening, they have applied quite a lot of pressure on every teacher. ... so research is important. ... but the way research is conducted is up to the commissioner really because the money's going that way, nobody's doing research for free, maybe somebody is but I don't know about it.
>
> (Lonergan, 2016, pp. 223–224)

Conclusions

In this chapter we aimed to unravel the multiple positionings of reflection, reflexivity, critical reflexivity and self-evaluation in teacher education, situating them as one of four positions along a spectrum of stances (Mordal-Moen & Green, 2014). This gave an understanding of reflective teachers acting as scientists, coaches, action researchers and/or as interrogating a critical reflexive positioning for a holistic reflexivity. The various positionings reveal whether good teaching is understood as a moral (apolitical) endeavour for the individual (teacher-as-scientist/coach), as a moral (apolitical) communitarian endeavour for securing the status quo and/or a moral and political orientation of a collective (yet non-identical) endeavour for education's social responsibility for public-interest values and emancipation, with capability to challenge the status quo for a vibrant and pluralist democracy.

As stated in previous chapters, our preferred view of democracy is for a strong democracy acting as a living system of vibrant exchange and dilemmatic spaces in the public sphere. This is different from passive views of democracy as assumed and given (e.g. electoral democracy) or compliant views of participatory democracy for securing the status quo in a diminished polity (e.g. where contrarian views and minority viewpoints are neither tolerated nor welcomed). This latter understanding of strong democracy, and teachers' democratic assignment, aligns with an evolving critical reflexive positioning. This fourth dimension of holistic reflexivity requires ongoing self-interrogation, rigorous analysis of practice and interconnectivity with wider moral, social and political issues of the day (Bleakley, 1999; Greenbank, 2003; Pillow, 2003). This connects teachers with a multidimensional cluster of value systems, multiple forms of knowledge, ethics, aesthetics, political awareness and activism, co-inquiry and co-intentionality. The inward-outward focus of critical reflexivity requires critical friendships as a shared endeavour among all policy actors, and extensive intellectual resources for teaching as an advanced practice rather than a debased mode of self-evaluation that is in bad taste and confined to the 'terrors of performativity' (Ball, 2003; Brady, 2016, 2019; Giroux, 1988).

We finish with a quote from Brady (2019), whose critique of self-evaluation used by the inspectorate of the *Department of Education and Skills* in Ireland leaves many unanswered questions: What is it that really matters in teaching? Of course, in a certain sense, technique, in the mechanical sense, is important. But is that all that teaching is, the employment of a specific technique? And if it is not, then can we measure teaching in the same ways that we would measure technique? These questions, seemingly lost in the urgency of policy, may open up a deeper discussion around what it means to be a teacher, and how we can more authentically evaluate good teaching, which goes beyond the kinds of performative anxiety that self-evaluation, unfortunately, seems to promote. Indeed, one might argue, that the teacher is anxious, should be anxious, and must learn to live, and work, well with this. What, indeed, is the measure of that?

Questions

1. What kind of spontaneous idea(s) did this chapter evoke in you? Can you put it into words using literature and concepts from this chapter as a point of departure?
2. Why might we need to turn to tensions between reflection, reflexivity and critical reflexivity and values to better grasp dilemmas in the present and to open new spaces for the future?
3. What do you think about the current notion of self-evaluation as a live reduction mechanism of complexity and plurality in relation to (teacher) education and democracy?
4. Can you see patterns of oppression for teachers who are partaking in systems that focus more on reflection and interrogation of self and practices rather than on critically reading the world?
5. What kind of philosophical struggles or ideas can you see in current reflection practices that you have taken part in that inspire you to critically question education and democracy?
6. In relation to what you have read in this chapter regarding the dangers of divorcing knowledge from knower dispositions and values, how would you handle this as a teacher?
7. What kind of dilemmas in relation to the topic discussed would you like to add, and why?

Supplementary materials

1. Associate Professor Wanda Pillow, Dr Sam Sellar and Dr Eva Peterson discuss critical and feminist views of education and policy:
   "Panelist – Lectures: Working the Ruins of Educational Policy", 21 July 2014. https://www.youtube.com/watch?v=MNcbzX36CR0
2. "Becoming a Reflective Teacher", 26 October 2012.
   Presented by Robert J. Merzano
   https://www.youtube.com/watch?v=UgrFx_gE89g
3. Dr Charlotte Meirdirk explains Schön's notion of reflection.
   "Schön's Reflective Practice", 13 July 2007.
   https://www.youtube.com/watch?v=Tzjz-l8L1lc
4. Professor Michael Fielding, author of *Radical Education and the Common School: A democratic alternative*. Manchester, UK: Manchester Metropolitan University, 14 September 2010.
   "Michael Fielding", 4 January 2014.
   https://www.youtube.com/watch?v=uvqcEVkwjcc

References

Apple, M. W. (2013). *Can schooling change society? Can society change schooling?* New York: Routledge.
Ball, S. J. (2003). The teacher's soul and the terrors of performativity. *Journal of Education Policy*, 18(2), 215–228.
Bernstein, B. (2000). *Pedagogy, symbolic control and identity: Theory, research, critique*. Oxford: Rowman & Littlefield.
Biesta, G. J. J. (2012). Giving teaching back to education: Responding to the disappearance of the teacher. *Phenomenology & Practice*, 6(2), 35–49.
Biesta, G. J. J. (2013). *The beautiful risk of education*. London: Routledge.

Biesta, G. J. J. & Miedema, S. (2002). Instruction or pedagogy? The need for a transformative conception of education. *Teaching and Teacher Education*, 18, 173–181.

Black, P. & Wiliam, D. (1998). Inside the black box: Raising standards through classroom assessment. *Phi Delta Kappan*, October, 139–148.

Bleakley, A. (1999). From reflective practice to holistic reflexivity. *Studies in Higher Education*, 24(3), 315–330.

Brady, A. M. (2019). Anxiety of performativity and anxiety of performance: Self-evaluation as bad faith, *Oxford Review of Education*.

Brady, A. M. (2016). The regime of self-evaluation: Self-conception for teachers and schools. *British Journal of Educational Studies*, 64(4), 523–541.

Brookfield, S. (1995). *Becoming a critically reflective teacher*. San Francisco, CA: Jossey-Bass.

Browning, C. R. (2018). The suffocation of democracy. *New York Review of Books*, 25 October issue, 65(16), 14–17.

Dewey, J. (1933). How we think. A restatement of the relations of reflective thinking and to the education process. Chicago, IL: Henry-Regnery.

Edge, J. (2011). *The reflexive teacher educator in TESOL roots and wings*. London & New York: Routledge.

Edling, S. & Mooney Simmie, G. (2018). Democracy and emancipation in teacher education: A summative content analysis of teacher educators' democratic assignment expressed in policies for Teacher Education in Sweden and Ireland between 2000–2010. *Citizenship, Social, Economics Education*, 17(1), 20–34.

Fielding, M. (2007). The human cost and intellectual poverty of high-performance schooling: Radical philosophy, John Macmurray and the remaking of person-centred education. *Journal of Education Policy*, 22(4), 383–409.

Freire, P. (1971). *Pedagogy of the oppressed*. Harmondsworth, UK: Penguin.

Giroux, H. A. (1988). *Teachers as intellectuals: Toward a critical pedagogy of learning*. Westport, CT: Bergin & Garvey.

Gray, D. (2007). Facilitating management learning: Developing critical reflection through reflective tools. *Management Learning*, 38(5), 495–517.

Greenbank, P. (2003). The role of values in educational research: The case for reflexivity. *British Educational Research Journal*, 29(6), 791–801.

Greene, M. (2017). *The dialectic of freedom. New introduction by Michelle Fine*. New York: Teachers College Press, Columbia University.

Hattie, J. (2012). *Visible learning for teachers maximizing impact on learning*. Abingdon, UK: Routledge.

Korthagen, F. A. & Vasalos, A. (2005). Levels in reflection: Core reflection as a means to enhance professional growth. *Teachers and Teaching: Theory and Practice*, 11(1), 47–71.

Lonergan, J. (2016). Teacher professional learning: Contextual understandings and perspectives of secondary school teachers in Ireland. PhD thesis. Limerick, Republic of Ireland: University of Limerick.

Lynch, K. (2015). Control by numbers: New managerialism and ranking in higher education. *Critical Studies in Education*, 56(2), 190–207.

Lynch, K., Grummell, B. & Devine, D. (2012). *New managerialism in education commercialization, carelessness and gender*. New York: Palgrave Macmillan.

Macbeath, J. with Schratz, M., Meuret, D. & Jakobsen, L. (2000). *Self-evaluation in European schools: A story of change*. London: Routledge.

McLaren, P. (2015). *Pedagogy of insurrection: From resurrection to revolution*. New York: Peter Lang.

Mooney Simmie, G. (2020). The power, politics and future of mentoring. In Beverly J. Irby, Linda Searby, Jennifer N. Boswell, Fran Kochan & Rubén Garza (eds.), *The Wiley international handbook of mentoring, paradigms, practices, programs, and possibilities* (1st edn.). Hoboken, NY: John Wiley, pp. 453–469.

Mooney Simmie, G. & Edling, S. (2016). Ideological governing forms in education and teacher education: A comparative study between highly secular Sweden and highly non-secular Republic of Ireland. *Nordic Journal of Studies in Educational Policy*, 1(32014), 1–12.

Mooney Simmie, G. & Edling, S. (2019). Teachers' democratic assignment: A critical discourse analysis of teacher education policies in Ireland and Sweden. *Discourse Studies in the Cultural Politics of Education*, 40(6), 832–846.

Mordal-Moen, K. & Green, K. (2014). Neither shaking nor stirring: A case study of reflexivity in Norwegian physical education teacher education. *Sports, Education and Society*, 19(4), 415–434.

Muller, J. K. (2018). *The tyranny of metrics*. Princeton, NJ: Princeton University Press.

Nussbaum, M. C. (2010). *Not for profit: Why democracy needs the humanities*. Princeton, NJ: Princeton University Press.

OECD (2013). *Reviews of evaluation and assessment in education. Synergies for better learning. An international perspective on evaluation and assessment*. Paris: OECD Publishing.

O'Neill, J. & Bourke, R. (2010). Educating teachers about a code of ethical conduct. *Ethics and Education*, 5(2), 159–172.

Palmer, P. J. (1997). The heart of a teacher: Identity and integrity in teaching. *Change: The Magazine of Higher Learning*, 29(6), 14–21.

Petersen, E. B. & Millei, Z. (eds.) (2016). *Interrupting the psy-disciplines in education*. London: Macmillan.

Pillow, W. (2003). Confession, catharsis, or cure? Rethinking the uses of reflexivity as methodological power in qualitative research. *International Journal of Qualitative Studies in Education*, 16(2), 175–196.

Ryan, M., Bourke, T., Brownlee, J. L., Rowan, L., Walker, S. & Churchward, P. (2019). Seeking a reflexive space for teaching to and about diversity: Emergent properties of enablement and constraint for teacher educators. *Teachers and Teaching Theory and Practice*, 25(2), 259–273.

Santoro, D. A. (2017). Cassandra in the classroom: Teaching and moral madness. *Studies in Philosophy of Education*, 36, 49–60.

Santoro, D. A. & Rocha, S. D. (2015). Review of Gert J. J. Biesta, The Beautiful Risk of Education. *Studies in Philosophy of Education*, 34, 413–418.

Schön, D. (1983). *The reflective practitioner*. New York: Basic Books.

Sellar, S. & Lingard, B. (2013). The OECD and global governance in education. *Journal of Education Policy*, 28(5), 710–725.

Sidorkin, A. M. (2016). Campbell's Law and the ethics of immensurability. *Studies in Philosophy of Education*, 35, 321–332.

Simić, N., Jokić, T. & Vukelić, M. (2019). Personal construct psychology in preservice teacher education: The path toward reflexivity. *Journal of Constructivist Psychology*, 32(1), 1–17.

Sundli, L. (2009). Mentoring – A new mantra for education. *Teaching and Teacher Education*, 23, 201–214.

Tan, E. (2014). Human capital theory: A holistic criticism. *Review of Educational Research*, 84(3), 411–445.

Thomas, M. A. M. & Vavrus, F. K. (2019). The Pluto problem: Reflexivities of discomfort in teacher professional development. *Critical Studies in Education*.

Whitehead, J. (1989). Creating a living educational theory from questions of the kind, 'How do I improve my practice?'. *Cambridge Journal of Education*, 19(1), 41–52.

Wiliam, D. (2014). Dylan William: Formative assessment. YouTube video clip. Retrieved from www.youtube.com/watch?v=sYdVe5O7KBE

8 Teachers' democratic assignment

Introduction

In the light of past knowledge humanity is characterized by seemingly endless struggles between various values, not least emancipation from different forms of oppression and the need to dominate others. The field of education and hence teacher education is not neutral, i.e. liberated from these social tensions, it is most certainly a product of it. Seeing that education plays a major role in preparing students for the future, questions like *what kind of future are we preparing them for?* is highly important to pose.

The purpose of teacher education institutions is to provide future teachers with whatever is deemed as important for children and young people to know in the society they live in today, while being aware that what is understood as important might change when student teachers graduate. This implies a symbiotic relationship between education and teacher education. Moreover, while teacher education is strongly regulated by the state, rendering aims such as qualification, socialization and emancipation to be discussed and negotiated on a political level (e.g. Hallsén, 2013; Öberg Tuleus, 2008; Krantz, 2009) it is at the same time regarded as an education for professionals based on autonomy, professional language, ethics, and responsibility. Teacher education is as such an interesting phenomenon in its position between various entities like:

- Teacher education/education
- Political governing forms/professionalism
- Teaching as something that is taught about (teaching as an object)/teaching that takes form by subjects for subjects (teaching as a practice)
- Teaching the familiar/unfamiliar
- Political order/individual and (professional) freedom.

A teacher (educator) caught in the web of policy regulations might say that 'I can't pose this question, since those in power have decided what to do for me'. Contrary to this stance and with regard to the broad field of knowledge about education and democracy we argue that there need to be spaces in education where these kinds of questions are asked and discussed.

Since the end of the World Wars and their horrors in the 20th century, democracy has obtained a crucial position in educational policy to secure peace, everyone's equal value, justice, and social well-being in general. Currently there are tendencies to reduce the space and meaning of democracy towards more technical and narrow interpretations (Edling and Mooney Simmie, 2018; Mooney Simmie & Edling, 2019).

Figure 8.1 A cloud/overview of value tensions and hence dilemmas discussed in the book.

At the same time it is important to remember that democracy in itself is not perfect and quite meaningless without an interpretation of what is meant by it. Democracy as an ideological governing form looks very different from country to country and even (teacher) education institution to (teacher) education institution. It is therefore important to gather a broad set of analytical tools that make it possible to interpret society around us and place these interpretations in relation to what is desirable.

A central driving force in this book has been *to take the democratic assignment in (teacher) education seriously* by starting from experiences of dilemmas by teachers and student teachers in a selected part of Sweden and the Republic of Ireland. Indeed, rather than providing a handbook with solutions locked into a tight echo chamber, we strive to open up in this book contradictory voices and tensions which are placed in relationship to **knowledge about, in** and **for democracy**.

The dilemmas in the book have evolved around seemingly dualistic values with the intention of showing that either–or solutions are not feasible due to the complexities residing in education as a human and relational practice and which involve a multitude of purposes. Here the values are presented as a cloud used as a springboard for discussion and debate (see Figure 8.1). Instead of accelerating into high speed, the situation pleads for slow driving and hence slow thinking (e.g. Kahneman, 2013).

The chapter is divided into three parts. In the first part we aim to summarize trends worldwide that risk harming democracy. In the second part we present strategies for democratic spaces based on the notion of the middle ground and a broad understanding of democracy and teacher professionalism. Finally the chapter ends with a conclusion.

Suffocation of democracy

In this book so far, we have explored interrelated concepts and big ideas in relation to education and democracy without any ambition to cover everything. We did this taking an overview of educational research, history, philosophy, empirical research and policy backgrounds to make meaning of why and how the construct of democracy is discursively reworked as a selection from culture and its historical roots. We have shown how democracy as an ideological governance form is nowadays mostly taken-for-granted in western democratic societies.

At the same time there are several predispositions in societies today that contribute to suffocating conditions for democracy, through narrow ideologies and world-views that influence the very features of education and the space for democracy in education. Ideologies that narrow down, conserve, fixate, separate, purify and aim to reduce or render doubt extinct come from various directions such as:

- Economy
- Politics
- Research
- Social debates and movements.

To put it differently, what they all have in common is their propensity to polarize, reduce complexity and curtail individual freedom and plurality which are necessary components for a vibrant education and democracy as a form of life. In this way, they ignore and/or overshadow the unavoidable presence of dilemmas that inevitably accompany the existence of people with various values and experiences.

Neoconservative turn and marketization

There is today a **neoconservative turn** to participatory democracy as a sense of moral duty and obligation to the status quo that elides any political notion of a pluralistic society of multiple hegemonies and the need for new associated forms of living for social solidarity, respect and tolerance (Hammersley-Fletcher et al., 2018). The ideal human is positioned by Human Capital Theory (Tan, 2014) as a logical rational utility-driven **homo economicus** with a claim to competitive self-sufficiency, not always matched by human needs and vulnerabilities (Bourdieu, 1988). The consequence of these types of actions is a diminishing of the nation state within a much reduced role of government, bending politics in an arc toward the primacy of the economy and business-like models of all public services, including commodification of higher education and schooling (Lynch, 2015; Tan, 2014). A resulting new politics of **inevitability** suggests that the social and political order is seen as something permanently fixed rather than being fluid and unchangeable (Snyder, 2018).

Within a new **politics of inevitability** (Snyder, 2018), there is no recognition or requirement for an 'us' or 'them' and the coexistence of multiple hegemonies, which is the essence of politics (Mouffe, 2000). Moreover differential social and power relations of a multiplicity of policy actors (e.g. voices of giant corporations, supra-national organizations, churches, state agencies) primarily involved in policymaking processes often remain hidden from view (see Chapter 3). A 'hidden hand' of the powerful (Bourdieu, 1988) becomes harder to identify as it lies within new superstructures, networks and assemblages which advocate for a view of extended professionalism for teachers. The teacher as an extended professional is understood not as a public intellectual or a knowledgeable other but as coaches and facilitators of other people's agendas. The disdain in which experienced teachers and their teacher unions are held becomes obvious when new efforts to work with teacher professional learning are provided less by face-to-face relational efforts as border-crossing dialogue, philosophical co-inquiry and deliberative democracy and more by online programs and e-learning platforms for a performative gaze (Giroux, 1988; Mooney Simmie & Lang, 2020).

What is more, it replaces the need for open vibrant public spaces for critical debate, for public interest values, for critical consciousness and for a just equitable society for all with new myths of liberal progressivism underpinned by biopsychosocial models for a **performative view** of the teacher in constant comparison with self and others (Ball, 2003; Brady, 2016, 2019a, 2019b; Muller, 2018). A new **depoliticized privatization** takes politics and philosophical co-inquiry off the agenda in schools and in higher education and shuts down spaces to question authority (Feldges, 2019; Lynch, 2015).

The concept of a **new ideal type of human** – and by implication a new ideal student, ideal teacher and ideal school leader and administrator – has become subjected to a policy make-over and is socially constructed as entrepreneurial competitive individuals operating within the 'terrors of performativity' in preference to any notion of existential emancipation and/or any view of a decent and vibrant democratic society (Ball, 2003; Brady, 2016, 2019a, 2019b).

While **reform policies** at global and national levels continue to make an urgent case for education and teaching to contribute to big societal and ethico-political tasks of associated living, such as, peace-building, multiculturalism and inclusion there are multiple views in how this task is envisaged and how it has rapidly changed in the last decade (Edling & Mooney Simmie, 2017; Mooney Simmie & Edling, 2016, 2019). In particular, while big societal and ethico-political tasks were once understood as a **shared responsibility** between policy actors, between the state, school and civil society, nowadays as a new market-led view of schooling and higher education takes hold these tasks are (re)framed as the **sole responsibility of 'quality' teachers** who, acting as collectives, provide policymakers and inspectors with continuing evidence that they have successfully achieved multicultural and inclusion outcomes for individuals in their classrooms and schools.

As a result, problems that were once considered wider societal, contextual and political issues are nowadays framed as problems of the individual and teachers are increasingly tasked with labelling and marking students in this regard (Ball, 2003; Muller, 2018). With the contemporary rise of entrepreneurship, far right politics and populism, democracy has been reduced to **electoral democracy** – where people generally consider their task is done after casting a vote (Snyder, 2018). Across the globe a neoliberal policy imaginary is buttressed by data analytics and a tyranny of **metrics fixation** (Muller, 2018). A 'narrow' or 'thin' (narrow/thin) view of democracy for a competitive individual is positioned as an entrepreneurial subject within a new flexible concept of the family and allegiance only to the flag and not to society. A slow **suffocation of democracy** removes politics from the agenda of schools and higher education for a new depoliticized privatization (Browning, 2018).

A **G-local turn** (Global-local) toward '**visible learning**' and nested systems of learning underscores a new quiet cultural revolution reshaping the global economy using decentralized notions and new partnership models, such as for **gentrification of cities** (Galvin & Mooney Simmie, 2017; Tan, 2014). Replacing former notions of the public good and equity in education with new soft sculpted notions based on data analytics and new seemingly benign modes of public-private partnerships and philanthropy (Galvin & Mooney Simmie, 2017).

Consequences of populism, extremism, and authoritarianism

The book has touched upon concepts such as **authoritarianism, populism** and **extremism** and it is argued that there is currently an increase in these phenomena in the world (McCarthy, 2019) from various ideological stances, which make it important to acknowledge and ponder about how they influence democracy and education. What we have argued for is that they impact on the popular debate about education and as such create tensions in teacher education that need to be acknowledged.

A government based on an authoritarian ideology has a strong central power that radically decreases people's possibilities to influence and at times comes to restrict all levels in society including the personal sphere such as people's thoughts, feelings, beliefs and actions (e.g. totalitarianism, see Chapter 2). Personal freedom (with frames and responsibilities) is a fundamental dimension of education (Biesta & Säfström, 2011), rendering authoritarianism to be a risk for education itself.

Populism is used by various groups (right, left, religious etc.) to trigger people and gain their sympathy and is quite efficient through its tendency to reduce complexity and its way of creating a distinct enemy that at times can take extreme and violent forms (see Chapter 2). For example, populist rhetoric from authoritarian directions tends to regard ethics, emancipation and social justice with contempt and as signs of weakness, hence dangerous for an ordered and strong society (see Chapter 6).

Moreover, the field of education has over the years been attacked for not delivering what it promises – not least through media – without arguing that all media is unnuanced. The critique for not reaching to high standards often comes from populism that harbours a specific form of idealism, e.g. simplified visions of a good society. One example of populism in relation to education is the way methods are treated as opposite to theory (e.g. Edling, 2014, 2015; Edling & Liljestrand, 2019). Theory is here considered as abstracted from reality, and teaching and learning instead become reduced to a technique (a belief that efficient methods from, for instance, neuroscience solve everything) or individual preferences (education is about making individuals content). **Idealism**, due to its simplified nature, is linked to unreachable demands and as such brands schools and teachers as constant failures and as being permanently weak in a sea of unrealistic demands (e.g. Biesta & Säfström, 2011; Edling, 2014).

Accordingly, a dominance of abridged debates and world-views expressed by politicians, media, students, student teachers, and (teacher) educators all risk decreasing the possibilities within education for critical thinking and democratic engagement. The tendency within authoritarian governing, populism and extremism to polarize, reduce complexity, individual freedom and plurality can also be found in research, and in a narrow interpretation within positivism.

Consequences with a narrow interpretation of positivism

While research based on positivism has contributed to a great deal of important findings to make our world better, we have argued that a narrow approach to positivism where ideals within positivism are seen as reality itself is harmful for people and for human diversity. Descartes' four principles which influence the ideas in **positivism** and **empiricism**: (a) the **principle of dichotomy**, (b) the **principle of everything's essence**, (c) the **principle about measurability, categorization** and **visibility** and (d) **the principle of the elimination of doubt** (see Chapter 2) are all problematic if they are treated as absolute reflections of reality. Positivism used in its narrow form harmonizes well with populism and idealism through its belief in polarization and the possibility of eliminating uncertainty and risk.

Today the talk about order, control, measurable aims and discerning the right answer to the question "**what works**" have increased drastically in education, teacher education and in society at large. A consequence of this is that the messiness, risks and complexities of education as well as a demand to see and handle these risks are decreased amongst teachers and student teachers (Mooney Simmie, Moles & O'Grady, 2019). Education becomes solely a practical field where practice means applying efficient methods rather than seeing it as a field of need of interpretation and hence theory (see Chapter 1, 2, 3, 4). The search for certainty and elimination of doubt can also be linked to an increased focus on legal documents and it is this to which we will now turn.

Juridification: the belief that legal documents can provide ultimate answers

Education within the nation state has always been regulated by legal documents since an education without legal documents and state interference can be compared to anarchy. However, what characterizes current trends is a belief that legal documents carry the possibility to drastically reduce and eliminate doubt entirely by increasing the notion that what is right and correct in society is already known and just needs to be correctly applied.

The upsurge of laws in education has been referred to as **juridification**, which means that teachers' judgements have become restricted by the expertise of lawyers and other legal representatives. In order to carry out their work they need to use a legal language and navigate in a terrain that legal representatives can themselves find problematic – ways that often make teachers feel insecure and afraid (see Chapter 3). Moreover, the strong focus on laws moves the attention from the dynamic field of education to filed complaints, bureaucracy, measures and punishments (e.g. Edling & Frelin, 2013; Hult & Lindgren, 2016; Lundström, 2018).

Without arguing that legal documents are unnecessary we suggest that the phenomenon places the spotlight on what kind of education and democracy are possible if and when teachers live in fear of doing wrong and/or being punished. Parallel with a desire to narrow down there is a tendency to create eco-chambers where world-views detached from the field of knowledge and societies at large can take form (see Chapter 5).

Alternative facts and eco-chambers

The term eco-chamber comes from the field of media and signifies how certain ways of thinking and believing are enhanced in closed systems, where other people say and think exactly as we do ourselves. It provides a sense of safety and security and gives reassurance that you/we are right while at the same time increasing bias through the distillation of pure ideas, i.e. the process of freeing ideas from complexities and dilemmas (e.g. Barberá et al., 2015; Hampton et al., 2017).

In the practices of narrowing public spaces, concepts like **alternative facts** (Wikfors, 2019) and **post-truth** (Rapacioli, 2017) have been created to describe a phenomenon where scientifically grounded knowledge is ignored or used in a limited and at times distorted way to enhance biased world-views (see Wikfors, 2019). An example of alternative facts or post-truth is the image of the good Sweden being destroyed by violent immigrants. One example is a tweet from the US president who referred to an event in Sweden that did not happen, creating huge confusion in Sweden and around the world (see for example Rapacioli, 2019). This propensity is not unique for our time or one ideology but can be found in history and in an assortment of groups with a variety of world-views. However, the presence of these and similar aspects in society tend to influence education and teacher professionalism in relation to democracy.

Teacher professionalism and a diminishing space for democracy and critical discussions

Within the contemporary global policy reform ensemble teachers are required to act as teacher-researchers systematically interrogating practices and providing evidence of success and achievement. This marks an understanding of good teaching not as a complex endeavour involving a messy narrative of change (Mooney Simmie, Moles & O'Grady, 2019) but rather as an atomized clinical practice positioning teachers as teacher-researchers. It opens a new 'scientistic' discourse of schooling and pedagogy as a science, rather than an art, of how young people learn.

As **action researchers**, and **researchers-in-action**, teachers are required, and often mandated to constantly provide external policy actors, such as inspectors, peers, school administrators, parents, guardians, with a perpetual stream of comparative data on each individual student while all the while demonstrating how this is related to or is a carbon-copy of what has already been described in policy terms as the new ideal teacher/student. In this way the teacher, school leaders and administrators are constantly on report and externally monitored.

This is supported by a new system which is testing school leadership so that the school presents as a **high-performance learning organization** where the communal-orientation is for the functional and exchange-value (Fielding, 2007). All the while theoretical and disciplinary knowledge forms are being eroded in the process (see Chapter 5). In Sweden, theory is a major dimension in student teachers' course syllabus but this is strongly questioned in media debates where it is argued that brain research and educational methods should exchange the use of theory (Edling & Liljestrand, 2019). While there is a point in adding methodology at teacher education institutions as a complement to theory, the debate tends to be either theory or methods. Generally though, in the last decade, teachers in both Ireland and Sweden are given far less access to the necessary intellectual resources needed to question authority (Beach et al., 2014; Beach & Bagley, 2013; Feldges, 2019; Nussbaum, 2010).

A **narrow/thin view of democracy** codifies teachers' democratic assignment as a straight-forward occupational role to develop a somewhat benign notion of a civic and cultural being for the expressed purpose of socializing young people into the existing culture and polity. Moreover, teachers' work practices are redefined as distinct roles: a **moral and caring person, generous expert**, an **instructional manager** and a **civic and cultural being** (Conway et al., 2009). The four stereotypic dimensions make it difficult to approach teaching and education as a more complex and messy business, where educators often express a myriad of different characteristics caught in a web of various, often contradictory, purposes.

The global world of education policy reform (see Chapter 3) appears to have opted for a **tyranny of metrics fixation** with standardized testing of young people through OECD PISA, TIMMS etc. and new low-stakes modes of teacher appraisal and school self-evaluation based on neoliberal *performative* principles of constant comparison (Brady,

2016, 2019a, 2019b; Muller, 2018). A reform policy ensemble of this type strategically prohibits mobility for the vast **majority** of the **marginalized** and **dispossessed**, it **institutionalizes poverty** while all the while presented as meritocratic intent to increase access of participation, only intended for a **minority** of the most able (McLaren, 2015). A departure emerges toward new forms of **biological determinism**, newly constructed bio-political determinism and eugenics in relation to **survival of the fittest**, a race toward best practice and the stratification in schooling and teacher leadership, see Gunter at Manchester University, UK (Gunter, 2001).

In Chapter 8, we have discussed how, over quite a short historical timeline policy, requirements have dramatically changed in relation to teachers' needs. What was previously understood as reflective practices for the moral goods of teaching have nowadays become constructed as low-stakes self-evaluation for teachers' clinical practices – a new entrepreneurial identity in accordance with a *performative* imaginary for new public modes of accountability and market-led cost–benefit principles.

Teacher's reflections are no longer understood as personal learning for necessary adjustments and self-moderation but instead have gone public under a new type of gaze and surveillance. A **neoliberal performative imaginary** involve teachers' show-casing continuing efforts at self-improvement through written documentation – such as keeping systematic personal journals, learning-logs, portfolios and/or writing reflection uploaded to electronic platforms – with new audiences of peers, students, parents and inspectors for a 360 degree gaze. Ball (2003) shows how teachers become neoliberal subjects not by having anything done to them by others but by being positioned in new spaces where there is an expectation that they must do it to themselves or risk losing employment prospects. In this regard, teachers' are given new freedoms and autonomy not for existential and emancipatory purposes but instead for (re)subjectification as neoliberal subjects and lifelong show-casers in constant public comparison with an existing ideal (Brady, 2019a, 2019b).

Indeed a deficit in teachers' democratic assignment means that **critical thinking** that involves critical consciousness, concern for social justice and questioning of authority is not only discouraged but is actively dismissed (Feldges, 2019) without claiming that differences between teacher education institutions and countries do not exist. A 'perfect storm' in the global education reform movement results in an ethical **suppression of teachers' voices**, their felt sense of demoralization with reforms that result in the loss of the moral goods of teaching, and turnaround classrooms and schools according to market principles and the needs of the economy (Santoro, 2018, 2017; Zipin & Brennan, 2003). Policymakers react quickly and decisively whenever teachers raise questions about proposed reforms. They call on experts, such as OECD experts, politicians, media presenters, career minded researchers to refute teachers' concerns. At the same time policymakers offer resilience workshops and mental health supports to teachers who are variously labelled as afraid of change, burned-out, stressed-out and/or otherwise unable to cope quickly with reform requirements of evidence-based clinical practices.

Strategies for a broad democracy and teacher professionalism

Whereas the section above focused on current challenges, this section aims to highlight overall strategies that stimulate the possibility for approaching democracy and teacher professionalism in broad terms. This stand-point is not value free but begins in an idea that a narrowing down (reducing) of education and democracy to be solely about (unrelated) fragments, absolute control, measurable knowledge, technique and procedures is not sufficient in order to handle the challenges we face today as human beings living together on planet Earth. Without arguing that technique, measurable knowledge, procedures, control and fragments are not important, they become problematic if people's use of these overlooks and/or suffocates individuals' freedom, plurality, dilemmas, and the ways in which people and the environment exist are complex, interrelated and interdependent.

In order to create possibilities for handling these tensions we suggest an awareness of the following, namely that:

1   Education is environmental and relational

- *In relation to what is desired (why) and for whom*
- *In relation to subject content, teacher, the student/students*
- *In relation to context and a practice in movement*
- *In relation to other (research) disciplines (eclectic/dialogue)*

2   Education involves handling difference
3   (mind the gap)

- *Difference between people*
- *Difference in people (embodiment)*
- *Difference in how the world is perceived*

4   (risk)
5   Education involves handling the existence of dilemmas

- *Middle ground*
- *Dilemmatic space*
- *Amor complexity/Dolores complexities*
- *What is/what is not*

6   Education and broad approaches to democracy and teacher professionalism

- *Democracy as procedure/democracy as a form of life*
- *Importance of oscillating between various phenomena*
- *Teacher perception and critical thinking.*

Education as environmental and relational

In 2004 the anthology *No Education without Relation* was published, edited by Charles Bingham and Alexander M. Sidorkin. The book puts the focus on the inevitable dimension of relations in education and what this might entail for the profession at large. The relational features of education also entail that education has an environmental (Dewey, 1916) and ecological dimension (Colwell, 1985; Dewey & Bentley, 1949), in the sense that relations created to peruse certain purposes in certain contexts (including non-biological aspects, like organizations and artefacts) also condition action.

This suggests that it becomes difficult to separate education from what takes place in society and the world at large since they intersect. In this book we have argued that the very presence of dilemmas that actors in (teacher) education face are created, not least due to these relations.

To begin with, education is always linked to certain purposes and these purposes are carefully interwoven with what a society at a given time in history finds as desirable as concerns way of being with others and as concerns what to learn (Englund, 1986). Research from various directions has shown that statements like 'they need to learn this', 'this is important knowledge', and so forth are in fact value statements that are interconnected with issues like: 'Why should these things be taught and not these? Who does the knowledge benefit? What kind of social citizens and social responsibilities does the knowledge chosen encourage/not encourage?' Subsequently, since education is always created in relation to desired purposes and values, it becomes important to take into account that there is no neutral or absolute objective education (see Chapter 1, 2 and 4) – without arguing that objectivity is not important. Generally, education has three purposes in societies, namely to provide qualifications, to socialize, and/or emancipate (Biesta, 2010; Edling, 2018). Since the content of and connection between these are far from obvious, they need to be constantly articulated and problematized in relation to what it is deemed to be desirable, for whom and for what: nationalism, democracy, economy, the personal, the environment, the global and/or so forth (see Chapter 4)?

Education is also relational in the sense that it is always linked to a specific subject content, those who learn (learning subject), and those who teach. Indeed, subject content does not just appear but is created and the process of this creation is important to scrutinize, just as the questions how, when and where it is to be taught and made meaningful for the subject. Who benefits?

As such, education always takes place in relation to a particular context and hence a practice in movement anchored in the present. Whereas the strong focus on measurable goals emphasizes the stable, controllable and predictable, teachers and teacher educators as actors in education are forced to exist and handle the flow of action. Relations here are moving and changing in the sense that people literally move in classrooms and corridors, address different people, relate to different perspectives and aims, alter their learning and hence focus, etcetera. A relational practice in education is not static but changeable, and subsequently in need of being taken into account.

The relational dimension is also expressed through the interdisciplinary and eclectic features of educational research (Boden et al., 2011; Haycock, 2007). This implies an awareness that the challenges education faces and the particular features of education require dialogue with a variety of research areas. At the same time, just as there are tensions between different groups in society there are tensions within the field of research itself (e.g. Hammersley, 2008; Oakley, 1999; Paraskeva, 2011; Lenz Taguchi, 2016; Wood, 2004). Whereas educational researchers tend to regard research conducted by psychologists, cognitivists and neuroscientists as dangerous and irrelevant for education, researchers within the fields mentioned are apt to regard research conducted within the field of education as quasi-research. We argue that in order to understand and navigate within the specific and complex field of education as a multidisciplinary field, relations to a range of disciplines are vital. These relations need to be guided by complexity approaches that can equally include and draw from both the universal and the particularity of education and the challenges residing there, rather than subjected to the dominance of a specific research tradition(s).

Education involves handling difference

Everything that takes form in education is influenced by relations taking form in educational environments and these relations are in turn influenced by people's differences, rendering them important to be aware of and handle. Consequently, difference is an unavoidable part in education, which does not mean that it has always been acknowledged or is acknowledged in the present time. Historically, difference has come to be treated in an essentialist and dualist manner. That is to say, poor, rich, boys, girls, foreigners, non-foreigners, homosexuals, heterosexuals, etcetera are naturally different from each other and need to be kept separate. In the light of past wars and current challenges, modern democracies have generally come to emphasize the positive and necessary dimensions of difference in the strife for securing ethical, just and peaceful relations (Edling, 2018).

One way of approaching difference is to regard it as a question of different groups and group culture (Brantefors, 2011). Difference is about existing with a variety of cultures and is frequently rendered equal with ethnicity: Somalis, Turks, Germans, Swedes, Irish and so forth. This way of grasping difference has been explored by intercultural pedagogy (Eklund, 2008). At the same time, a wide range of research shows that group difference also has to do with the uniqueness of individuals implying that there is an unavoidable gap between people and their perceptions rendering it difficult to merely treat people as homogenous groups (e.g. Biesta, 2003; Caine & Caine, 1991; Caine, Caine, McLintic, & Klimek, 2005; Gilkey, 2014; Lévinas, 1981).

Besides that difference existing on a group and individual level, it also exists in people. Research about embodiment emphasizes the ways people exist in their bodies rather than as floating heads. This entails that thinking, no matter how rationally or objectively conducted, is interlaced with emotions, expectations and desires that colour language and influence our actions towards others, rendering it important to pay attention to (e.g. Aldama, 2003; Arturo & Arteaga, 2003; Kristeva, 1984).

There is a lot of evidence that people are radically different from each other and that a suppression of and ignorance of this difference risks harming people and impedes learning processes (see Chapter 2 and 4). This does not entail that all difference is good in itself or easy to handle, mainly that it exists and causes dilemmas that plead for attention.

Education involves handling the existence of dilemmas

It can at times feel tempting to be seduced by promises aiming to terminate uncertainties, conflicts and risks, and hence gnawing anxieties. Strategies to polarize, narrow down and reduce complexities are far from a new phenomenon. History shows that these tendencies are all present when major conflicts and war arise. However, just as difference exists whether we want it or not, complexity does too.

People have an inclination to think using two extreme stand-points; 'either–or' (Dewey, 1916). For example, difference/plurality is good or it is bad or complexity is good or it is bad. A central thread through the book has been how to problematize these either–ors, not least in relation to complexity. The elimination and fear for complexity referred to as *dolor complexity* exists for instance in authoritarian governing, extremism, populism, technical views on education, whereas *amor complexity* stresses a more positive view on complexities (e.g. Bakker & Montesano Montessori, 2016). Rather than simply embracing either–or, we have argued for the need to keep these in tension when education and democracy are discussed and approached in everyday life.

There is a point in regarding education as a *field of challenges and possibilities*, which can appear frightful and promising at the same time. The field of challenges and possibilities requires people to face tensions even though they are difficult. It is through exposure to complexity and tensions that the possibility for fronting social challenges lies. This can be compared to Fransson and Grannäs's (2013) *dilemmatic space* in education that highlights the unescapable presence of dilemmas, and Biesta's (2012) term the middle ground that requires grown-up behaviour (see Chapter 1).

Conclusion: broad approaches to democracy and teacher professionalism

Threading through this book is the notion of broad democracy and inside-out-professionalism that are not to be seen as opposites to narrow democracy and outside-in-professionalism, but rather signal a starting-point that includes everyday life aspects in teachers' judgements. From this it follows that it is not enough with methods and techniques, teachers need to interpret what takes place in a practice that is in constant movement (Edling, 2016) while being professionally present (Frelin, 2014).

The problem at the heart of teaching in diverse democratic societies, where diversity and minority viewpoints are given recognition is that teaching needs to be mediated with the wider world and cannot be hermetically sealed into a closed system that only requires teachers to interrogate themselves and their practices. While the practice of self-interrogation and interrogation of practice is necessary, it is not sufficient for democratic plurality. Democracy as a living breathing organic entity must be experienced at first hand by students, student teachers and all teachers if they are to emulate this way of associated living with young people in their classrooms and schools. In this way, teachers act as cultural workers and public intellectuals, within the paradoxical dilemma of acting as guardians of inherited culture and at the same time allowing affordances for something new to burst through and emerge. As such, teachers need to constantly oscillate between what is known beforehand and what takes place in front of and around them while making space for an unknown future (Edling, 2016).

The hallmarks of a democratic way of associated living require feeling that one has a stake in the process and that one can make a valued contribution to the school and/or society. The power to influence with honour is a key innate driver for many teachers who, acting as shaper-planners and moral agents, make a real difference in the lives of the young people they teach. As we discussed in Chapter 7, teacher self-interrogation involves deep critical reflexivity that is often uncomfortable (Bleakley, 1999; Pillow, 2003). It is based on the premise that teaching is heart-work and takes place at the fragile intersection of the personal and the public. It is only through embarking on the journey of getting to know ourselves at a deep level, and embracing our 'unfinishedness' (Freire, 1970), that we are able to encourage others to join in a life of inner contemplation and action (Steel, 2018).

Ben Ferencz, a prosecutor in the Nuremburg Trials, speaking on a BBC Hard Talk Interview with Zeinab Badawi, claims that the world has yet to learn the lessons from the atrocities of the Second World War (Ferencz, 2017). He asserts that the world lives in constant danger of repetition of new forms of eugenics, particularly state annihilation, censorship and even killings in relation to any perceived threat to the economy, religion or the nation state. This and other references make for sobering reading in a global world where there is no shortage of evidence of uncritical knee-jerk reactions using the principle of retaliate first and ask questions later.

Biesta (2015) argues that democracy requires us to learn to live well with people who are not like us. This not only requires peace-building and community building it also requires capability for active debate of contrarian views, to embrace deliberative discussion that seeks to go well beyond agreement (Mooney Simmie & Lang, 2018, 2020). This begs a form of agonistic deliberation which respects multiple hegemonies and allows the global world to move beyond narrow chains of logic and repression (Mouffe, 2000).

In this way, living well with others who are like us and those who are not like us in truly vibrant democratic societies that are culturally diverse will require many societal efforts in addition to teachers' democratic assignment for 'thick' democracy and plurality to emerge. The alternative is to remain perpetually trapped in the slow suffocation of democracy that is currently besetting governance across all public services, including schooling and teacher education.

References

Aldama, A. (2003). *Violence, bodies, and the color of fear*. Indiana: Indiana University Press.
Arturo, A. & Arteaga, A. (2003). *Violence and the body: race, gender and the state*. Indiana: Indiana University Press.
Bakker, Cok & Montesano Montessori, Nicolina (2016). *Complexity in education. From horror to passion*. Rotterdam, The Netherlands; Boston, MA & Taipei, Taiwan: Sense.
Ball, S. J. (2003). The teacher's soul and the terrors of performativity. *Journal of Education Policy*, 18(2), 215–228.
Barberá, Pablo, Jost, John T., Nagler, Jonathan, Tucker, Joshua A. & Bonneau, Richard (2015). Tweeting from left to right. *Psychological Science*, 26(10), 1531–1542.
Beach, Dennis & Bagley, Carl (2013). Changing professional discourses in teacher education policy back towards a training paradigm: A comparative study. *European Journal of Teacher Education*, 36(4), 379–392.
Beach, Dennis, Bagley, Carl, Eriksson, Anita & Player-Koro, Catarina (2014). Changing teacher education in Sweden: Using meta-ethnographic analysis to understand and describe policy making and educational changes. *Teaching and Teacher Education*, 44, 160–168.
Biesta, Gert (2015). Freeing teaching from learning: Opening up existential possibilities in educational relationships. *Studies in Philosophy and Education*, 34(3), 229–243.
Biesta, Gert (2010). *Good education in an age of measurement: Ethics, politics, democracy*. Boulder, CO: Paradigm.
Biesta, Gert(2004). "Mind the Gap!" Communication and the educational relation. In C.Bingham & A. M.Sidorkin (eds.). *No education without relation*. New York:Peter Lang.
Biesta, Gert (2012). The educational significance of the experience of resistance: Schooling and the dialogue between child and world. *Other Education. The Journal of Educational Alternatives*, 1(1), 92–103.
Biesta, Gert & Säfström, Carl Anders (2011). A manifesto for education. *Policy Futures in Education*, 9(5), 540–547.
Bingham, Charles W. & Sidorkin, Alexander M. (2004). *No education without relation*. New York: Peter Lang.
Bleakley, A. (1999). From reflective practice to holistic reflexivity. *Studies in Higher Education*, 24(3), 315–330.
Boden, Daniel, Borrego, Maura & Newswander, Lynita K. (2011). Student socialization in interdisciplinary doctoral education. *Higher Education*, 62(6), 741–755.
Bourdieu, P. (1988). *Homo academicus*. Cambridge, UK: Polity Press.
Brady, A. M. (2019a). Anxiety of performativity and anxiety of performance: Self-evaluation as bad faith. *Oxford Review of Education*, 45(5), 605–618.
Brady, A. M. (2016). The regime of self-evaluation: Self-conception for teachers and schools. *British Journal of Educational Studies*, 64(4), 523–541.
Brady, A. M. (2019b). The teacher-student relationship: An existential approach. In T. Feldges (ed.), *Philosophy and the study of education. New perspectives on a complex relationship*. Abingdon, UK: Routledge, pp. 104–117.
Brantefors, Lotta (2011). *Kulturell fostran. En didaktisk studie av talet om kulturella relationer i texter om skola och utbildning*. Uppsala, Sweden: Acta Universitatis Upsaliensis (AUU), Uppsala Universitet.

Browning, C. R. (2018). The suffocation of democracy. *New York Review of Books*, 25 October, 65 (16), 14–17.

Caine, Renate Nummela & Caine, Geoffrey (1991). *Making connections: Teaching and the human brain*. Alexandria, VA: Association for Supervision and Curriculum Development.

Caine, Renate Nummela, Caine, Geoffrey, McLintic, Carol & Klimek, Karl (2005). *Brain/mind learning principles in action. The fieldbook for making connections, teaching and the human brain*. Thousand Oaks, CA: Corwin Press.

Colwell, Tom (1985). The ecological perspective in John Dewey's philosophy. *Educational Theory*, 35(30), 255–266.

Conway, P., Murphy, R., Rath, A. & Hall, K. (2009). *Learning to teach and its implications for the continuum of teacher education: A nine-country cross-national study*. Maynooth, Republic of Ireland: The Teaching Council.

Dewey, J. (1916). Democracy and education [Elektronisk resurs]. Retrieved from https://en.wikisource.org/wiki/Democracy_and_Education

Dewey, John & Bentley, Arthur F. (1949). *Knowing and the known*. Boston, MA: Beacon Press.

Edling, Silvia (2014). Between stereotypes and task complexity. Exploring stereotypes of teachers and education in media as a question of structural violence. *Journal of Curriculum Studies*, 47(3), 399–415. Retrieved from www.tandfonline.com/doi/abs/10.1080/00220272.2014.956796

Edling, Silvia (2016). *Demokratidilemman i läraruppdraget. Att arbeta för lika villkor* [Democracy dilemmas in the teacher mission. To strive for equity]. Stockholm: Liber.

Edling, Silvia (2015). Två förhållningssätt till teorier på (lärar)utbildningar i relation till lärares förutsättningar att motverka våld [Two strategies to theories at (teacher) education in relation to teachers' assignment to oppose violence]. In C. Ljunggren, I. Unemar & T. Englund (eds.), *Kontroversiella frågor i samhällsundervisningen*. Malmö, Sweden: Gleerups Utbildning AB, pp. 114–134.

Edling, Silvia (2018). *Vilja andra väl är inte alltid smärtfritt. Att motverka kränkning och diskriminering i förskola och skola*. [Wanting others' wellbeing is not always painless. To oppose violence and discrimination in preschool and school]. Lund, Sweden: Studentlitteratur.

Edling, Silvia & Frelin, Anneli (2013). Doing good? Interpreting teachers' given and felt responsibilities for the pupil's well-being in an age of measurement. *Teachers and Teaching: Theory and Practice*, 19(4), 419–432.

Edling, S. & Liljestrand, J. (2019). Let's talk about teacher education! Analysing the media debates in 2016–2017 on teacher education using Sweden as a case. *Asia-Pacific Journal of Teacher Education* (Online). Retrieved from www.tandfonline.com/doi/full/10.1080/1359866X.2019.1631255. doi:10.1080/1359866X.2019.1631255

Edling, S. & Mooney Simmie, G. (2018). Democracy and emancipation in teacher education: A summative content analysis of teacher educators' democratic assignment expressed in policies for Teacher Education in Sweden and Ireland between 2000–2010. *Citizenship, Social, Economics Education*, 17(1), 20–34.

Eklund, Monica (2008). *Interkulturellt lärande – intentioner och realiteter i svensk grundskola sedan 1960-talets början* (nr 36) [Intercultural learning – intentions and realities in Swedish elementary school since the 1960s beginning]. Luleå, Sweden: Luleå Tekniska Universitet.

Englund, Tomas (1986). Curriculum as a political problem: Changing educational conceptions, with special reference to citizenship education. Dissertation. Uppsala and Lund, Sweden: Studentlitteratur.

Feldges, T. (ed.) (2019). *Philosophy and the study of education new perspectives on a complex relationship*. Abingdon, UK: Routledge.

Ferencz, B. (2017). BBC World Service – HARDtalk. Ben Ferencz, Prosecutor at the Nuremburg Trials, talks to Zeinab Badawi. 25 December 2017. Retrieved from www.bbc.co.uk/programmes/p04xd4pq

Fielding, M. (2007). The human cost and intellectual poverty of high-performance schooling: Radical philosophy, John Macmurray and the remaking of person-centred education. *Journal of Education Policy*, 22(4), 383–409.

Fransson, Göran & Grannäs, Jan (2011). Dilemmatic spaces in teachers work – Towards a conceptual framework for dilemmas in teachers work. Paper presented at the American Educational Research Association, New Orleans, LA.

Freire, P. (1970). *Pedagogy of the oppressed*. New York: Herder.

Frelin, Anneli (2014). Professionally present – Highlighting the temporal aspects of teachers' professional judgements. *Teacher Development: An International Journal of Teachers' Professional Development*, 18(2), 264–273.

Galvin, M. & Mooney Simmie, G. (2017). Theorising participation in urban regeneration partnerships: an adult education perspective. *Journal of Education Policy*, 32(6), 809–831.

Gilkey, Joseph William (2014). Brain and Learning. *Journal of Arts and Humanities*, 3(1), 50–56.

Giroux, H. A. (1988). *Teachers as intellectuals: Toward a critical pedagogy of learning*. Westport, CT: Bergin & Garvey.

Gunter, H. (2001). Critical approaches to leadership in education. *Journal of Educational Enquiry*, 2(2), 94–108.

Hallsén, Stina. (2013). *Lärarutbildning i skolans tjänst? En policyanalys av statliga argument för förändring* [Teacher education in the service of schools? A policy analysis about state arguments for change]. Uppsala, Sweden: Uppsala University.

Hammersley, Martyn (2008). (IN RESPONSE) Paradigm war revived? On the diagnosis of resistance to randomized controlled trials and systematic review in education. *International Journal of Research & Method in Education*, 31(1), 3–10.

Hammersley-Fletcher, L., Clarke, M. & McManus, V. (2018). Agonistic democracy and passionate professional development in teacher-leaders. *Cambridge Journal of Education*, 48(5), 591–606.

Hampton, Keith N., Shin, Inyoung & Lu, Weixu (2017). Social media and political discussion: When online presence silences offline conversation. *Information, Communication & Society*, 20(7), 1090–1107.

Haycock, Laurel (2007). Interdisciplinarity in education research. *Behavioral & Social Sciences Librarian*, 25(2), 79–92.

Hult, Agneta & Lindgren, Joakim (2016). Med lagen som rättesnöre i lärares arbete mot kränkande behandling [With the acts as guidance in teachers' work against violating treatment]. *Utbildning & Demokrati – tidskrift för didaktik och utbildningspolitik*, 25(1), 73–93.

Kahneman, Daniel (2013). *Thinking, fast and slow* (1st pbk edn.). New York: Farrar, Straus and Giroux.

Krantz, Joakim (2009). *Styrning och mening – anspråk på professionellt handlande i lärarutbildning och skola*, Acta Wexionensia No. 181/2009 [Governing and meaning – claims on professional action in teacher education and school]. Thesis. Växjö, Sweden: Växjö University Press. Retrieved from www.diva-portal.org/smash/get/diva2:232831/FULLTEXT01.pdf

Kristeva, Julia (1984). *Revolution in poetic language*. New York: Columbia University Press.

Lenz Taguchi, Hillevi (2016). 'The concept as method': Tracing-and-mapping the problem of the neuro(n) in the field of education. *Cultural Studies Critical Methodologies*, 16(2), 213–223.

Levinas, Emmanuel (1981). *Otherwise than being: Or, Beyond essence*. The Hague, The Netherlands; Boston and Hingham, MA: Martinus Nijhoff; Distributors for the US and Canada, Kluwer Boston.

Lundström, Ulf (2018). Lärares professionella autonomi under New Public Managementepoken [Teachers' professional autonomy under new public management]. *Utbildning & Demokrati – tidskrift för didaktik och utbildningspolitik*, 27(1), 33–59.

Lynch, K. (2015). Control by numbers: New managerialism and ranking in higher education. *Critical Studies in Education*, 56(2), 190–207. doi:10.1080/17508487.2014.949811

McCarthy, James (2019). Authoritarianism, populism, and the environment: Comparative experiences, insights, and perspectives. *Annals of the American Association of Geographers*, 109(2), 301–313.

McLaren, P. (2015). *Pedagogy of insurrection from resurrection to revolution*. New York: Peter Lang.

Mooney Simmie, G. (2020). The power, politics and future of mentoring. In Beverly J. Irby, Linda Searby, Jennifer N. Boswell, Fran Kochan & Rubén Garza (eds.), *The wiley international handbook of mentoring, paradigms, practices, programs, and possibilities* (1st edn.). Hoboken, NY: John Wiley, pp. 453–469.

Mooney Simmie, G. & Edling, S. (2016). Ideological governing forms in education and teacher education: A comparative study between highly secular Sweden and highly non-secular Republic of Ireland. *Nordic Journal of Studies in Educational Policy*, 2016(1), 1–12.

Mooney Simmie, G. & Edling, S. (2019). Teachers' democratic assignment: A critical discourse analysis of teacher education policies in Ireland and Sweden. *Discourse Studies in the Cultural Politics of Education*, 40(6), 832–846.

Mooney Simmie, G. & Lang, M. (2018). Deliberative teacher education beyond boundaries: Discursive practices for eliciting gender awareness. *Teachers and Teaching Theory and Practice*, 24(2), 135–150.

Mooney Simmie, G. & Lang, M. (2020). *School-based deliberative partnership as a platform for teacher professionalization and curriculum innovation*. Routledge Research Teacher Education Series. London & New York: Routledge.

Mooney Simmie, G., Moles, J. & O'Grady, E. (2019). Good teaching as a messy narrative of change within a policy ensemble of networks, superstructures and flows. *Critical Studies in Education*, 60(1), 55–72.

Mouffe, C. (2000). *The democratic paradox*. London: Verso.

Muller, J. K. (2018). *The tyranny of metrics*. Princeton, NJ: Princeton University Press.

Nussbaum, M. C. (2010). *Not for profit: Why democracy needs the humanities*. Princeton, NJ: Princeton University Press.

Oakley, Ann (1999). Paradigm wars. Some thoughts on a personal and public trajectory. *International Journal of Social Research Methodology*, 2(3), 247–254.

Öberg Tuleus, Marianne (2008). *Lärarutbildning mellan det bekanta och det obekanta. En studie av lärares och lärarstudenters beskrivningar av levd erfarenhet i skola och högskola* [Teacher education between the known and unknown. A study of teachers' and teacher students' descriptions of lived experience in school and higher education]. Örebro Studies in Education 23. Dissertation. Örebro, Sweden: Örebro University.

Paraskeva, João M. (2011). *Conflicts in curriculum theory: Challenging hegemonic epistemologies*. New York: Palgrave Macmillan.

Pillow, W. (2003). Confession, catharsis, or cure? Rethinking the uses of reflexivity as methodological power in qualitative research. *International Journal of Qualitative Studies in Education*, 16(2), 175–196.

Rapacioli, Paul (2017). *Good swede, bad Sweden. The use and abuse of Swedish values in a post-truth world*. Stockholm, Sweden: Volante.

Santoro, D. A. (2017). Cassandra in the classroom: Teaching and moral madness. *Studies in Philosophy of Education*, 36, 49–60.

Santoro, D. A. (2018). *Demoralized why teachers leave the profession they love and how they can stay*. Cambridge, MA: Harvard University Press.

Snyder, T. (2018). *The road to unfreedom*. London: Penguin Random House.

Steel, S. (2018). Revisioning philosophy instruction in competency-based B.Ed. programs. *Interchange*, 49, 417–431.

Tan, E. (2014). Human capital theory: A holistic criticism. *Review of Educational Research*, 84(3), 411–445.

Wikfors, Åsa (2019). *Alternativa fakta: om kunskapen och dess fiender* [Alternative facts: about knowledge and its enemies]. Stockholm, Sweden: Fri Tanke Förlag.

Wood, Elisabeth (2004). A new paradigm war? The impact of national curriculum policies on early childhood teachers' thinking and classroom practice. *Teaching and Teacher Education*, 20(4), 361–374.

Zipin, L. & Brennan, M. (2003). The suppression of ethical dispositions through managerial governmentality: A habitus crisis in Australian higher education. *International Journal of Leadership in Education*, 6(4), 351–370.

Index

Page numbers in *italics* refer to figures, those in **bold** indicate tables.

academic knowledge 102
academic language 92
action-researcher, teacher as 156–7, 172
active reformer, teacher as 104–5
adiaphorization 133–4
Aggestam, K. and Höglund, K. 31
Allodi, M. 87
Allport, G. W. 132–3
alternative facts 171–2
Amor complexitatis 11–12, 176
Apple, M. W. 39, 60, 101, 110, 115, 151, 152, 158
Arendt, H. 129
assimilation and respect 67
authoritarianism: populism and extremism 170; *see also* Nazism and Second World War
authority: and autonomy 83; and obedience studies 143–4

Bakker, C. et al. 12
Ball, S. J. 2, 4, 5, 54, 57, 60, 66, 85, 101, 105, 152, 153, 161, 169, 173; et al. 13, 56–7
Bauman, Z. 27, 133–4
behaviourism 66–7
Bernstein, B. 45, 46, 99, 102, 107, 108–9, 142
Biesta, G. J. J. 12, 31, 54, 64, 66, 75, 78, 99, 109, 113, 153, 154, 177; et al. 78; and Miedema, S. 108, 114, 158; and Säfström, C. A. 102, 170
Bildung spaces 101
biological determinism 123
Black, P. 113; and Wiliam, D. 113
Bleakley, A. 154, 156, 158–9
body and emotions 135–7
brain research and human complexity 137–40
Bretton Woods Agreement 28
broad democracy: conditions for promoting knowledge and 105–7; and educational environment 81–3; narrow vs 78–81, 113–14, 172; strategies 173–8
Browning, C. 129–30, 144

Browning, C. R. 3, 32, 38, 66, 108, 137, 158, 169
bureaucratic demands 65–6

Cartesian perspective *see* Descartes, R.
certainty, teleology of 4, 40
civic and cultural person, teacher as 34–5, 68, 77, 160
coach, teacher as 155–6
Cochran-Smith, M. 101–2; et al. 104; and Fries, M. K. 100; and Lytle, S. L. 3, 103–4, 113
cognitive research and human complexity 137–40
commodification of knowledge 107
communitarian notions of reflection 151–2
complexity 1, 11–12, 176; cognitive research and 137–40; and complication 76; images 130–1; theory 65; *see also* knowledge
conflictual consensus 33
constant comparison method 152–3
constructivism 105, 112, 155–6
controversies 6
critical debate 4
critical discourse 5
critical pedagogy 109–10
critical realists 111–12
critical reflexivity/reflection 152, 157–9; in practice 160–2
critical thinking 173
curriculum theory 9–10

Darwinian strength *see* weakness vs strength
deep vs shallow learning 89, 100–1
dehumanization and humanism 131–5
democracy: democratization process 28–9; and dilemmas 4–6; forces influencing education and 2–4; suffocation of 167–73; *see also* broad democracy
Descartes, R. 41–6, 78–9
Dewey, J. 4, 12, 29–30, 32, 43–4, 78, 79, 82, 83, 150

difference, handling 175–6
dilemmas: cases of 9; democracy and 4–6; handling 176–7
disciplinary order 60
discourses 4–5, 141–2; performative 65; vertical and horizontal 102
Discrimination Act, Sweden 80
discrimination and distancing 133–4
Dolor complexitatis 11–12, 176
dualism: principle of 42, 45; teacher professionalism 83–5; *see also* weakness vs strength
duck and rabbit image 90–1

Early Childhood Care and Education (ECCE) 125
Edling, S. 1, 2, 4, 5, 10, 11, 13, 29, 45, 57, 61, 64, 67, 75, 78, 80, 83, 85, 100, 103, 121, 125, 136, 142, 176, 177; and Liljestrand, J. 3, 36, 56, 68, 80–1, 105, 172; and Mooney Simmie, G. 2, 8–9, 29, 55, 64, 66, 67, 68, 100, 101, 158, 166, 169
Eichmann, A.O. 129
elimination, principle of 42–3
Elliot, J. 41
Elmgren, M. and Henriksson, A. S. 90
emancipation: philosophies 29–31; and praxis 99; struggles 28–31; subjectification as 78
embodiment and emotions 135–7
empathy and care 92, 129
empiricism 41
enactment, policy as 57
entrepreneurial, managerial and democratic reform 104
environmental and relational aspects of education 174–5
epistemology: dominance of OECD 66–7; and epistemic justice 105–6
equal treatment 75, 76–7
essentialism 43–4, 45, 67–8, 123
ethics: of alterity 130, 133, 134; codes 111; principles 83
ethnopluralism 27
European Convention on Human Rights 36–7
everyday language 92
everything's essence, principle of 42
Excellent Education (Håkansson and Sundberg) 85–8, **89–90**

fast vs slow thinking 85, 91, 137–9
feelings 92; embodiment and 135–7; masculinity and 125–7
femininity and masculinity 124–30
feminist perspective 111
fixed democracy/order: vs living entity 79–81; vs process 32–9
Fjelde, H. 31–2
form of life, democracy as 4, 78, 79

Frankfurt School 30
free speech and political correctness 36–7
Freire, P. 30, 106, 115, 122, 124, 130–1, 177
French Revolution (1789) 29

Galvin, M. 105–6
genocides 131–2, 144
Global Education Reform Movement (GERM) 60, 99, 112–15
global policy reform: impacts of 172–3; national and local policy tensions 58–66
globalization 56
Gloria Effect 140, **141**
Green, M. 90
Greenbank, P. 153, 158
Gunter, H. 5, 69, 115

Habermas, J. 30
Håkansson, J. and Sundberg, D.: *Excellent Education* 85–8, **89–90**
Hargreaves, D. 40
Hattie, J.: *Visible Learning* 85–8, **89–90**
hegemonic masculinity 126–7
hidden content-meaning of knowledge 77–8
hidden curriculum 76
historical background: politics 24–32; present 44–7; research 39–44
Hitler, A. 122–3, 124, 129, 131
Human Capital Theory (HCT) 2, 58–9, 152
humanism and dehumanization 131–5
humanistic discourse 5
hyper masculinity 127

ideological governing forms 24–5; and nation/'people' 25–8
implementation, policy as 57
Inside the Black Box 57–8, 113
inside- and outside-groups 132–3
inside-out-professionalism 92; vs outside-in-professionalism 84–5
instrumental discourse 5
instrumental values 79
intellectual vs technician, teacher as 85
international comparison in education systems 152–3
intersectionality 140–3
intrinsic values 79
Ireland 7–9; and Sweden, policy cycle 67–9

Jackson, P. W. 76
Johansson Heinö, A. 5–6
judgement and interpretations, importance of 89–92
juridification 61–4, 106, 171

Kahneman, D. 87, 91, 137, 139, 140
Kant, I. 28

Keane, M. G. 106–7
knowledge 99–100, 115; active reformer role 104–5; conditions for promoting broad democracy and 105–7; demands for complex 100–2; Global Education Reform Movement (GERM) 99, 112–15; overview of dilemmas **100**; practical and theoretical 102–4; schools of thought 107–12
knowledge assignment 75; and socialization 76–8; *see also* qualifications
Kvernbekk, T. 103–4

language: everyday, academic and professional 92; and meaning 90; new, of learning 64–6; of professionalization 83
leadership: and policy directives 62–4; training study 106–7
legal regulation *see* juridification
Levinas, E. 130, 133
Lonergan, J. 84, 160–1, 162
Lynch, K. 56, 158, 168; et al. 59, 60, 92, 114,

majority and minority groups 27–8, 80, 132–3; *see also* inside-out-professionalism
managerial, entrepreneurial and democratic reform 104
market economy/marketization 39–40, 64–6, 107, 108–9, 130, 152, 156, 168–9
Marx, K. and Engels, F. 30
masculinity and femininity 124–30
McLaren, P. 2, 173; and Jandrić, P. 12, 27, 60,
media influences 3, 45, 171–2
mental weakness 122
Milgram, S. 143–4
Mooney Simmie, G. 61, 66, 87; and Elding, S. 5, 43, 68; Edling, S. and *see under* Elding, S; et al. 13, 85, 108, 171, 172; and Lang, M. 5, 78, 177
moral agency 111, 114
Mordal-Moen, K. and Green, K. 150–1, 152, 159
Mouffe, c. 5, 27, 33, 78, 80, 168, 177
multinational corporations 2, 60
Murphy, D. 125

naïve consciousness 25
nationalism 25–8, 33
Nazism and Second World War 122–3, 124, 127, *128*, 129–30, 131, *132*
neo-conservatives/neoliberalism 2, 168–9; *see also* market economy/marketization
New Quality Management 59
norms and policy enactment 57

obedience studies 143–4
OECD 60, 66–7, 114, 152, 154
official recontextualizing field (ORF) vs pedagogical recontextualizing field (PRF) 109

Ofstad, H. 122–3, 124
order and disorder 37–9

pedagogical (PRF) vs official recontextualizing field (ORF) 109
perennialism 43
performative discourses 65
Pillow, W. 2, 14, 124, 130, 150, 158
pilot metaphor of teacher 57–8, *59*
plurality 5–6, 27, 33; and adiaphorization 133–4; assimilation and respect 67; Cartesian anxiety and principles 41–2, 45–6; elimination of 33–6
policy actors 59–60
policy cycle 2, 54–5, 69; epistemic dominance of OECD 66–7; global, national and local tensions 58–66; Ireland and Sweden 67–9; overview of dilemmas **56**; various 56–8
political correctness 36–7
politically defined assignments 75–8; *see also specific assignments*
politics and political science 3
populism, authoritarianism and extremism 170
positivism 41, 46, 153; consequences of narrow interpretation of 170–1; notions of reflection 152
post-truth phenomenon 171–2
pragmatism 30, 107–8
private and/or public good 60–1
procedure, democracy as 78, 79
professional language 92
professionalism *see* teacher professionalism
progressivism 44
purity 27
purposes of teacher education 1, 11–13; *see also* politically defined assignments

qualifications 11, 55; *see also* knowledge assignment
qualitative research 65

Rancière, J. 30–1
realists and critical realists 111–12
reconstructivism 44
reflection/reflexivity *see* teacher reflexivity/reflection
relational and environmental aspects of education 174–5
research: cognitive 137–40; historical background 39–44; over-reliance on scientific 153–4; qualitative 65; teacher as action-researcher 156–7, 172
respect and assimilation 67
responsibilities and juridification 62–3
Rydgren, J. 27, 123

Santoro, D. A. 111, 150, 161, 173; and Rocha, S. D. 111, 114
Schön, D. 84
scientific discourse 5
scientist, teacher as 154–5
Second World War 122–3, 124, 127, *128*, 129–30, 131, *132*, 143, 144
seeing and interpretations 89–91
shallow vs deep learning 89, 100–1
Sheehan, c. 62–4
Simić, N. et al. 154, 155
Simon, R. 131–2
slow vs fast thinking 85, 91, 137–9
social constructivism 105, 112, 155–6
Social Investment State 60
social order, democracy as 79
social welfare state 28, 60
socialization 11, 55, 75–8; gendered 126, 127
sociologists of education 108–9
STEM subjects 112
Stradling, R. 6
strength vs weakness *see* weakness vs strength
subjectification 11, 55, 75, 78; equal treatment as 75, 76–7
supranational agencies 2, 60, 66, 152
Sweden 7; and Ireland, policy cycle 67–9
Swedish Council for Higher Education 7
Swedish National Board of Education 13

Tan, E. 2, 39, 43, 59, 69, 168
teacher democratic assignment 166–7; broad democracy strategies 173–8; and critical approaches 158, 160, 173; and narrow view of democracy 172; and policy cycle 57, 69
teacher professionalism 10–13, 74–5, 93; demands and approaches 83–5; and global policy reform 172–3; judgement and interpretations 89–92; meta studies 85–9; overview of dilemmas **75**; politically defined assignments 75–8; vs professionalization 83; *see also* broad democracy
teacher reflexivity/reflection 124, 150–1, 162; constant comparison method 152–3; contemporary notions of reflection 151–2; dilemmas in practice 160–2; over-reliance on scientific research 153–4; overview of dilemmas **151**; positions of reflection 154–9
Teaching Council, Ireland 8
technician vs intellectual, teacher as 85
technologization 56
theory and practice: knowlege 102–4; tensions between 83–5
Todd, S. 135

UNESCO 3, 4
'unfinishedness' 124, 130–1, 140
universal methods 13
universal vs practice oriented teaching 83–4

vertical and horizontal discourse 102
violence 122, 123, 124, 127–8, 129–30, 131–2
Visible Learning (Hattie) 85–8, **89–90**
von Humboldt, W. 101

Watson, C. 67
weakness vs strength 122–4, 144–5; authority and obedience studies 143–4; cognitive research and human complexity 137–40; complex images 130–1; embodiment and emotions 135–7; humanism and dehumanization 131–5; intersectionality 140–3; masculinity and femininity 124–30; overview of dilemmas **122**
Westphalian peace agreement (1648) 29
Wiliam, D. 57–8, 113
Wittgenstein, L.: duck and rabbit image 90–1

Young, I. M. 44–5
Young, M. 112, 114–15